Unreal City:
A Priest in the Square Mile

by Peter Mullen

First Published 2016
Text Copyright © Peter Mullen 2016
Peter Mullen asserts his moral rights to be recognised as the author of this work.

permission of the publisher:
Bretwalda Books, Unit 8, Fir Tree Close, Epsom, Surrey KT17 3LD
info@BretwaldaBooks.com
www.BretwaldaBooks.com
ISBN 978-1-910440-33-9

Printed and bound in Great Britain by
Marston Book Services Ltd, Oxfordshire

Unreal City: A Priest in the Square Mile

"Unreal City,

Under the brown fog of a winter dawn,

A crowd flowed over London Bridge, so many,

I had not thought death had undone so many."

The Waste Land - T.S. Eliot

For Alexander Boot

I

After my public execution, they performed an exorcism of my spirit. They? I mean the church authorities. They are very thorough. It was like this...

In 1998, Richard Chartres, Bishop of London, appointed me to two parishes in the City of London: St Michael's Cornhill and St Sepulchre-without-Newgate. Both were moribund. The Bishop's commission was for me to revive them. St Michael's is a Wren church of 1672 with a tower by Hawksmoor, added in 1722. But there had been a church dedicated to St Michael there long before that. Documents of the Roman occupation state clearly that a pagan temple on the corner of the forum became a Christian church in AD 179. There were relics and recollections which haunted the church, clinging historical evocations. We had long possessed William Cowper's walking stick and this was displayed in a glass case – until it was stolen. Daniel Defoe was baptised in our font. And there was an outstanding musical tradition. William Boyce had been Master of the Music for thirty-two years in the 18th century, before being sacked for drunkenness. Harold Darke was organist from 1916-1966. This is the Harold Darke who composed Christina Rossetti's poem *In the Bleak Midwinter* – a piece of such limpid melancholy and translucent joy that, as the choir sang it at the climax to the carol service every year, the congregation always seemed to be holding their breath throughout. It makes Holst's setting of the same poem sound competent but dull. This was also the Harold Darke of the Evensong responses known as *Darke in F* – always referred to by choristers as 'effin dark. Darke played a Monday organ recital for the whole of his fifty years here, clambering through the bomb craters during the Second World War Moribund. A huge empty mausoleum, echoing to loud choral singing, mostly of the turgid Edwardian sort – what you might call Come into the Garden Lord music. At the parish Eucharist on my first Sunday, All Souls Day, 1998, there were three in the congregation and ten in the choir. This desolate scene was the inheritance of years of civil war between my predecessor-but- one and the Director of Music, mainly about money and fees for the musicians. That Rector had been given a pay-off to retire. A new man was appointed in the hope of a resurrection. But he stayed only a few months, having received a better offer in the shape of an administrative job in the Diocese of Europe. He raised St Michael's several inches up the liturgical candle by introducing incense and providing a choral service at the end of the week for the City called Thank God it's Friday Mass.

St Sepulchre, that is the church of the Holy Sepulchre, is on Holborn Viaduct, across the road from The Old Bailey whose golden statue of justice I could see through my rectory window – until Merrill Lynch built a new bank which blocked the view. History galore. In a glass case the execution bell which the parish clerk used to ring when there was a hanging nearby. Very popular these occasions were, days out for the whole family who would crowd into the area between St Sep's and Newgate prison, drink beer, eat pies and watch the show. Shakespeare mentions the bell in *Macbeth*:

It was the owl that shrieked, the fatal bellman which gives the sternest goodnight.

Naturally, the officers at St Sep's were quick to notice the pulling power of the bard and had printed out his words in sham antique script and stuck them on a pillar next to the bell. A sort of aide-macabre to go with the pies and the family glee. Our tower houses the twelve bells of Old Bailey of the Cries of London nursery rhyme. On the south side there is a stained glass window featuring the three little ships in which Captain John Smith, late of this parish, set sail to found the colony of Virginia in 1607. He is buried here. One of his men married Pocahontas and brought her back to England and the poor girl, before she knew she would one day be Disneyfied, died at Gravesend. St Sepulchre's also has a notable musical tradition. Opposite Smith's three little ships is the Musicians' Chapel, centrepiece image of Sir Henry Wood – his acolytes Handel and Bach – on either side showing that Henry certainly knew his place in the scheme of things. He is interred here. But before that, he learnt the organ in St Sepulchre's and there are delicious stories: that, for example, his teacher would set him a piece to learn and then disappear across the road to the Viaduct Tavern. Young Henry, displaying early the talent for tactlessness and bumptiousness which he brought to full fruition in adulthood, would race across to the pub, catch his mentor at his ale and conversation and exclaim, "I've finished already, Sir. Now what should I do?" It is reliably reported that his teacher told him exactly what to do. There are windows to Nellie Melba and John Ireland in the Musicians' Chapel too as well as a memorial to Roger Ascham, tutor to Queen Elizabeth I.

All these glories had passed away. Now St Sepulchre's was deader even than St Michael's. At least St Michael's had heating and lighting. St Sep's was dark and cold and locked up. It was opened only a couple of times in the year: once for the Royal Fusiliers Remembrance Day Parade, and for something else, quasi-masonic, which I can't recall. It was as dank and depressing as the old Newgate prison over the road. There was a churchwarden who wanted to keep it that way, a peevish jailer of a man. St Sep's was his jail and by God he was going to keep the public out.

The Rectory was called The Watch House, built in 1791 and now reconstructed in its original style. It was called The Watch House because its tenant – some said the Rector – was paid £30pa to keep an eye on the grave robbers who stole corpses from our graveyard and sold them £10 a time to the doctors from St Bartholomew's hospital, a building not obscured by the new Merrill Lynch HQ. I looked out on it from my dining room. Female corpses were in demand and this presented difficulties as the surgeons were only allowed the bodies of executed criminals for dissection. But the doctors craved understanding of the female anatomy. Step up St Sep's graveyard then whose back side (so to speak) was full of the remains of prostitutes who plied their trade in the nearby Cock Lane – the street which Dr Johnson visited to dispel the locals' disquiet at the supposed appearance of a ghost. Anyhow, there was no more body-snatching by the time I got there and so I never got the thirty quid.

Chartres had asked me what I proposed to do in these City churches. I said, "I want to set up a Theological Foundation, a sort of sane version of the beads, joss sticks and feminist fairy lights at St James Piccadilly."

The bearded wonder nodded agreeably at this. He had not yet deliquesced into the fully paid up modern churchman he is today.

But theology and philosophy had to wait. The pressing business was getting some heating and lighting, which meant interminable meetings with the bureaucratic wretches in the London Diocese and the pedantic (and tasteless) aesthetes in English Heritage. There was no money at St Michael's either. How could there be when there was no congregation? And what cash there might be all went into the coffers of the choir and the wonderful Director of Music. I decided I would do the only thing I knew how to do: concentrate my energies on making a go of the Parish Eucharist on Sunday mornings, trying to establish sound theological teaching, as an antidote to the touchy-feely, you and yours, jogging- for-Jesus humbug that passes for worship in so many places. And for all the problems, to raise money for the music, dispatch the Come into Garden Lord sugar lumps and get in some Mozart and Haydn. And to develop a pastoral and convivial ministry: not just look after people myself, but encourage the people – if we could get any people in – to look after one another. By convivial, I meant a proper social life in the parish. None of that eighth sacrament instant coffee in the vestry after the Eucharist, but red and white wine and avid conversation persisting for an hour and more in the garden. And that followed by small gangs of us drifting off for long theological lunches in the City restaurants. By some special grace of the divine providence, this actually came to pass and not only persisted but increased and strengthened over the years.

I know that's one of the reasons why the authorities were so eager to enforce my retirement at the statutory age of three score years and ten. Traditional theological teaching? The bishops don't like it. But the people do. And they started to come to St Mike's in pretty good numbers, for the *King James Bible* and *The Book of Common Prayer*, to belong to a place where prayer was valid, where theology had not been entirely divested of all meaning and where people actually believed the Creed; where there was fellowship of the non-mawkish sort. And for the wine and the jokes.

Unreal City. A three-quarters of a mile walk from my house adjoining St Sepulchre's to my other church of St Michael. Out through the front door on to Giltspur Street, walk between Barts hospital and the Old Bailey, along Newgate Street past St Paul's cathedral and the Stock Exchange. These things were of my parish. Along Cheapside and past St Mary- le-Bow down to Bank station, the Lord Mayor's Mansion House and the Bank of England. Lombard Street and down King William Street to where St Mary Woolnoth kept the hours with a dead sound on the final stroke of nine. The bank where Tom Eliot worked is in the parish. I met a man over the Champagne in a livery company reception whose grandfather had known Eliot. He said, "And it was all true – those

lines about St Mary's in *The Waste Land*. Eliot
morning at the bank but he would refuse to e
of nine, standing there with his arms outspre
altar."

The City streets are narrower than you i
is claustrophobic. There is a sort of controll
bankers, risking their lives to run across t
cardboard cups of undrinkable *Starbucks*. Exquisite young women,
City workers, immaculately coiffeured and tailored in peerless black
suits. These are goddesses. Until they open their mouths: "Well, it was
like I didn't know what to tell him, like. He was like, like, like…well,
I mean. Like it was no like contest." (I probably missed out a couple
of "likes") But that's only the syntax. The tone and articulation is
all corncrake. The nymphs are departed through the photosynthetic
haze. And the wine bars sempiternal. And, as you return from a City
banquet around 11pm, you may see some of these goddesses, sitting,
lying, cursing, pissed as arseholes and crying their eyes out on the
kerb edge in Cornhill and Threadneedle Street. When lovely woman
stoops to folly…There is clearly much pastoral work to be done.

I suppose, apart from my meetings with Chartres, I was never
truly interviewed for the job – except I was. But all in that way of the
City, hints and guesses style. St Michael's Patrons are the fabulously
wealthy and terrifically self-regarding Worshipful Company of
Drapers. They have been Patrons since 1503, having bought the
living from the Bishop of London "for a quantity of wine." I asked
Chartres if he still got the wine. "'Fraid not."

"That makes two of us. I don't get the thirty quid for keeping an
eye out for the dealers in dead whores."

But, to the interview, such as it was… The Court of the Drapers
– livery courts are effectually the companies' boards of directors –
invited me to lunch in that glorious room they have with the 19th
century painting of the lovely lady revealing more than she ought.
(I always thought it was a bit daring of Drapers, and really out of
character with their customary strait-lacedness, to have such a treat
on show). This private luncheon was an opportunity, you might say,
for the Patrons to inspect my table manners. Champagne. The livery
companies float on the stuff. Twenty-four eminent men around
a courtly table. Chandeliers mixing their magical light with the
sunlight peering in through the high windows.

me butter, Peter. All this stuff about clogging up the
a load of bollocks."

my other side sat the Master and I asked him about the
pany's treasures. He said, "Oh yes, I dare say after lunch we
ight find someone to show you around."

It was he himself, a kindly, gentle man, who showed me round. I
had never seen anything like it all since the day I went on that school
visit to the Crown Jewels in 1958. And that was it – the interview.
No one asked one word about my plans for St Michael's, whether I
was high church, low or broad, how long I intended staying. Only,
"Would you like another glass of burgundy before we move on to
the port?"

That was it and I was in. And that Master contributed generously
every year throughout my time as Rector to the St Michael's
Foundation – once I had got it, as one of the exquisite young ladies
in black would have said, "Like, up and running like innit?"

There wasn't an interview of any sort for the St Sep's job, but I
was asked to sit around a table over a glass of claret with the
churchwardens, one of whom was the jailer I mentioned earlier. One
of them – not the jailer – said, "What order of service will you use?"

"There's only one as far as I'm concerned and that's *The Book of
Common Prayer.*"

This was met with quiet squeals of satisfaction, like feeding-time
for the piglets. All except the jailer:

"I won't go anywhere near that dreadful book. I'll help see you in
and then I'll retire."

Chartres had said, "The atmosphere at St Michael's is tricksy, but
St Sepulchre's is benign."

I'll talk about St Michael's tricksiness in due course, but he was
right about St Sep's. The first time I entered the building was for
that meeting with the churchwardens. A glorious place. It stands
so calmly and elegantly on the opposite corner to the Old Bailey.
A garden with plane trees and benches where City workers would
come and eat their sandwiches. It was the way it stood: it spoke pure
reassurance, as if to say, "You have nothing to fret about. You can
trust me. I've been standing here for centuries and I've seen it all."

There was a gentleness about the place, but nothing pusillanimous.
The tower foursquare as a castle. The 15th century porch like a cave
full of exquisite carvings – the oldest part of the church. I walked

through that porch for the first time on my way to the meeting with the churchwardens. Straight ahead and, once inside, turn right. The extreme beauty of the interior comes as a shock. The high roof. The soft light. The tall, wide pillars in white stone and then, so far away, the sanctuary, the broad altar with the red lamp indicating the place of the Blessed Sacrament and the west window's image of Christ over the City of London. Suddenly I was in a panic: "O God, don't let anything happen to prevent my coming here!"

All the coloured windows in the church are new, replacing the originals blasted out by Herr Hitler. And sensibly, they left some plain, so the place was full of light. The morning light miraculous, throwing golden shafts across the altar as if you were in heaven already. There was a 1905 Steinway grand with its blue cover, the same colour as the long aisle carpet. Two pulpits. St Sepulchre's is the largest church in the City – almost twice as capacious as any of the others.

St Michael's, befitting its dedication to the warrior archangel, the archistrategos, the General Officer Commanding, has a more rugged beauty, The atmosphere volatile, as if the place were permanently on the move. By the font a huge image of the pelican, adopted as an emblem of Christ, because it was thought to feed its young on its own blood. And behind the pelican, the spiral stone stairway to the ringing room and the tower. There was a nasty scar on the stonework halfway up and the story had it that this was the work of St Michael himself, a fiery dart cast at the devil who was trying to enter from the top of the tower. I preached a sermon about this and afterwards over drinks a visitor scorned my credulousness: "It was owing to a lighting strike!"

"Of course. Doesn't everybody know that the first item of weaponry in the archangel's armoury are lightning bolts?"

And that tricksy atmosphere? There certainly was something unsettled and unsettling. You could feel uneasy entering alone in the dark. The director of music told me, "I've heard some strange noises when I've been practising late in the winter evenings. So when that happens, I switch to playing Bach and everything calms down."

The strange noises did not always wait for the cover of darkness. There was one September Sunday with the sunlight streaming through the high windows on the south side during the Choral Eucharist. It was just after the Offertory, the hymn had finished and I was arranging the sacred vessels on the altar. From the back of the church came a great rattling and thumping and my first thought was that we were possessed by an unruly child. But I was told afterwards:

"No, the noises came from the pew just in front of me and it was quite empty. Everybody near the back at that side was startled - scared, if I'm honest."

This happened more than once. And there was one little church-going dog that would squeal and shudder at the presence.

As if to compensate for this disturbance, we were also visited by a friendly ghost. Tiny John Gaze, parish clerk, the smallest chap in the City but with the loudest "Amen," told me about it. John owned an icon shop in the Piccadilly arcade: a self-made man in every way, risen to wealth by the sale of these icons which some said were acquired in rather dubious circumstances from Orthodox monasteries which had been forcibly closed during the Soviet era. John was an east-ender, but as his social star ascended he took to boasting his Huguenot roots and removed himself from Spitalfields to Chelsea. Chain-smoking, aficionado of the Carlton Club. God knows why he chose that Tory bastion as his hideout, since he always claimed to be a communist. Where others drank water, John drank gin. He said,

"It was a Sunday morning and I was in early dressing the altar. Out of the corner of my eye, I saw a priest walking down the south aisle towards the sacristy, so I came down the short way to cut him off. I got close and had a good look at him. Then he disappeared! I realised it was the priest on that photo in the vestry – one of your predecessors, Peter, a man called Ellison. I described him to Bishop Ellison who was our visiting preacher a week or two later and he confirmed it: 'Yes, that was my father.'"

Some pregnant women are induced. All Rectors are inducted. I am a Rector and therefore I was… This little syllogistic nicety was borne in on me as, unlike the pregnant ladies, I went about arranging my own induction. They make you come into church in the presence of the bishop and the area dean and swear stuff: such as that you will avoid all seditious ambition against her Majesty. Now, of all the vices which the authorities might have had cause to invite me to adjure, treason was never one of them. Then you have to say you will accept the authority of the bishop. Well, yes. I suppose all the befuddled legal apparatus has to be gone through, but really the Induction is an excuse for a party, for the provision of a memorable church service and an opportunity to welcome the latest example of that notable species, the new priest, so enchantingly described by Anthony Burgess as "His Arse-holiness the Rectum."

There is always accidental amusement. Receiving the proofs of the order of service from the printer, I discovered that where we had asked for "Agnus Dei," we were given instead "Angus Dei" – as if the Lamb of God were some captain of the grouse moors, The Laird in fact.

My inducement, "or wha'ever," as those City girls would say, occurred at noon on Friday 30th October: the day before Halloween. The bell-ringers rang a peel of bells, sustaining their effort for three hours and twenty-two minutes, and afterwards presented me with a wonderful certificate to say that this is what they had done in my honour. It was pretty humbling for a Yorkshire country parson, which was what I had been for the previous twenty years. On that matter of leaving the shires, I had wondered what to do about my two weekly journalistic columns: the one for *The Yorkshire Evening Press* and the other for *The Northern Echo*. I had decided the decent thing to do was to resign. The York paper accepted my offer, with what measure of alacrity I know not. But that gentleman Peter Barron, editor of the renowned Darlington daily, sparked a flash of imagination and asked me to keep writing my Tuesday column as "our man in the Smoke." I am writing this on 21st July 2014, two years into my retirement in Eastbourne. And I'm still turning in that weekly piece.

I told you: three in the congregation on my first Sunday 1st November. But the preceding Friday's event might have looked to an unschooled observer as evidence of a religious revival. There were two hundred in St Michael's. My family and friends, the officers of the parish, the Alderman for Cornhill, Sir David Howard Bt, other Aldermen, members of the Court of Common Council, the Secondary (that is the manager) of the Old Bailey, Masters and Clerks of many livery companies, a representative of the Stock Exchange and another of the Bank of England and as many bods and bodesses off the street as you could shake a crozier at.

Speaking of which, in comes the bishop and the organ roars. The choir, paid for today by our Patrons the Drapers, sets off with something magnificent. The area dean got me to do all the swearing bit and then Chartres preached in his thespian style, surely one of the last of the great 19th century hams. There was little content in what he said – there never is - but – as Sir Thomas Beecham said of the English people's enthusiasm for music – "They don't know what it means but they sure like the noise it makes!" These City ceremonial occasions have little to do with Christianity. They are religious nonetheless. There are prayers from the Prayer Book and lessons from the Bible, but the essence is the cult of the local tribe: in this case, the City reflecting itself in the corporate myth of solidarity.

When it was all over, the whole congregation adjourned, across Cornhill to Throgmorton Avenue for what is officially and municipally known as the piss-up. This is the way of the City. All ceremonial occasions float on that ocean of Champagne. The attentive, uniformed male waiters and their crisp, agreeable female colleagues greet you with a whole tray of the stuff. And for the next few hours the flow is uninterrupted. As a St Michael's chorister put it, "Even when you've fallen to the floor dead drunk, they come with a funnel and pour it down your throat."

We were in the huge hall – there are so many – at Drapers. Such an extravagant setting for such extravagant hospitality. My friend the civil engineer Robin Osborn described it as "the most over-the-top Victorian interior in the world." Drapers have learnt the knack of making a few bob on the side by hiring the place out to movie-makers. Scenes from *The King's Speech* were shot here. It was the most spectacularly grand occasion I'd witnessed since the Coronation – and I only saw that on the telly.

They don't chuck you out of Drapers' Hall. But one minute the whole room is a chattering burlesque and the next – say around four o'clock – there is a near silence. The company has evanesced. It had been a fine party, the sort of thing of which I might once have written that everyone had been so very gay. Actually there were gays a-plenty in both senses. Tons of gay in the new sense among City musicians. I remember once asking the director of music if we could have the hymn *O Strength and Stay* to the Dykes tune and he quipped, "That should please the sopranos!" All good natured, live and let live. A whole lot of old mates from Yorkshire and a few new ones from London dragged ourselves from the fleshpots and drifted through the start of the rush hour along London Wall. Already the City workers were finding their way into the wine bars. Thank God it was Friday indeed. A slow and dozy stroll up past Guildhall into Gresham Street, crossing St Martin- le-Grand and cutting round the back of Bart's hospital into Giltspur Street, piling into The Watch

House for beer, tea, coffee, whisky and the day's anecdotes. Then they were all off on buses, tubes and trains and the evening closed in, replete, delighted, exhausted. The usual night of sirens from the ambulances coming and going to the station at the end of our street and into West Smithfield, and contrapuntal sirens from the cop cars around Snow Hill Police Station. The rest was silence until the crapulous dawn and the City Saturday, desultory, litter-strewn, deserted. They had all gone, if not under the hill, then at least to the leafy suburbs for the weekend: the clerks, the brokers, the bankers and the Almanac de Gotha. The weekend: I had not known the weekend had undone so many. I went into St Sep's which was a dusty cavern of All Saints' Eve low sunshine and played a Mozart ditty on the 1905 Steinway. Then set about my first sermon

But – I began with the mention of my public execution and the subsequent exorcism. What could I have possibly meant by that? Only to say that canon law obliges beneficed clergy to retire when they reach the age of seventy. Of course the bishop has ultimate discretion and has been known to let trusties stay on for a couple of years or so. In 2011 I, sound in wind and limb, had asked Chartres if I might hang around a bit longer. (In fact in forty years of priestly ministry I had missed only one service owing to illness or indisposition of any kind). But no, he couldn't wait to get rid of me. I had, after all, spent a proportion of the previous fourteen years building up a traditional congregation and generally knocking the illiterate new forms of public prayer to be found first in *The Alternative Service Book* and then in its execrable successor *Common Worship*. I drew particular attention to the fact that when the Synod introduced the *ASB* in 1980, they trumpeted it as "The greatest publishing event in four hundred years." Twenty years later they actually banned it – yes, banned it. Church Bans Books. What a headline. Worthy of the Nazis. And then there were other inanities such as *The London Challenge* – of which more later – an ecclesiastical pantomime up there with *Monty Python*.

Chartres, posing as a traditionalist in 1998 – or perhaps he really had been a traditionalist of sorts in those days? – said he had appointed me to say the things that he couldn't say and that he would back me for saying them. Somewhere in that short space of years, he modernised himself and joined the touchy-feely set. Here we had not just the vicar of Bray but the Bishop of the whole bloody diocese of Bray. The world including the church was, as they say, moving on. And Chartres was determined it would not leave him behind. So my retirement was enforced on the dot as soon as I reached three score years and ten. The parishioners wrote countless letters telling Chartres what a fine thing we had going at St Michael's. But a newly-trendy bishop doesn't want a crowd of intelligent, informed, devoted traditional believers causing trouble in his backyard. So he would not. And effectually I suppose I was sacked – though all was legal and above board of course. The St Michael's people voted with their feet.

That was the public execution. The exorcism went like this...

I had been appointed to revive two City churches and to celebrate the traditional faith. Mission accomplished. But the Bishop of Bray had new fetishes and new masters. So, after my departure, at St Sepulchre he appointed a coterie of numbskull happy-clappies, aisle-dancers, guitars and overhead projectors devotees. I met my successor once. It was enough. On the short walk to the war memorial from St Sep's on Remembrance Sunday, his whole conversation was a supplication: could I get him any livery connections in the City and in the Old Bailey? Social-climbing *in excelsis.*

Chartres is Patron of the Prayer Book Society which exists to uphold *The Book of Common Prayer.* And nobody laughs. He replaced me at St Michael's by appointing an old mate of his who is or was Chairman of the Liturgical Commission, the philistine outfit that chucked out *The Book of Common Prayer* and invented all the new Noddy language services.

Well, I've told you about how it all started and how it all ended up. The rest of this book will tell you what happened in between.

II

The trouble with the hair of the dog is that it can so easily turn into another dog. And so it was in the scheme of things that the day after my Induction was the annual dinner of the Ancient Society of College Youths. bell-ringers, in other words. From all over the world they came for a weekend's ringing in City belfries and pints in City taverns. They had been doing this for three hundred and sixty-three years. And they kindly invited me – to Accountants' Hall, a sparse, minimalist building, rather draughty. The impression was of being inside a 1940s wireless set. You needed stamina, for it started at 5pm with a choice of drinks: pints of beer or halves of beer. Over these early drinks I experienced one of those moments – not uncommon in the City – of otherwise quite extraordinary charity and grace.

Having been a country parson for the last twenty years, I did feel rather like a bumpkin in this gaudy metropolis with its rules, conventions and taboos. In particular, there was a dress code. Not at ASCY dinners of course. These ringers were all proper lads and wouldn't have cared – or even noticed – if you'd turned up wearing only a loin cloth. But how should the City priest disport himself at the more formal banquets? I was nervous. Step up Fr David Rhodes, genial Vicar of St Giles Cripplegate – or, as politically-correct protocols suggested we should refer to it – St Giles Differently-abledgate. I didn't have the full clerical fig at that time – the frock coat, the funny trousers and the varnished shoes. David said, "A priest is always properly dressed in his cassock. Just turn up to the fleshpots in your cassock, as if for Evensong." Then he added, "But, for a touch of class, go to *Wippells* clerical outfitters in Westminster and get yourself a cincture." That's a wide belt with a tassle. Looks as if it means something hierarchical, but it's just an ornament. So I did and began to feel at home.

There were many other such gracious moments. Early one evening I was sitting watching the news when the doorbell rang and I opened up to find Fr David Burgess of St Lawrence Jewry, the Guildhall church, standing there with a bottle of wine. We sat together for an hour during which he gave me a bit of very welcome schooling into the best way to survive in the City:

"Sometimes you will have a lunch and a dinner in the same day. Of course, if you've enjoyed a fillet steak at lunchtime, you might prefer something a little less filling in the evening. So when they come round with the huge portions of flesh, just say, 'Would you mind if I had a little piece of fish?' And they'll bring you a delicious – and light – plate of sea bass. The same with puddings. If you're full, just tell them you'd prefer a piece of fruit and immediately you will be presented with the most glorious fresh fruit salad."

Manners maketh man.

The belli-ringers' evening was cheerful and lively. In fact it was like being in Victoria station at rush hour. All those conventions about not getting up for the loo until after the Loyal Toast might never have been heard of. There was wine on the table, but what these lads craved was ale. And so, whenever the thirst came upon them – say every five or six minutes – they would leave their places at the table and charge into the bar, coming back with trays bearing half a dozen foaming pints, holding them aloft virtuosic as a circus act. And laugh? The cascade of raucous glee held no pauses. Or chaps would just get up and walk to another table to talk to infrequently-seen mates from distant parts of the globe. And behold, I show you a mystery....

There is an historic feud – how serious I've never been able to work out – between ASCY and a rival group of ringers known as The Cumberlands. There were even some Cumberlands in the hall and I'm sure they had been properly invited. But they were extravagantly disdained as if they had been fifth columnists. At about half past nine there was a religious interlude. Non-denominational. Nothing doctrinal about it. It was the moment of the hand-bells. Ten minutes of mellifluous, melodic softness. The whole raucous evening paused for this short period of meditative, you could say contemplative, musicality. And then the Wurlitzer started all up again with a guest speaker – ordered to be as cheeky as he dare. (I found myself doing it one year, but of course I had no notion of such possibilities on this my initiation). But the evening ended strangely. After all the cheerful commotion, everyone settled down while the Master for the year read his annual report, and this always entered the realms of unsearchable obscurity – not one halfpenny of accounting passed over without justification. Not one proposition or resolution however insignificant – such as the provision of a new light bulb for the cloakroom in the ASCY HQ – unacknowledged. Many slept. Some snored. Then that blessed moment when the speaker says, "I end with…"

And everyone charged off in search of more beer.

From the mightily convivial to the fantastically pretentious. One day the following week I was invited to the new Lloyds building – the one that indecently displays its innards on the outside – to be part of what was described as a "select" audience to hear a lecture by its designer Richard Rogers. Now, I have worked in the civil service and trained as a linguistic philosopher, but this man's jargon was impenetrable. And everyone knew it. But no one would say it. Talk about the king's new clothes. He spoke for an hour and said nothing. The apotheosis of arrogance. At the end, questions were invited and one was asked. Rogers didn't even attempt to answer it but just continued as before with his inane solipsistic prattle. After this, we were taken on to the trading floor for drinks. This was a vast claustrophobic area with no breathing space, no windows, a low ceiling which, like the walls, was painted black. Our compere, host for the evening, said, "More workers from Lloyds building than from any other building in the City commit suicide each year."

Gerraway!

Back at the day job, we were trying to get some electric light in St Sepulchre's. You have to go though "processes" involving the Diocesan Advisory Committee (DAC) – those letters having provoked many variations on the theme of what they might stand for – and the polite mechanicals in English Heritage. This is what happened… The committees trailed laboriously around the church and looked at the proposal which Alan Frost our architect had put forward. They rejected it. Not immediately, you understand: disappointment and the dashing of hopes have to take due process too. So we proposed another scheme. After a long silence this also was rejected…. In favour of, guess what? The original scheme. Frustrated, I was told that this sort of thing is not at all unusual.

My first month in the City. Sundry surrealities. The Archdeacon came round to perform his statutory inspection of my living accommodation. He declared all in order, went out into the garden, picked an unripe fig and ate it. Subsequently, he was made a bishop. Keith Robinson, secretary of the Stock Exchange took me out for lunch at The City Pipe, a restaurant off Gresham Street whose rooms were like so many old-style railway carriages. I arranged visiting preachers for the Advent Sundays: Professor David Martin, Professor Dennis O'Keeffe and Dr James LeFanu – the author of the doctor's column on the *Daily Telegraph*. We doubled the congregation and on Christmas Day itself there were eighteen in the pews. Some of our attached livery companies came for their carol services and these were well-attended: The Water Conservators, The Woolmen, The Guild of Air Pilots and Air Navigators (GAPAN). Always a supper afterwards in a local hostelry. I was honoured to be invited to become Chaplain to GAPAN and at the drinks reception after my first Court meeting, I approached a tall, lean, wiry, sprightly, mischievous youth in, I suppose, his mid-sixties.

"Good evening, padre. I suppose you think this croak in my voice means I've got some awful cancer? Well, I haven't. I was chief test pilot on the Harrier and things went wrong. I pressed the button and the ejector worked but the bloody roof didn't open. So I went right though, taking it with me. It was three months before I was able to get airborne again!"

Surrealism wasn't in it. There was one occasion of such outlandish absurdity that we might have been in something by Pirandello. The Upholders Company came to St Michael's for their carol service with their chaplain Fr John Cowling. Except that John didn't turn up at the start, so we began without him. The Upholders, by the way, are by trade upholsterers. The name derives from their having been in earlier times the tradesmen who upholstered coffins and put in that little raised platform so that the head of the deceased is lifted from the horizontal. Anyhow, John arrived just in time to preach his sermon. He began mysteriously, "I'm sorry I'm late – but I'm not going to tell you why I'm late." Then he got into his stride. "I'd like you to know about a man I once met who operated a workshop for people who had lost proper control of their limbs and muscles. So he installed an electrical circular saw…"

The congregation were flabbergasted. But that was only the warm-up. John soon rose to his spiritual theme: "So I would conclude by saying, whenever you find something you want to do, put your hand to it and work at it with all your might."

I confess to having whispered to a nearby chorister: "Now we know why he was late!"

Another regular Advent "do" at St Michael's is the Merchant Taylors' Vernon Service. Vernon was a prominent early benefactor and he left money in his will to pay for a service and lunch every Christmas in his memory in perpetuity. The money long since ran out of course but the MT's keep the ball rolling. They all pile in at lunchtime: liverymen, their wives and concubines and pupils from the Merchant Taylors School – bringing their choir. The church is full and the whole thing is a whirlpool of delight. Not without its queasy humour. When it comes to that Rossetti hymn *In the bleak midwinter*, there has to be censorship and so we all sing "a cup full of milk and a cradle full of hay." I wondered why and was told by the MT's choirmaster, "We tried singing the original, 'a breastful of milk' but it sends the lads potty."

The Merchant Taylors are one of the most benign and generous, cheerful and self-effacing livery companies in the City. They do nice things – such as their summer party in the garden behind the Hall in Threadneedle Street with course after course of delicious canapés and Pimms poured down your neck all night. Moreover, the Company bestowed enormous generosity on me. Out of the blue I got a letter from their Clerk saying that they had followed my writings for a long time and wanted to make a contribution to any fresh literary project I might be embarked upon. This came with a cheque for £3000. I wrote my book *A Partial Vision* and delivered six copies to MT's Beadle. About three months later, I bumped into the Master in Cornhill and asked him if they'd got the copies. "Not only have we got the book, Peter; we're reading sections aloud in Court meetings."

I was asked to try to revive the new Year City Service which historically used to be held at St Michael's but which had fallen off during the years of – what shall I say? –the troubles. It was traditionally held at noon on the second Friday in January, so this didn't give me much time. I was determined it should not go off half-cock. We must fill the church with City people, with the Sheriffs from the Old Bailey and representatives from the Aldermanic Court and the Mayoralty. The Drapers generously offered to provide a grand luncheon reception, so that would surely encourage a few to turn out. The theme should be English Traditional. An anthem by Elgar or Parry, the majestic hymns *I vow to thee my country* and Blake's *Jerusalem*. Readings from the Authorised Version. Now I needed to find a star preacher. Surely not an imported bishop or dean, but someone substantial and in the public eye. This was going to be difficult because speakers usually expect a few months' notice, but I had only four weeks. A stray inspiration flitted into my mind. The substantial person I would invite was Ann Widdecombe MP. She was the lively, controversial, colourful character who would bring them in. She had just converted to Roman Catholicism and she was in the papers a lot, talking about it. It was a long shot and I hardly dared to hope. *Carpe diem*. I picked up the phone:

"That's very intriguing, but Miss Widdecombe is out until later today. I will put your request to her when she comes in."

I put the phone down and the long shot seemed to have got suddenly longer. Then at half past five: "Ann Widdecombe here. I'd love to come."

Well now!

I was full of smug satisfaction as City folk marvelled at my disgusting minor triumph. But, as Tom Eliot said, between the idea and the reality falls the shadow. Churchwardens and Parochial Church Councils are hard to please. At 11.50am on the day I was getting complaints that the church was too full: "Some people will have to stand!"

OK, that's like what legs and feet are for innit!

Ah but, also by 11.50 there was no show from Ann. 11.55, still a blank, High noon came and went and I knew I had to start. What could I do? I dare say I could get into the pulpit, put a bag over my head, as they say, and make some sort of noise. But the gathered hundreds had not come to hear me. We began. The gorgeous, frosty, tender Epiphany hymn *O worship the Lord in the beauty of holiness*. Bidding prayers. And, by the choir, that soaring Psalm 8 which has all creation singing and dancing for joy: *O Lord our Governor, how excellent is thy name in all the world…*

No Miss Widdecombe though.

The prophet Isaiah in his most reassuring mood: "Comfort ye, comfort ye my people…"

No comfort for the Rector though. Still no show. The whole congregation – and what a sound tit made! – praying the General Thanksgiving: "…for the means of grace and for the hope of glory."

For the hope of Miss Widdecombe. That'll teach me to be smug! Oh but the disgrace: NEW RECTOR OF ST MICHAEL'S DOES BIG PROMO ADVERTISING ANN WIDDECOMBE WHO, HOWEVER, FAILS TO MATERIALISE.

Another hymn: "Bring me my sword… my chariot of fire…" I was ready to fall on my sword or to be burned in my chariot. Then at 12.23 precisely I caught sight of the sacristan leading a small figure down the south aisle – the one where John Gaze had espied Ellison's ghost – and I was spared. Ann was so small in the pulpit. Reminded me of the story about the tiny parson who was inducted to a Yorkshire village and he began his first sermon, "I am the light of the world…" And a voice from the back, "Well, turn thi' wick up a bit lad!" But she preached a most competent sermon – not a political diatribe but a considered reflection on the parable of the Good Samaritan.

Nothing could go wrong after that. We all went over to Drapers' Hall and the City networkers networked, crowding around Ann, or I should say towering over her. It was particularly engaging to notice her in conversation with our churchwarden and Alderman, Sir David Howard who stands about six foot four. He was bent almost double.

While I'm on the subject of the City Service, I might as well record what happened the following year and then it's done with. Of course I had plenty of time to think about who might be willing to give the address. Frederick Forsyth, I thought, a true Englishman and a Eurosceptic. Let me take just one line to tell you the horrible truth:

Where Ann had been twenty-three minutes late, Freddy was twenty-five minutes overdue. I had to wonder, was this going to become a feature every year, a sort of necessary part of the order of service? Rubric: "Then shall the preacher arrive just in time to save the Rector from his nervous breakdown."

Freddy was remarkable. He had told me: "I can't speak off the cuff and I can't bear to read an address, so what I'll do is memorise it and recite it." Which he did with affecting cadences and eloquent inflection. But it was what he said which caused the riot:

"The regime was totalitarian. It pretended to freedom but really the people were enslaved. Now, you must be wondering why I'm telling you about my time in East Germany in the 1960s. But actually I'm not. I'm talking about life in Europe today under the EU dictatorship…"

And afterwards they all with one accord said the boy done good. Except – in the crowded luncheon buffet, the Master of the Drapers, John Padovan, rebuked me blisteringly, "What did you mean by engaging that Forsyth fellow? I am to entertain a visitor this week - Romano Prodi, just appointed President of the European Commission!"

I heard from my spies that this had been such a big deal that Padovan came within a whisker of severing all contact between Drapers and St Michael's for the duration of my incumbency. But John was a bigger man than that. Things went very quiet for a while and then he invited me to a private lunch at Drapers with himself and the Clerk. Don't mention the war.

"Now, Peter, I'd like to do something to help your Theological Foundation. What would be best?"

"I'm hoping to put on a St Michael's Festival – music and lectures – during the summer."

"Would £5000 be any use to you?"

Music. I was surrounded by music, drowning in ecstasy. And all the better because at both churches we made our own music. It was a rare privilege to sit down with the director of music at St Michael's and say such as, "I wonder if this term we could have Masses by Tallis and Byrd, Beethoven's Mass in C, Schubert in G and on Easter Sunday Mozart's Coronation Mass?" Yes we could. And we did with much else besides. Vaughan Williams' gloriously rustic-mystical Mass in A-minor, Haydn's St Nicholas, Lassus, Palestrina, the excruciatingly loud Langlais and even some very early settings which had not been heard in St Michael's before.

The City opened the door on all possibilities. The finest singers and instrumentalists would come to us – all I had to do was ask. For example, I heard the lyrical tenor Robert Tear one day in *Figaro* on Radio Three and asked him if he would come and sing at one of our services.

"No, but I'd like to come and preach!"

That was a turn up. He did preach too at our Ash Wednesday Evensong. Vaguely Buddhist, was Bob, very let-go-and-live. He was well-received. Afterwards he said, "My heart sank when I saw the old lady in your choir who was to sing the Allegri *Miserere*. But my God, I've never heard it better: top C and all!"

That was Ruth and she sang the piece every year until she was at least seventy-five. This was the start of a ten-years' friendship with Bob, ended only by his death in 2011. He was a past president of The Arts Club in Dover Street – Algernon Charles Swinburne's old haunt - and I became a member through Bob. Regular lunches together of such outrageous hilarity we often came close to being chucked out. Plainly, Bob was a genius. A genial genius. I watched him give a master class to two young sopranos – on Schubert songs. Their performance of these songs by the time he'd finished with them bore no comparison to the enthusiastic but rough and ready style of their initial rendering. And all Bob had seemed to do for the whole hour was gently flirt with them both!

His sense of humour and of the ridiculous - particularly his own ridiculousness, that was the most lovable part – was boundless and legendary. The deputy director of the Royal Opera House told me how Bob constantly played practical jokes on his fellow musicians. One day a long-suffering orchestral player decided enough was enough. Bob was due to sing the premier of some hideous new piece – the sort that is known among seasoned musicians as three whistles and a fart. The orchestral player glued together the sheets of Bob's copy of the score. He hadn't practised. He was just going to wing it, sight-read.

"When it came to the performance then, what did he do?"

"He just made it up. Few if any were the wiser."

When it came to the music programmes, we were, to use Ezra Pound's phrase, regularly "refreshed with shards of ecstasy."

The celebrated, now emeritus, Master of the Music at York Minster, Francis Jackson came to stay for the inside of a week at The Watch House, bringing his wife. If anything, Francis has an even more cheeky twinkle than Bob Tear. Around the dining table he was incorrigible. One evening I had to be at St Michael's for a rehearsal and I came back and joined Francis when it was all over.

"What music did you have this evening, Peter?"

"Practice for Sunday. Mozart – The Coronation."

In that faux weary high alto of his, he said, "Never heard of it!"

I produced the score from the piano stool and Francis promptly sat down and – you know all those fast quaver passages in the Agnus Dei? – he played them in octaves. There were giants in those days. Francis is a giant about five feet in his high heels. And as I write this recollection of him, he's still playing three organ recitals a week anywhere in the world and making mischief. He's only ninety-seven.

Ralph Vaughan Williams was sometime director of the St Michael's Singers and his widow Ursula invited me to tea. Silver tray. Done proper. Ursula was every bit as talented as Ralph, an original poet speaking in her own voice. She wanted to talk about him:

"He was so amusing. He told a charming tale about how he and Elgar were once coming back from a City banquet, having dined well.

They saw a rather forlorn figure slumped across a doorstep. They were in that twilight zone, that mood of sentimental philanthropy. So they decided to open the front door and shove the bloke back inside. Congratulating themselves on their fellow-feeling, Edward and Ralph resumed their course – only to see a little boy at the upstairs window and hear him call out, 'Oi mister, that's not my dad!'"

A couple of years later Ursula came to a concert at St Sep's. It was crowded and she was an elderly lady, so I thought she might like to avail herself of The Watch House loo in the interval. Seeing her through the sitting room, I asked, "Would you like anything to drink? Cup of tea? Coffee?"

"Oh no thank you. Nothing at all."

"Gin and tonic?"

"Yes, please – and make it a large one!"

Music. Music and literature. I made a thing about getting some Eliot read every Ash Wednesday. The obvious, but one year I thought we might go for *The Waste Land*. Who to read it then? I asked Diana Rigg and she replied immediately, "Yes, please. But I'll have to have a good look at it first. I really don't know the poem very well."

Such was her commitment that she took herself off for several tutorials with an Oxford professor of English. On the day, I was walking towards St Michael's in good time for the service when I caught sight of Diana in a coffee bar across the road, swotting her lines. I rescued her and took her into the vestry. John Gaze asked, "Will you want the sound system?"

The resonance of her articulation showed at once that she wouldn't. And so she ascended the pulpit.

"April is the cruellest month, breeding lilacs out of the dead land…"

From the first line there was that stamp of indubitable authority. Eliot would have loved it. He couldn't read like that. Afterwards, Diana was anxious to be off to the West End where her daughter was making her debut in a new play. It's the very devil to get a taxi around 7pm in the City. One of our PCC members flagged down one that was already engaged, opened the door and enquired, "Would you chaps mind sharing a cab with Diana Rigg?"

She had no trouble after that.

I just pause for breath now and to try to correct any – very understandable – conclusions I might have placed in your mind.

Being a City Rector was not all wine and roses. And, having just spent twenty years as a country parson in Yorkshire where the hospitality quotient was a couple of pints of Sam Smith's in The Boot and Shoe, I was by no means accustomed to a milieu that floated on Champagne. Just pints of Yorkshire beer now and then. I was used to the same frugality in music too: the village choir, not all this ubiquitous, high-octane, wall-to-wall Palestrina and Purcell. I enjoyed the wine and the roses – and the music – of course I did. But I like to think I didn't take it all entirely for granted. And in any case it wasn't a matter of meandering from this posh reception to that sublime concert: there was a heavy routine. And, looking back into my diaries now as I write, I sometimes wonder how I stood the pace. There were endless committee and business meetings concerned with renewing the fabric at St Sepulchre. Interminable. Think of the myth of Sisyphus. I seemed to have to roll that particular boulder up the hill four times every week. And all the hours spent money-raising. The music didn't grow on trees and had to be paid for. Not cheap. There was the director of music's stipend – not inconsiderable – to provide for. And his commuter ticket from his house in Surrey. Ten in the choir. Forty quid a head per service. Go figure, as they say.

And there was the regular schedule of services. Sunday, of course. Then lunchtime Mass (said with one minute sermon) Wednesdays and Fridays at St Michael's, Thursdays at St Sepulchre. Choral Evensong at St Sep's every Tuesday. And the usual run of pastoralia: christenings, weddings, funerals – to which we must add that City favourite, the Memorial Service. This is how it works. An old banker decides to shuffle off his mortal coil. He worked in the City but lived in Sevenoaks. So the funeral is held in Sevenoaks with his family. His mates in the bank want to pay their respects too, and naturally to have a good nosh and booze up in his memory. So they book a City church and pack it out with cronies. The usual format is much like the City Service with traditional readings and warhorse hymns, to which are added short (we hope, though I have known differently!) addresses by said cronies paying tribute to old Jack who was, by all accounts…well, I'll go into more detail a bit later on.

There were the annual services, Masters' election services and carol services for our attached livery companies: six attending St Michael's and three at St Sep's. All these things came as big surprises to me. And there was another thing which struck me as curious… I had been used to visiting parishioners in their homes or in hospital when they were ill. I'd not been more than a few weeks in the City when I heard that one of our churchwardens was in the Royal Free. So I got on the bus and went to see him. He was recovering from surgery, relaxing in his dressing gown. I knocked at the door and he opened, saying, "Rector – what do you want?"

He looked about as pleased to see me as if I'd been the grim reaper himself.

"Well, I heard you were in dock. I'm your friend and parish priest. I've come to see you."

"That's extremely kind of you, Peter." And he cried. Blimey – don't City types expect their priest to care about them?

There were other entertainments. I wrote occasionally for a think tank called The Social Affairs Unit, an institution which takes a traditional line on public affairs. This was 1999 and Blair's New Labour had been ruling the roost for a couple of years. Blair had said that his government was going to be different from previous Labour administrations – hence the "New". There wasn't going to be any of that Clause Four nonsense or a blank cheque for welfarism. Frank Field, the principled MP for Birkenhead, had been commissioned to "think the unthinkable" and rationalise the welfare and social support system. Frank duly reported to his master Tony who promptly told him that his proposed reforms were, after all, uncongenial to the socialist ideologues who still wielded the power, despite that "New." Frank was understandably disgruntled. He had invited a small gang of us from the SAU - Digby Anderson, Ken Minogue, Dennis O'Keeffe and one or two others – to discuss the government and public life. Frank opened: "Actually, I haven't asked you come to talk about social affairs. I just want to tell you what it's like to be a cabinet minister on a typical day under the Blair regime."

There followed a hilarious-horrific account of spin-doctoring, PR, wheeler-dealing and all manner of chicanery. As Frank said, "Government is now a branch of the advertising industry."

III

At St Sepulchre, our musical heaven seemed frequently set in a physical hell. Choirs, instrumental groups and even whole orchestras based in the City began to apply to use the church – with its resonant and forgiving acoustic – for rehearsals and performances. George Bernard Shaw said that hell is full of musical amateurs. But even amateurs need to go to the lavatory, and the church had only one loo. In fact this loo was not even in the church. It was the downstairs facility for the occupants of The Watch House and right outside my kitchen door. Whenever there was a musical event, there would be a constant procession of performers and members of their audience through the connecting door from the church to the rectory – with noises off that can well be imagined. And while they attended to their comfort, they would practise their scales or gossip loudly among themselves as they queued. That was not all, or even the worst of it. Musicians who had booked the church, and again their audiences, would not actually enter the church by the porch but ring the doorbell of The Watch House and there was a constant procession throughout the evening. Meanwhile the colossal overuse of the lavatory meant that it was often blocked with…sundries.

We needed the rental money if ever we were to revive the church according to the original plan. We needed the money just to pay the extortionate annual diocesan tax known as The Common Fund.

We inaugurated a Wednesday lunchtime recital, often given by advanced students from the Guildhall School of Music and Drama. And thereby hangs a very sorry tale. The bishop told me at my appointment that negotiations between himself and his agents and the authorities at GSM&D were well-advanced for the school to make St Sepulchre their main rehearsal space and indeed their concert hall. This would have solved the church's financial problems at a stroke, for the school was flush with endowments and grants, most conspicuously from The City Corporation who regard the GSM&D as their flagship. However, at my first meeting with the principal, I was told abruptly that the school had received a better offer and they were reneging on the agreement. So St Sep's was going to have to make its own way and we determined to enhance our reputation for music, as befits The National Musicians' Church, with musical virtuosi of world renown: Sir Colin Davis, the pianist Imogen Cooper playing Mozart piano concertos and, the most glorious of the lot, The Sixteen conducted by Harry Christophers. Whenever they came in to rehearse, there was nothing for it but to stop whatever I was doing and creep into church to listen. It was not too much of an agony to cast aside the relentlessly futile diocesan paperwork. Bu I was also trying to produce a book to be published by the Foundation, *Words from St Michael's*, a collection of sermons on the Sunday gospel readings. And I had a deadline.

And, by the way, the latrine at St Michael's – which was actually in the church – resembled something out of a TV promo concerning dread diseases in equatorial Africa. Just a step above a hole in the ground. We managed to raise the cash to have decent loos, a kitchen and some accommodation for the choir, much of this owing to the benign influence of my friend Keith Robinson at the Stock Exchange who blessedly *leaned on* the diocesan authorities on our behalf. What vengeance I was thereby stoking up for later years was a matter of indifference to me at the time. I was determined to make these once glorious, now moribund, churches sparkle. The congregation for the Parish Eucharist at St Michael's now numbered around fifty

Under the auspices of the Theological Foundation – for which I was also fully occupied trying to raise funds – I tried to engage a series of talks and lectures at St Michael's. It soon dawned on me that the chief employment of those who run City churches was neither pastoral nor sacramental, but consisted in fund-raising and unblocking lavatories. I was fortunate indeed to have someone who performed that service for me. But the fund-raising was all mine.

I was delighted when Michael Brearley, the former extremely successful England cricket captain, agreed to speak to us – but not about cricket or even about leadership on which he had published a bestselling book. Mike was a psychotherapist, in fact a psychoanalyst, as it turned out a rather doctrinaire Freudian. The church was full of cricket fans, but they were captivated in any case by Mike's informed, intelligent and easy-going style. I had arranged through the good offices of John Gaze, to take Mike and a couple of guests to the Carlton Club for dinner. It was a hot night in that interminably torrid summer of 1999. The City is unbearable in these conditions. The huge office buildings crammed into narrow streets act as storage heaters and you can actually feel their radiation as you pass by. The damp tarpaulin sky holds in the heat, liberally flavoured with traffic fumes. The noise seems only to increase the temperature.

It was stickily hot in the Carlton too and Mike and I took off our jackets. So here comes the steward (to Mike): "I'm sorry Sir, we have a dress code and gentlemen must wear their jackets at dinner."

Mike is one of the least bolshy, least antinomian men I have ever met, and he poured forth gallons of apologies and put his jacket back on. I put mine on too. The steward (to me this time) "Oh Father, you don't need to do that. A priest is always regarded as correctly dressed in his clerical shirt and collar." I kept my jacket on anyway by way of solidarity. Mike was full of glee, just loving the outrageous farce of it all. A very nice dinner. All I wanted to do was to ask the great cricket captain how he managed robust characters such as Ian Botham and what it was like facing Dennis Lillee on that glassy fast track at the WACA. But Mike had discovered that I had published a book *Being Saved*, which was a comparison of Christian doctrine and the categories of Jungian psychology. So there was not so much about Lillee's bouncers and a lot more about the archetypes of the Collective Unconscious. Unfortunately.

Following Mike we were addressed by Fay Weldon, one of the gentlest and most humane characters I've ever come across. She spoke vehemently, in her quiet way, in favour of *The Book of Common Prayer*. My aged aunt Doris from New Zealand was holidaying with us at the time. Fay is a Kiwi. They giggled together inseparably for most of the evening. Then Melanie Philipps, the erstwhile ferocious feminist turned social conservative - and with a vengeance - explained to a bemused lunchtime audience in St Mike's how men are the downtrodden sex nowadays. After her, Peter Hughes, the curator of the Wallace Collection who was followed by the deputy director of the National Gallery, Ian Robinson on Shakespeare and, last of the term, to me the highlight of the season, Professor John Macquarrie.

Fifty- five people had turned up to hear him. Macquarrie was a theologian of the first rank. I first came across him at college in the mid-sixties, from his celebrated 1956 book *An Existentialist Theology* which was a comparison of the metaphysics of Martin

Heidegger and Professor Rudolf Bultmann of Marburg who was attempting to "demythologise" the gospels. John's talk was memorable for one remark he made in answer to a question:

"D'you think God really exists?"

"God does not exist: God is that which allows everything that does exist to exist."

I took him - John, not God – next door but one to the City University Club for lunch where he repeated the remark. I asked him if he thought it possible to reconcile an existentialist theology with the whole panoply of Catholic doctrine and ritual.

"Of course. Why don't *you* do it, Peter?"

Well, I never tried to write a big book about it, but Macquarrie's remark provoked me to a particular tactic in theological interpretation, in my sermons for example. It was a very practical device, since I have never thought much of theories, or academics if it comes to that. Reminding me of the definition of an academic as a man whose mind is so fine that it has never been penetrated by a single idea. As Orwell said, "Eschew jargon." I have made such eschewing my life's work. For a thing to be said at all, it must be said plainly. Orwell again: "Don't say, 'Objective consideration of contemporary phenomena compels the conclusion...' say, 'I looked and saw...'." The Bible and the real prayer book have no trouble with plain words. In fact, whenever these books are aiming to instruct us in the deepest matters, they invariably resort to words of one syllable: "With this ring I thee wed"; "Man that is born of a woman hath but a short time to live"; "This is my body...this is my blood..." What I learnt from that casually fertile remark of Macquarrie's was always to relate the personal religion of individual encounter with God to the full complement of the Catholic faith as expressed in the magisterium of doctrine. As Coleridge said, "I am weary of evidences. Only make a man *feel* the truth of his religion." He wasn't talking about touchy-feely either, but about incarnation. Words made into things. I would go so far to say that that is the whole task of the teacher and the preacher. No one was ever saved by means of a *formula*.

My first Easter in the City provided an interesting pastoral diversion. A young insurance broker, a dapper eccentric , always in a double-breasted blazer and with his black hair sleeked back – he might have been a minor character from P.G. Wodehouse -Jason, took to attending the Friday lunchtime Mass at St Michael's but, since he was not Confirmed, he was unable to receive the Sacrament.

"We can put that right at once, Jason. The bishop is holding a Confirmation Service at St Paul's on Easter Eve. Shall I ask him to add your name to his list?"

We arrived just before 6pm – Jason (without his Argonauts) and me with Jason's father, an old sea dog affectionately known as Curly. A minor canon called Lucy Winkett was in charge of the choreography. I had never met her before but knew her by repute. She had been the central character in a recent television documentary about the canons when much had been made of the alleged persecution Lucy had experienced by misogynistic male clergy. Later I discovered that the reality had been almost exactly the reverse. Among the modernists and lefties who constituted the cathedral chapter, there was one exception, Canon, Dr John Halliburton, an outstanding scholar from whom in due course I came to learn a lot, who was constantly made to suffer by all the others for his principled doctrinal objections to the ordination of women. These modern, so called "liberal" Christians are liberal in the reduced sense that they tolerate only those who agree with them. For "liberal" read "totalitarian."

Of course I didn't mention any of this to the photogenic and excitable Minor Canon Lucy. I asked her how she was enjoying being a priest at the cathedral. She was very candid, "I'm making progress, I hope. But if I find I really can't settle in the priesthood, I can always go back to my singing."

"Wow, what a profound sense of vocation!" Well, I thought it, but resisted saying it. Lucy has certainly made progress. She was subsequently made Rector of that phantasmagoric New Agey shrine St James Piccadilly which I mentioned earlier. And she is an occasional doyenne of *Thought for the Day*. I am writing this a week after the Synod voted in favour of appointing women to the episcopate and it is generally supposed that Lucy is one of the fair sex being fast-tracked for an early mitre.

The Confirmation Service was according to the new worship book. Noddy language. As if they had replaced The General Thanksgiving with The General Infantilisation. That one of our great national churches should so despise the miraculous text of *The Book of Common Prayer* and opt for banalities perfectly demonstrates the quality of the minds of those who run the place. In the sermon the bishop's booming rhetoric was well up to his usual standard. The trendy establishment at St Paul's explicitly hates the old prayer book and the old Bible. I say explicitly, because they told me in as many words. It was like this…St Sepulchre's did not have a lectern edition of the *King James Bible* and it occurred to me that St Paul's might have one to spare which I could borrow. The canon I spoke to on the phone could not have been more obliging:

"Borrow it? You can have it. We never use *The King James Bible* here except when Royalty come – awkward people like that!"

Anyhow, Jason was made kosher and Curly was shiningly proud of him.

Jason's dad was a former merchant seaman and, according to his son, "a rambunctious old bugger." He was religious in the sense that he kept regular observances. Every morning he went to his wife's grave and sat there for a while, had a smoke then went on to the pub for six pints of beer and three glasses of whisky. Then home to cook Jason's supper.

His bronchitis, always a trouble to him, got worse and, after a mercifully short period of distressing illness, he died. Jason wanted to do things right for the old man, so he hired a coach and horses and decorated the cortege with ostrich feathers and the coffin with the Red Ensign in honour of his dad's sea-going days. We must have looked like a scene out of Dickens as we set out on our way to the church – making sure that the coach passed the pub where Curly had for so long and with such diligence done his boozing. The procession stopped at another of the hostelries which the old man had frequented over many years. Jason had promised his father that the cortege would make a formal halt here. The old man was duly laid out in state in the four ale bar, his usual pint on top of the coffin. A toast was proposed and bizarrely we drank to the health of the deceased.

The church service was a simple family affair – heartfelt with unpretentious short speeches from the family and the clergy, including a very amusing one from Jason himself. Then we were off across the road to the cemetery. It was a brilliant blue and golden January day and there was still frost on the ground at one o'clock. We meandered to the graveside and began the words of committal. The praying finished, the undertaker's men stepped forward to lower the coffin into the earth. Embarrassingly, it would not go into the hole. It was stuck. The men angled and shoved and grunted and grimaced, but still it would not go in. By some mischance or miscalculation, the grave had been dug too small.

Nothing for it then but for one of the men to take off his frock coat – to reveal a t-shirt with the skull and crossbones on the back and an advertising slogan on the front FCUK – and start to dig. Digging graves is hard work at the best of times, but trying to remove frosted earth requires the strength of Hercules and the patience of Job. Twenty minutes later and after three more attempts to get the old man to his last rest, the substantial congregation were clearly bemused and embarrassed. It was then that Jason relieved the tension by calling out in a loud and cheerful voice: "Ah well, dad, y'old bugger, you were always too tight…" He meant tipsy, not stingy – "…when you were alive, and now you're too tight to fit into your own grave!"

That did the trick. One more shove and Curly slid into his neat little patch of winter's earth and the rest of us went back to his local to spend the afternoon in gleeful recollection of the unusual manner of his departing.

There were legendary figures among the City clergy and none more renowned and revered than Fr John Paul of St James Garlickhythe, headquarters of The Prayer Book Society. John was an Aussie, about five foot-three and one of the most powerful and influential priests the City churches have ever seen. In the early 1990s the Church of England in the diocese of London found itself in the not unaccustomed situation of being critically short of money. So what do you do? Try to raise the money? Exhort priests and people to pull out all the stops? No, this is the Church of England, so you set up a committee, get some bigwig to front it and call it a Commission. They hit upon Lord Templeman for the smoke and mirrors job and the Commission's "findings" were that most of the City churches should be closed. The Templeman plan envisaged only four or five churches to be left open, the number of clergy drastically reduced and the ecclesiastical organisation remodelled on something that looked like Berlin before the breaking down of the wall: four sectors with a senior clergyman in overall authority and a few assistant, and mainly non-stipendiary – that's "unpaid" in ordinary English, isn't it? - under him. Worthy of Stalin himself.

John was having none of this defeatism and bureaucratic take-over. So he wrote to the Lord Mayor, the Corporation and all one hundred livery companies and told them what was afoot. He gathered about him a small group of highly intelligent and motivated people and produced his antidote to the Templeman reductionist defeatism, typically following St Paul and calling his report *A More Excellent Way*. He booked the Guildhall and assembled all the movers and shakers in the City to gainsay the Stalinist scheme. And he won, enlisting a huge City-wide commitment to keep open and working as many of the City churches as possible.

John ran a thing called the Advanced Sunday School, a cross between a theological seminar and a think tank. He invited me to speak. Lunch first, prepared by John's wife Lynette. The food was delicious and I ate so much I knew I was in danger of falling asleep during my own sermon in defence of *The Book of Common Prayer*. In the course of my address, I remarked that I had heard of a modernising bishop who, in his previous incarnation as principal of a theological college, and at the time of the promotion of the ghastly *Alternative Service Book*, had encouraged his students in a ritual pantomime in which they burnt a copy of the *BCP*. In my lily-livered way, I said, "I suppose I'd better not name him."

Up sprang John from the pews and exclaimed in his wide-open Aussie twang, "Oi'll nime him. Colin Buchanan."

John was not, as he appeared, a small man. He was a giant.

Meanwhile, twenty-five yards from my front door they were laying the foundations for that new Merrill Lynch HQ. Pile-driving for eight hours, five days a week. Every two seconds the heavy whatsit thudded into the ground and The Watch House shook on its own foundations. It was like living inside some metal canister while someone caned the outside with an iron bar. Merrill Lynch had a PR man in the shape of a community relations officer. I asked him over for a cup of tea.

"There's nothing we can do, I'm afraid," he explained, smiling enchantingly. "But the pile-driving will be finished inside a couple of months."

What he didn't tell me was the pile-driving would be followed by three months of steel-erecting. It was the same pandemonium, only at a higher pitch than the whatsit's thud. And, when the three months were up, there came the procession of cement-mixer lorries – all day long for a further nine weeks. Something must have registered with the community relations officer, for one morning there was a letter in a very upmarket envelope inviting me, on behalf of the chief executive no less, to Merrill Lynch's topping out ceremony on the new roof. The chief executive greeted me over the Champagne: "I'm so sorry – it must have been very disquieting for you all these weeks."

"Disquieting"? He was certainly a man for the *mot juste*.

I said, "Well, at least when it's done it'll be finished." It was all I could think to say.

"Not for long. Modern companies like to change their iconic signatures regularly. They'll knock it down and put something else up in twenty years or so.

"Disquieting." "Iconic signatures." The man was a walking thesaurus.

I lived three hundred yards from the palatial Smithfield meat market. Literally palatial, for the main hall with its fifteen tons iron gates was modelled on a renaissance palace. I walked along Giltspur Street into West Smithfield most days, calling at my newsagents, the Iraqi escapee Mr Shakir whose iconic signature was, "You can't win!" Occasionally I would slip into *The Bishop's Finger* for a pint of *Spitfire*, then on to Trevor the butcher who, seeing my dog collar, immediately fired off a salvo of filthy jokes. The only antidote was to retaliate with jokes that were even more scurrilous. Shakir and Trev were good mates for all the fourteen years of my sojourn in the City.

It's odd, but when I was a country parson in Yorkshire I used to hate to have to travel up to London to meet a publisher or a newspaper editor. The great sprawl seemed too dirty, too noisy and just too big, a place colonised by demons. I couldn't wait to get business over and be back on the train from King's Cross. But actually living here was quite different and, after a year or so, I was coming to love my life in the Square Mile. I speak of the City, but really it is a tale of two cities: the Monday to Friday pandemonium of 70,000 workers commuting in and out; then the weekend when there was no one around and what few shops there were all closed. Mr Shakir never opened his newsagents on Saturdays and Sundays. Why should he when it was very likely that I would have been his only customer? Apart from the Barbican – all beautiful within but the exterior, post-war concrete brutalism - hardly anyone lived in the Square Mile. I said to my friend Alex Boot, who was born and raised in Moscow, "The Barbican's like the bloody Lubyanka."

He sniffed and looked towards one of the concrete towers: "The Lubyaka is a palace beside that pile of…"

The character of the City when I was there would have been unrecognisable to a banker or broker from thirty years back. We've all seen the newsreel pictures of the City in the 1940s, and the photographs in *Picture Post*. The City men in their uniforms: bowlers, formal jackets, striped trousers, umbrellas and with neatly folded copies of *The Times* under their arms. A crowd flowed over London Bridge, so many. I had not thought death had undone so many. And when any one of those bankers arrived at his office – at about 9.45, just in time for a cup of coffee – he would first spend ten minutes with his secretary to recap the order of the day.

"You have a meeting with Sir Brian Taylor. I've booked the table for you at *Simpson's*."

Look at the post, make a few phone calls and perhaps dictate a couple of letters. Then it's pretty well time for lunch. An enlivening amble from King William Street to *Simpson's* in The Strand. There would be people you stopped to talk to on the way. Perhaps Sir Brian would be in the restaurant already. That's fine. He would have been shown to your usual table, and be saying Good morning to his gin and tonic. Two or three courses as a rule. At least one bottle of claret or burgundy. And the port. A black cab back to the office at a quarter to four. All this was not merely sybaritic – not at all, in fact. Long lunches were where the business was done.

"Any messages?"

Sign the letters dictated during the morning and then pick up the bowler and *The Times* and back over London Bridge heading for, as it might be Haywards Heath or Three Bridges.

It's not like that now. The uniform has been discarded, or rather it has been exchanged for a different uniform: expensive smart casual – not every man wearing a tie. Not so many copies of *The Times* either but more likely one of the free sheets *Metro* or *City AM*, picked up at the station or even discovered on the train. And now there are women too - thousands of them – in their slick black suits and carrying designer handbags. I'm not talking about that 9.45 tempo either. They are all in by 6.30 or 7.00 at the latest. Maybe half an hour in the bank's gym and then to the desk and the computer screen, there to sit all day with a sandwich at one o'clock. No long lunches. No "alcohol," as wine is disdainfully described by the prefects in this new Puritan order. And no leaving for the train at 5pm. No one wants to be the first to quit that desk – or rather to be seen to quit the desk. Eventually, around 7pm one will wimpishly give in and, after offering a paltry excuse for leaving so early, make his way shamefacedly to the exit. Only then will others follow, ones and twos, slowly, unsmiling. This is the new regime, only slightly different on the last working day widely observed as "dress down Friday," when it's jeans and t-shirts, and a brightly coloured skirt for the lady and a white silk blouse. Friday five o'clock is "alcohol" time – and with what vengeance. The flight to the pubs and wine bars. The noise of the jollity is terrific. After the week's tortuous overworking, it's as if the workers have all blown their corks, and I don't just mean the Champagne bottles. There is a custom which I've not seen anywhere else and that is for whole hordes of workers to take their booze outside and crowd the pavements. The atmosphere of Thank God It's Friday – and the drinking – might continue until midnight and beyond.

Just before Christmas 1999, I took a phone call from David Conway, professor of philosophy at Middlesex: "Peter – would you like to come and see me in the New Year? I have a proposition." So I went one January morning to David's house in north London.

"The university has a scheme in which we offer doctorates on the basis of a chap's record of work. I believe it used be called his *oeuvre.* I've been reading your books and you would qualify for the PhD – so long as you're prepared to submit a 30,000 words summary of what your books are about."

So I went back to The Watch House and began work, slotting it in, as it were, where it would fit among the services, the livery courts, the dinners, the committees, the fund-raising and the rubbish tip of ludicrous paperwork. Just before Easter I phoned and told David the summary was done.

"Good. Now you need to come in for your *viva voce.*"

There were three of them in the classroom at the university. Professor Roger Homan from Brighton, David himself and another whom I knew not. It was not the grilling I'd expected but really a rather friendly and fascinating chat about matters which, after all, had been my life's interest. Some agreeable banter here and there too:

"Peter, you say that in Jungian terminology - and in western art, of course - the Virgin Mary wears blue because she is the Earth Mother clothed by the Sky Father. But Mary was never pictured in blue until we hit upon lapis lazuli."

"Well, I think if we discover a Lady has been wearing the same colour dress for eight hundred years, we might expect to recognise her in it."

I was pleased that they were nice about my summary, but...

"You really ought to give us more footnotes."

I said, "I did think about putting more in, but then I thought footnotes which are surely necessary in a fellow who's twenty-three ought to be invisible by the time he gets to be fifty-eight!"

I put them in anyhow, turned up in July in my hired red robe to receive my scrap of parchment, watched by my aged aunt Doris, from New Zealand, who was holidaying with us.

Roger Homan is a man of great charm, subtlety and wit. He is also nearly blind and sadly becoming more so. I invited him to come and preach at St Michael's where he told a delicious story:

"I was on holiday in Rome and I wandered into a church, as far as I could see up the aisle to the chancel step. I was dimly aware of a priest's surplice touching my arm. Only it wasn't a white surplice, it was a white dress, worn of course by the bride!"

No harm done, and Roger ended up being invited to join the Reception.

In June 2002 I dedicated a Sunday Parish Mass in thanksgiving for the Queen's Golden Jubilee. I know the proper anniversary of the Accession is 6th February, but it is better to arrange a garden party in the summer rather than during the late winter gloom. Throughout my ministry I have been grateful for the kindness of local businesses. If you ask nicely, most will give you what you want. So, for our Jubilee party, Fuller's - brewers of *London Pride* – donated a gross of cans of their best bitter. And the sun shone.

It was wonderful to see millions turn out in towns and villages all over the country to show their love and gratitude to Her Majesty, and so to see off all those dreary media prophecies about the Monarchy as doomed. Instead, it was the left wing pundits in the press and the BBC who were doomed, as the crowds lined The Mall in their hundreds of thousands. Of course the usual suspects in the Church of England crawled out to perform their usual spoiling act. For example *Church Times* – a sort of ecclesiastical *Pravda* these days – gave a page to the Reverend Dr Kenneth Leech who used the space to write, "Monarchy is opposed to the Christian tradition of equality." What equality is this when in fact the church itself is hierarchical with its archbishops, bishops, priests and deacons? The only equality in the Christian religion is in the true doctrine that we are all equal in the sight of God. Leech peevishly referred to Her Majesty as "… that child of God whom some people call the Queen." *Some people.* Quite a lot of people, Ken, to judge by the tens of thousands of street parties nationwide. He said, "The Jubilee stands for the preservation of inequality, privilege and injustice."

Shame on the editor of *Church Times* for letting this class warrior and East End apparatchik loose to spit on the celebrations. His article drips with malice and hatred: "At every point, monarchy is opposed to the Christian tradition of equality and solidarity." But nothing shows more equality and solidarity than Richard Hooker's definition of the Anglican Settlement: "Every man of England a member of the Church of England under the Monarch." I suppose Ken would prefer the equality for which socialism was renowned under Lenin, Stalin, Chairman Mau and a score of dictatorial and shambolic regimes in eastern Europe and South America? I was brought up – and so was Leech, if he would but face facts – in a Christian tradition that declares "Fear God and honour the King" (1 Peter 2:17); in which the Sovereign is Defender of the Faith and Supreme Governor of the Church; and in which the Monarch, in the Royal declaration annexed to *The Book of Common Prayer*, says, "We hold it most agreeable to this our kingly office and our own religious zeal to maintain and conserve the church committed to our charge." Or Article Thirty-seven of the Thirty-nine Articles where it says, "The King's Majesty hath the chief power in this realm of England of all estates of the realm, whether they be ecclesiastical or civil." The Queen is not above the law, as the socialist dictators were. She is the embodiment of the democratic, principle providing the focus of unity for all her subjects regardless of their divergent political opinions – only so long as these opinions are not anarchical or treasonous.

All this was beyond our Ken.

Leech asked us to pity him and his cronies: "In 1974 a small group of eight socialist Anglican Catholics met at St Matthew's Bethnal Green. We felt isolated in the church because we were on the Left." This must be some sort of paranoid, sick joke. Now that the Berlin wall has come down, there are more lefties in the General Synod than there are in Russia. It is they with their socialist policies who have ruled the church for these last thirty years – or would Leech have us believe that it was not the Synod but the Tory Party at prayer which advocated unilateral nuclear disarmament in its official publication *The Church and the Bomb* and devised the Marxist policy document *Faith in the City*? The Synod, and particularly its Board for Social Responsibility, is dominated by socialists and collectivists who constantly issue their reports on every aspect of public life and policy.

IV

"How do you cope with all those dying people and the funerals? "

It's the question I'm asked more than any other. There are two answers, I think. First, we have rituals and forms of words in prayers for the sick and the Burial of the Dead in *The Book of Common Prayer*. And, contrary to what's generally supposed, the burial service is one of the more cheerful rites in that book. The Marriage Service – properly called *The Solemnisation of Holy Matrimony* – can be rather depressing with all its talk of "fornication...carnal lusts...brute beasts with no understanding...those who have not the gift of continency..." and so on. But the funeral starts with the resurrection of the dead: "I know that my Redeemer liveth and that he shall stand at the latter day upon the earth." It goes on, relentlessly confident, "Though worms destroy this body, yet in my flesh shall I see God." The firm belief that God loves us and that therefore we have nothing to fear because we are in his hands resounds throughout: "Thou knowest Lord the secrets of our hearts." And supremely the climax, the words of the Son of God himself: "Come ye blessed children of my Father, receive the kingdom prepared for you from the beginning of the world."

There, does that make you feel any better?

Of course it helps if you actually believe it. The confidence expressed in the old funeral rite is overwhelming, even outrageous. The service starts with the melancholy tolling of a bell. Then here comes a man leading in a corpse. Yet the first words he says are the plain declaration that this person now dead will at the end stand up and see God. But is it true? It's too much of a tall story for many. St Paul does not lack confidence: "If in this life only we have hope in Christ, we are of all men most miserable." But St Paul is far from miserable. Rather he chooses the subject of death in his Epistle to the Corinthians – the lesson prescribed to be read at the funeral – and makes of it a long ecstatic poem celebrating life:

"O death where is thy sting?
O grave where is thy victory?
The sting of death is sin
And the strength of sin is the law
But thanks be to God which giveth us the victory
Through Our Lord Jesus Christ."

Yes, I admit it is a tall story and the funeral service itself agrees, saying: "In the midst of life we are in death." But the point is that *The Book of Common Prayer* is unfailingly accurate when it describes human nature. It knows that we are sinners – deviants from the will of God. It understands our weakness and lack of faith, our selfishness, lust, covetousness, envy, hatred and malice. And a book which has us bang to rights in every aspect of our lives is surely not suddenly to go wildly wrong when it speaks to us of death? The astounding truth of the Gospel is that no matter how rotten you feel – no matter how rotten you *are* – Jesus Christ has redeemed you. And, as Dr Johnson used to say, "There's an end on't."

Unfortunately, there are many in the clergy who don't believe it. They think that the Christian faith consists of social work among the poor. In fact it's worse than that, for they don't even have a realistic notion of who the poor are, but instead merely ape and mouth the secular fantasies about "equality," "diversity," "inclusivity" and all the associated claptrap. I don't know how much the modern clergy love the poor, but I do know that they hate the rich. So what do they do, these secularist politicos in cassock and surplice, when it comes to the divine and supernatural parts of the Gospel which are the foundations of it all? They treat these stories, these doctrines – the Virgin Birth, The Resurrection and Ascension – as metaphors. They are the ones to whom St Paul's words apply precisely: "If in this life only we have hope in Christ, we are of all men most miserable." They are futile.

I have read countless books and articles by modern theologians which assert that the miracles never happened: they are only "acted parables." But As G.K. Chesterton said, "They don't deny the resurrection because their liberal Christianity allows them to doubt it, but because their very strict materialism doesn't allow them to believe it." In other words, they are all Enlightenment men. But the secular dogmas of the Enlightenment are, I suggest, more dodgy than any clause in the Nicene Creed. Why start doing philosophy as late as the 18th century? The modern theologians forever remind us that "Jesus was a man of his time" – while forgetting the fact that *they too are men of their time.* And so they come close to supposing that anyone who lived a long time ago must have been stupid and that we were all in the dark until that 18th century arrived. Well, that word "Enlightenment" says as much explicitly.

So how do I cope with all the death and the funerals? By believing the promises of Jesus Christ. When you do this, you will be dismissed by the modern types as a "fundamentalist" – to which the appropriate response is, "Very well, but *something* has to be fundamental and I would rather believe in the words of Jesus Christ, who never once showed himself to be untrustworthy, than in all the implausible dogmas of materialism. And when a priest *does* believe Christ's promises – to which should be added the spiritual and philosophical insights of such as St Paul and St Augustine – he has a context into which to set the facts of suffering and death. Once the profound theological truths are grasped and accepted, the pastoral work flows on from them perfectly naturally. At the graveside, throwing earth on the coffin, or at the bedside of a dying man, the believer does not see the same scene as that perceived by the unbeliever.

Some of the priest's most rewarding – and occasionally hilarious experiences – happen in the close presence of death. A friend and parishioner, Richard Lewis was dying and his son asked me to come to the hospital and say prayers – the prayers which are commonly referred to as the Last Rites. There is nothing gloomy or macabre about these prayers. We are living in the presence of God, not in a Dracula film. These prayers are the Our Father, the Absolution: "Pardon and deliver you from all your sins and bring you to everlasting life." And the most beautiful of all:

"Go forth on thy way O Christian soul, in the name of God the Father, who created thee; in the name of Jesus Christ, Son of the living God, who suffered for thee; in the name of the Holy Ghost, who was poured forth upon thee; in the name of the glorious and ever blessed Virgin Mary, Mother of God. And may the cherubim and seraphim and all the holy angels receive thee this day into heaven with Lazarus who once was poor."

Richard had suffered a distressing final illness and he had not spoken or moved for a week. I stood by the bed and began the prayers. When I was nearly at the end, he moved his arm very slightly and made a soft sound which was remarkably like, "Thanks."

Moving. How about hilarious? Our parish treasurer at St Sepulchre was in an expensive private nursing home and nearing the end after a long period of suffering. His wife asked me to give him the Last Rites. He was deeply unconscious and had been so for some time. Certainly, he was not expected to live more than a day or two. I said the prayers, blessed him and left the hospital ward. Later that day, I took a phone call from his wife to say that Andrew was sitting up and cheerfully asking for something to eat. The hilarious bit was what she said next: "Thank you for coming, Peter. But I don't think you should come again!" (That nursing home was *very* expensive)

The Royal Regiment of Fusiliers' Memorial Chapel is on the south side of St Sepulchre's, and I was invited to be Chaplain to the Fusiliers' Association. Every year, names of old soldiers recently departed this life are inscribed on oak panels extending the whole length of the south wall and the Chaplain dedicates the new panels at the Remembrance Sunday Parade. Is as event of surpassing dignity and honour, beginning at the war memorial at Holborn Bar. A poignant mix of solemn recollection, pride, triumph, thanksgiving and hope. *Dulce et decorum est pro patria mori* is out of fashion in an age that forms its opinions about war from *Blackadder* and subscribes to the slogan "lions led by donkeys." The memorials and the hymns speak of our Glorious Dead, but you frequently hear it said that there's nothing glorious about war. Of course there is. It's just that there's much else about war that is far from glorious: the slaughter of the innocent, the destruction of whole lands and lives and the bitterness which persists long after the guns have fallen silent. What glory remains is in the courage and self-sacrifice demonstrated by so many who are called out of quiet obscurity to rise to duties and displays of character they never imagined they were capable of. And the comradeship of the regiments.

Sniffer dogs have inspected the church for evidence of impending sabotage or terrorist activity. The traffic is halted. Assembled by 10.45 are serving soldiers, cadets and the ever-diminishing company of veterans. The barked orders. The wreath-laying. Binyon's "Age shall not weary them, nor the years condemn; at the going down of the sun and in the morning, we will remember them." And the response from the whole parade together with hundreds joining in from the pavements: "We will remember them." We notice that it does not go, "We *shall* remember them" but "We *will...*" for the sincere act of memorial requires a parallel act of volition and intent. The Last Post. The drums beating the four hundred yards march across Holborn Viaduct to church and the soldiers' hymn *O Valiant Heart*. Scores of extra chairs have had to be brought in to accommodate the congregation of four hundred. The Chaplain takes his place in the sanctuary and four veterans slow march up the aisle carrying the Regimental colours. The Memorial Chapel contains colours from long ago – the oldest from about 1750, ragged now, fretted and falling apart. But they must never be removed, however tattered. For old soldiers never die, they only fade away.

What to say in the sermon on such an overwhelming occasion? I feel inadequate for I have never been a soldier. But my father served in the RAF during the Second World War and my father-in-Law at El Alamein. I have numbered soldiers, sailors and airmen among my dearest friends and colleagues all through my career. In all this time, I have never met a soldier who wanted to go to war. Yet every soldier I have had the honour to meet always knew the truth of Edmund Burke's saying: "The only thing necessary for the triumph of evil is for good men to do nothing."

And I have long been sickened to see how Remembrance Sunday has been hijacked in the schools by trendy teachers and in the churches by the sackless pacifist clergy. The only war poetry that gets read is the maudlin, cowardly stuff by Wilfred Owen. And in most churches on Remembrance Sunday, the prayers are always about the horror of war and the evil of war. Now every soldier knows more than these armchair politicos about the horror of war and the evil of war – because it is the soldier who has to fight it. But what the soldier also knows is that there are worse evils than warfare. Worse than warfare is non-resistance in the face of the aggressor who would kill or enslave you, your family, our nation.

I have had plenty of opportunity to get acquainted with the York Quaker pacifist ladies. Let me tell you, this sort is not harmless. They are not merely picturesque, quaint, high-minded eccentrics flitting between the tea shops in Stonegate. Pacifism is the enemy of peace, because it is the enemy of justice and righteousness. For pacifism always prefers the triumph of evil to necessary resistance. Pacifism and the appeasement of the aggressor always leads to more trouble in the long run. If you appease the crocodile, don't think he won't eat you. He will just eat you *last*. If the governments of the allied nations had listened to Churchill, Harold Nicholson and Duff Cooper in the 1930s instead of to the treacherous Lord Halifax and the lying Rab Butler, Hitler could have been stopped in his tracks and millions of lives would have been saved.

The soldier-poet T.E.Hulme, killed by one of the last shells to fall in the First World War, succinctly describes the reality: "The pacifists' incapacity to realise the consequences of defeat arises from a relativist, utilitarian ethic. They live securely and comfortably, finding a sufficient support in a sceptical rationalism. But individuals in a condition of danger, when the pseudo-absolutes melt away into a flux, require once more a real absolute to enable them to live."

And the pacifist churchmen forget that Christ who said, "Blessed are the peacemakers" also said, "I come not to send peace but a sword." I am tired of having to listen to the slander by those clergymen and schoolteachers who make up today's liberal establishment in which they speak of patriotism, the love of one's country and the willingness to lay down one's life as "jingoism." I cannot abide the fact that the memory of our valiant dead is ungratefully insulted in this way. And they foolishly – or deliberately? – misinterpret Johnson's definition of patriotism as "the last refuge of a scoundrel" to suggest that it is patriotism which is scoundrelly. That's not what he meant at all. He meant that the scoundrel is such a cad that he will even pretend to patriotism to further his own ends.

In short the Christian believes that death is not the worst thing that can happen: worse, far worse, than death is the triumph of wrong. This is why the Thirty-Nine Articles of Religion in *The Book of Common Prayer* – Articles which all the clergy are obliged to recite and affirm – contain these words: "It is lawful for Christian men, at the commandment of the Magistrate, to wear weapons and serve in the wars."

Greater love hath no man than this: that he lay down his life for his friends.

Afterwards, outside the porch, as I was saying Good Morning to the worshippers on their way to lunch, the Brigadier whispered, "Thank you, Padre. You're the first parson in years I've heard with a ******* good word for the army!"

Colonel George Pettifar, chairman of the Memorial Chapel Committee and his vivacious wife Beverley, invited me to the Regiment's HQ at the Tower of London to witness the Ceremony of the Keys. This has been performed every night at the Tower since the 14th century. At precisely 9.53pm, the Chief Yeoman Warder, dressed in Tudor watch-coat, meets a military escort made up of members of the Tower of London Guard and together they secure the main gates of the Tower. Upon their return down Water Lane, the party are challenged by the sentry to identify themselves:

> Sentry: "Halt! Who comes there?"
> Chief Warder: "The keys."
> Sentry: "Whose keys?"
> Chief Warder: "Queen Elizabeth's keys."
> Sentry: "Pass Queen Elizabeth's Keys. All is well."

After this, the party makes its way through the Bloody Tower Archway into the fortress, where they halt at the bottom of the Broadwalk Steps. At the top of the Steps, under the command of their officer, the Tower Guard present arms and the Chief Warder raises his hat, proclaiming:

> Chief Warder: "God preserve Queen Elizabeth."
> Sentry: "Amen!"

He then takes the keys to the Queen's House for safekeeping and the Last Post is sounded. I did wonder for a moment if I was now locked in for the night with the ghost of Anne Boleyn, "with 'er 'ead tucked underneath 'er arm." George and Bev showed me my way of escape.

The livery companies are various. The ancient ones were medieval trades guilds, each dedicated to a saint and many to the Virgin Mary, Ironically, it is some of the ancient companies which have lost their original character – for example, I don't think there are many liverymen of the Drapers who earn their living as drapers – and it is the more modern liveries whose members are hands on, so to speak. All members of the Air Pilots and Air Navigators are pilots or navigators and I know that most members of the Worshipful Company of Chartered Secretaries and Administrators are what they say they are. Which reminds me of an incident...

I was asked to be Chaplain to the Secs and Admins – known by their acronym WCCS&A – to be Company Chaplain. Delighted, especially as you get to turn up to dinners wearing a Chaplain's whatsit that hangs round your neck with the image of a secretary bird on it. My first duty was to say Grace at the annual banquet. Well, I worked up something that I hoped was mildly amusing, while expressing due thanks, of course:

"With reference to yours of 22nd
We accept this feast to which we're beckoned
To give thanks for fellowship and food
To the Maker and Preserver of all that's good:
We are much obliged that our thanks are heard –
Signed – in triplicate – Secretary Bird."

It was received with a round of applause and some prolonged laughter. So I was not displeased, thinking to myself that, whatever might follow, I had at least got off on the right foot. But things are only rarely what they seem. Three months later the Master Elect for the following year came to see me and asked if I would arrange the annual service and again say Grace at the dinner.

"Of course, it will be a pleasure."

"Only, just one thing: we don't want any levity. A few complained after last year that your Grace had been too jokey."

Then, hand on his heart, he added, "Not me, of course. I have a good sense of humour. But certain of the Past Masters are, shall we say, a bit stuffy."

Oh well! But what to say this year?

"O Lord, we beseech thee, remove from our hearts every tincture of levity; let joy be not once mentioned among us. And we ask this for Past Masters' sakes. Amen."

I was tempted. In the end I decided to say it in Latin, so most of the diners wouldn't know whether there was any levity in it or not.

I was – still am – Chaplain to both the Woolmen and the Fuellers companies in which most of the chaps are hands-on. So are the Master Mariners – and what a treat they are. They hold their service at St Michael's, first Friday every June. The church full of old sea dogs from the Merchant Navy. We always sang the great ocean-going Trinitarian hymn *Eternal Father Strong to Save* and the lesson from

The Acts of the Apostles about St Paul's shipwreck which one year was read so beguilingly by the Master that the whole congregation was almost sea-sick. But again, what to preach about? I have not spent as much time on the sea as I should have liked, but the saltiest thing I know is Ezra Pound's first *Canto*. So I read them a good chunk of that:

"And then went down to the ship,
Set keel to breakers, forth on the godly seas, and
We set up mast and sail on that swart ship,
Bore sheep aboard her, and our bodies also
Heavy with weeping, and winds from sternward
Bore us out onward with bellying canvas,
Circe's this craft, the trim-coifed goddess.
Then sat we amidships, wind jamming the tiller,
Thus with stretched sail, we went over sea till day's end.
Sun to his slumber, shadows o'er all the ocean,
Came we then to the bounds of deepest water,
To the Kimmerian lands, and peopled cities
Covered with close-webbed mist, un-pierced ever
With glitter of sun-rays
Nor with stars stretched, nor looking back from heaven
Swartest night stretched over wretched men there.
The ocean flowing backward, came we then to the place
Aforesaid by Circe…"

I have never seen a congregation – or an audience, come to that – so transfixed. But these were old sea dogs and Uncle Ez was a notorious elitist wasn't he?

After the service we piled on to the coach along Upper and Lower Thames Street…

"This music crept by me upon the waters
….up Queen Victoria Street.
O City, City I can sometimes hear
Beside a public bar in Lower Thames Street
The pleasant whining of a mandolin

And a clattering and chatter from within
Where fishermen lounge at noon where the walls
Of Magnus Martyr hold
Inexplicable splendour of Ionian white and gold."

....past Blackfriars to the livery hall of the Master Mariners for lunch. A ship, no less. Tne "HQS Wellington" moored at Temple Stairs. And so you go aboard for Champagne on the top deck and then into the bowels for asparagus, spring lamb, fruit salad and ice cream. The gentle swaying of the dining room on the tide is novel, reassuring and soporific.

My first acquaintance with the good ship Wellington was in May 1999 after I had solemnised the marriage of the daughter of the Clerk to the Master Mariners, John Maddock. It was a benign, motionless evening and, for once, the ship didn't sway or roll – reminding me of Coleridge's painted vessel in the poem. But the sky! It put to death once and for all those critics who said that J.M.W. Turner exaggerated. Clouds like tropical birds. Archetypal Westminster buildings poking through the warm mist.

I mentioned Coleridge, so I shouldn't forget his friend Charles Lamb, whose bust is on the front of The Watch House. This has its disadvantages, for it meant that I was regaled many an evening by City Guides loudly lecturing the tourists with legends of the City literati. Lamb was a wit of the surreal sort, with a broad taste in black humour. He once said, "Anything awful makes me laugh. I misbehaved once at a funeral." He's not the only one! Lamb was extremely sociable, clubbable and seemed always to be at a dinner somewhere with literary and artistic friends. At one of these gatherings, Sam Coleridge was holding forth as usual. In the course of his disquisition, he paused and turned to Lamb for support:

"I've been asked to preach in the cathedral. I've preached before, you know. You've heard me preach, haven't you Charles?"
"I never heard you do anything else!"

Wordsworth was forever trying to entice him to the Lakeland Fells, but Lamb would have none of it:

"You can keep your mountains. I love to live in other men's minds. I love reading. I cannot sit and think. Books think for me."

A pub landlord in the Lakes told me how his great grandfather, who had first managed the pub, entertained Wordsworth one day along with his whole family.

"What was he like – the great poet."

"Miserable bugger! He went off and left the children by themselves while he mumbled his verses into the wind. Miserable bugger – it were t'poetry that did it!"

When Lamb did stretch his legs, he paced himself in an extraordinary and idiosyncratic manner, never measuring by the mile but by how much drink he had earned for the distance he had walked. So once he said to Thomas Hood, with whom he rambled often, "Now, Tom, I have walked a pint."

Hood said of him, "Walking with Lamb was like going for a walk with Izaak Walton – minus the fishing."

So I was delighted to welcome the Charles Lamb Society to St Sepulchre to present talks about their hero. Twenty or thirty men and women of a certain age, avid, agreeable, enjoying the outing. It is these little societies that do more than anything else – and certainly more than the academic pursuit of literature – to keep the love of English letters alive. The first time they came, I led them in procession and blessed Lamb's memorial, sensing that he would have approved. Lamb's statue came to us from Christ Church Greyfriars which was the church traditionally attended by Christ's Hospital School where Coleridge and Lamb were pupils. Christ's Church had been almost completely destroyed by Hitler's bombs. The shell of it was in our parish, so it seemed right that the memorial should come to us.

Long ago, the school moved out of the City to Horsham, but they returned to St Sepulchre for their service to mark the 450th anniversary of their founding. It was a treat to have all those talented boys and girls in church, their singing and instrumental playing a fair height above that usually achieved by schoolchildren. Altogether an enchanting occasion: pupils, masters, parents, the boys in blue blazers, the girls in summer dresses. The only blemish on the event was that the music master made them play and sing the Te Deum to a setting by John Rutter. As everyone knows, the Te Deum ends with the anxious plea, "Let me never be confounded." And surely only Rutter could so score his musical setting that that the word "confounded" occurs on a fortissimo! What, for heaven's sake, is this supposed to indicate – triumphant despair, or the good news of our damnation?

Better was the two act drama by Leslie Irons, a member of the Lamb Society, called *My Gentle-hearted Charles*. It received its first performance in St Sepulchre. This is the sort of thing for which you think City churches were intended. It brought Lamb home where he belongs and his words shone all through Leslie's clever script. As the late afternoon sun filtered dustily through the west window, you could imagine you saw gentle-hearted Charles in the shadows, applauding discreetly. Lovable Lamb who once said, "The greatest blessing anyone can receive is to do a good action by stealth and have it found out by accident."

Just across the road, behind the Old Bailey in Warwick Lane, is Cutlers' Hall and hanging on the outside wall the Company's famous emblem, the elephant. In the past, ivory was used for the handles of high quality knives. Cutlers asked me to be their Chaplain and my first engagement was to say Grace at an annual event called the Surgical Awards Dinner. Here the prize-winners – young surgeons who were deemed to have made an outstanding contribution to medical science - were feted and presented with a significant cheque. Naturally, the award-winners would then propose a vote of thanks to the Company. This particular year the prize was given to two young Australians who confessed they didn't know anything about City livery companies and so would welcome some sort of steer to help them compose what they ought to say:

"Well, a livery company is rather like a club."

Alas, the young Aussies' idea of what constituted a club and what the Clerk to the Cutlers had in mind when he advised them were at some considerable variance. The young surgeons got to their feet and spoke as if they were doing stand-up in an ale house for sheep-shearers. The jokes were good jokes – but not so good as to make me stuff my hanky in my mouth to prevent my completely letting the side down. What did make me stuff my hanky in my mouth were the looks on the faces of the assembled liverymen and their ladies.

The jokes were filthy. Of course, nobody laughed. So the young docs thought they were not quite pulling out all the stops. They put that right by telling jokes that were even filthier – off the Richter scale. I suppose this was a good example of the educational function of the livery companies.

It was after the Surgical Awards dinner that I was the recipient of a generous gesture:

"Is your doctorate in theology, Peter?

"Philosophy"

"Do you get any – you know – regalia with it."

"I hired the red robe and mortar board for the degree ceremony."

"Well, the Company with buy them for you if you'll agree to wear them at our lunches and dinners."

They did and I have.

There is another summer event at Cutlers' Hall known as The Captain Boot Dinner. Francis George Boot was an employee of the Bank of England and Master of the Cutlers in 1894. He left £42,000 in his Will to the Company without conditions but with the hope that some of the money would be used to endow a dinner in his memory at which part of his Will would be read aloud. This is the part they read every year: "The wines and appointments should be the best of their kind and hospitality should be dispensed with no niggard hand."

It causes some funny looks, that "niggard."

V

In the millennium year, I was surprised – no, I was shocked incredulous – to receive an invitation to serve as Chaplain to the Lord Mayor. Brought up in Armley, a scruffy suburb of Leeds, notable perhaps only for its black castellated jail, I had of course seen on television the Lord Mayor's coach, but never imagined I would get to ride in it. Sir David Howard Bt, a churchwarden at St Michael's and Alderman for the ward of Cornhill, was to be elected to the Mayoralty that year. David was unique: the son of a Lord Mayor who himself was the son of a Lord Mayor. Before I recount my adventure further, I should say something about the governance of the City of London, an ancient and powerful institution which has been known to pick fights with medieval monarchs and win them. There are two courts: the Court of Common Councilmen, each elected to a ward in the City and the Court of Aldermen likewise. The Common Council is, as it were, the Commons and the Aldermanic Court the Lords. Then there are the two sheriffs: the Aldermanic Sheriff and the Lay Sheriff and these live and work in The Central Criminal Court - the Old Bailey - where a notable feature of their responsibility is to provide lunch in the Bailey each day, while the Criminal Court is in session, for the judges and their guests. The Sheriffs pay for this out of their own private resources. I've been to one of these lunches and it's the briskest of all formal meals in the City. It starts with a choice of drinks - gin or tomato juice – and proceeds at a pace. All done in three-quarters of an hour, then back into court, guests invited to take their places in the public galleries.

At the summit of this feudal pyramid of governance, sits the Lord Mayor. Literally feudal: the first man to occupy the office was Henry Fitz Aylwin in 1192. To say that the Lord Mayor is elected is quite true, in a sense. In reality it amounts to buggins' turn. The position always goes to one of the Aldermen on the principle of seniority, but the Aldermanic Court is a Machiavellian stockpot of factional interests and political "persuasion" – some of this friendly, some of it not. Despite the sectional interests, the Aldermen always contrive to come together in a unity of power on those occasions – and these are not infrequent – when they regard the candidate for the Mayoralty as "unsuitable."

As soon as the letter arrived, I went shopping for a pair of shoes with silver buckles and a tricorn hat. By the time I'd paid for the fancy shoes, there was nothing left in the kitty for the hat. By chance I came across one in a joke shop in Salisbury and it was mine for £1.50. Large brown envelopes began to arrive every day from Mansion House, setting out the various duties of the Chaplain: duties festooned with their traditional – quaint – protocols. Some of the lunches and dinners I was required to say Grace at were merely formal and so you put on the usual evening dress. Others, such as the Lord Mayor's Banquet at Guildhall, were designated "State" and these commanded the Chaplain to wear such an array of clothes that the aptest comment would be to say that even Solomon in all his glory was not arrayed like me. Not just a black cassock, but over it scarf and a Geneva gown. White gloves, preaching bands, the hat of course and Papageno's twinkly shoes.

Everyone on the Court of Aldermen knows at least three years beforehand who the next Lord Mayor is to be, but the election ceremony is held anyway in Guildhall. Representatives from more than a hundred livery companies fill the great hall and listen to orations from the Town Crier and the senior judge at the Old Bailey - known as the Recorder – and other bewigged and gowned officials with romantic titles such as the Remembrancer – which sounded to me like the name of a character from *Brave New World*. First, the name of the person who hopes to be Lord Mayor several years hence is called out and the chorus of liverymen answers back, "Not yet." Then the name of the next year's Lord Mayor, and the response is "Later." At last the real Lord Mayor is acclaimed by a unanimous "Aye." And that's what passes for the election.

Following the election, there is a further formality, a piece of pure theatre called the Silent Ceremony, when the Guildhall is once again packed with Aldermen, Common Councilmen and liverymen to witness in utter quiet while the incoming Lord Mayor subscribes to the Declaration of Loyalty. There is much exchanging of hats between the new Lord Mayor and the one outgoing, unnervingly entitled the Late Lord Mayor. A solemn pantomime and the silence in that cavernous hall so intense it seems to hiss.

In the very early morning, while it was yet dark, of the first Friday in November in the Year of Our Lord 2000, I put on my State costume and walked the half mile from The Watch House to Guildhall for a rehearsal of the Lord Mayor's procession the next day. The wet cobbles like a rocky shore at low tide. By the tall tower of Christ Church Greyfriars a single tree illuminated by the street lamps was the only dash of colour in the clinging blackness. City ceremonials invariably start with a drink, continue with several more and end with another, so that some participants have been known to be not only in State but in a state. But at 5.30am there was a rare concession to abstemiousness and the drink on offer was coffee. Parked outside Guildhall. like a scene from Cinderella, stood the 17th century State Coach and we practised getting into it. The only people who get to ride in the coach are the Sword-bearer in his fur hat, the Mace-bearer, the Chaplain and the Lord Mayor himself. The ceremonial Sword and Mace are taken in there as well, so it is a rather cramped elegance. The procession of State Coach, marching Pikemen and the two Sheriffs in their coaches, led by the City Marshal on horseback, set off for Mansion House, provoking a mixture of intrigue and irritation among the early motorists.

Bumping and rolling through the ancient streets of London town with their resounding names – Gresham Street, Cheapside and Poultry – awe is what one feels, awe and cramp. The Sword-bearer leant forward and whispered, "Tomorrow you'll have carrots under your seat for the horses. It's traditional." Once outside Mansion House, the Lord Mayor's official residence, we stopped and rehearsed getting out of the coaches and on to the balcony from where, next day, we would watch the decorated floats and the uniformed and costumed marchers. A triangle of weighty history: the Bank of England – that Old Lady of Threadneedle Street – the Royal Exchange, the Stock Exchange and the Cornhill branch of Lloyds where T.S. Eliot had once laboured in the foreign exchange department. By now the traffic had increased around our civic parade and car drivers were giving us uncivil black looks.

Lord Mayor's day dawned with a drenching and a gale. We sat under the striped canopy on the balcony of Mansion House while less privileged souls stood beneath in the wind and the rain to watch the pageant – under the direction, appropriately, of the Pageant Master: the regiments with their military bands, Life on the Ocean Wave…Men of Harlech…pride and nostalgia. Then the steel bands from Hackney and Brixton and the whirling dancers exotically under-dressed for the weather. The Fire brigade and the Red Cross, Police, Pensioners, Postmen. A single Lancaster bomber roared the RAF's fly past. Tremulously, I led the procession down the external staircase and got into the coach for the short ceremony on the steps of St Paul's and then on to the Law Courts. The Mace-bearer leant forward and said, "It's OK, I've got the carrots!" It teemed down all the way, but still thousands from all over London and beyond crammed the pavements and waved their flags. It wasn't a case of oiks doffing their caps to toffs. Those cheering, drenched people were celebrating something which gave them their own sense of identity. Despite the great egalitarian brainwashing which has gone on since the end of the Second World War and which has reached insane proportions recently, people still have the urge to defer to something or someone they esteem and value. And the nature of what you value shows you what you're worth. People will revere *something*. Better a nine hundred years mayoralty than a grade three celeb.

The Law Courts are pure Gilbert and Sullivan and on this historic but light-hearted occasion the exalted legal principals grinned like characters from one of the Savoy operas. The new Lord Mayor was presented to the Lord Chief Justice and to the Recorder whose speeches were all erudite banter and name-calling incorporating the more salacious remarks of the ancient Greek orators. Things were running late and I had ten seconds before the coach left for the journey back to Mansion House to grab two glasses of Champagne to refresh my Lord Mayor before he must be out in the street again acknowledging the greetings of his public. In fact things were running very late and the Sword-bearer said that, if we didn't get back to the delayed luncheon reception soon, he would eat the ceremonial carrots provided for the horses.

On the Monday following the presentation, there is always the Lord Mayor's Banquet at Guildhall. The Chaplain is made to stand behind the throne in State while the hundreds of guests are received, chief among them the Prime Minister and the Archbishop of Canterbury. There are many other such banquets in the Mayoral calendar and I was told by a member of staff that they reserved the finest wines for the dinner attended by all the bishops and archbishops. I was at that dinner. Mansion House a blur of purple and twittering ecclesiastical niceties with lashings of St Aubin Premier Cru Bourgogne washed down with gallons of Chateau Malartic-Lagraviere Pessac- Leognan 1993.

Quiet a contrast is the dinner which the Lord Mayor provides for the mayors of all the other London boroughs. Respectable toy-town civics for the most part, with just a dash of class warfare. Many of these mayors are from south of the river and some of them regard the City as the Great Satan that will be cast down when the revolution comes. When these types are presented, they approach the chair with smiles like acid indigestion and make their deep bows with cynical obsequiousness and sideways grins towards their fellow-travelling comrades. Towards the end of the dinner I passed some of this party as they staggered on the stairs. Most were on their way down (and out), but a few were tenaciously pressing back upwards into the main hall. Conversation as follows:

"Aren't you going home?"

"Not just yet. We're sticking around for a drop more of this f****** capitalist booze!"

You see quite a bit of the lumpen intelligentsia as the year rolls on – particularly among the clergy. A woman priest, all ironical and post-modern, with clanking earrings and a sanctimoniousness of which Caiaphas would have been proud, bumped into me at the Lord Mayor's Breakfast in the crypt at Guildhall. She was new to the City and she looked a bit lost, so I took my plate of scrambled eggs over to where she was picking at her bowl of muesli and asked if she were enjoying herself:

"Oh, it's all so white and middle class and male!"

"Oh dear, Esmeralda Salmonella, what did you expect – cans of lager, punk rock and bongo drums?"

I didn't say it. For all her high-minded misgivings, she still drank the Lord Mayor's mulled wine and scoffed his breakfast cereal even as she sneered. Another clergyman, with a resplendent complexion and a handshake cold as the living dead, told me with earnest ferocity: "I regard myself as a prophet to the City. The City is the enemy you know!" This from a man who is out to a livery dinner twice a week and whose church receives generous financial support from City institutions. Their hubris is terrifying. Their self-righteousness exceeds that of the Scribes and Pharisees. If they don't like the City, why the hell do they come to work here? Presumably to convert us all to their more excellent way. Count me out.

By the way, when I speak of the hospitality provided by the Lord Mayor, I mean to say that it really is his doing. The LM does receive a grant towards the cost of his year from the City Corporation but this doesn't pay for even a tenth of the total bill. The Lord Mayor has to be (as we say in Yorkshire) "Not short of a bob or two." Nothing wrong with that. It's commendable that a man should distribute his personal resources to civic causes and the general good.

I don't understand the leftie parsons. They don't seem to see the deeply paradoxical nature of their position. Here they all are, privileged members of an elite establishment, yet they talk as if they're living on a diet of locusts and wild honey. Worse, they completely lack any insight into their own political prejudices. All these social-gospellers, class warriors and liberation theologians – personal composites of Uriah Heep and Jane Austen's Mr Collins. And the Lord Mayor himself: it's not as if he spends his year floating from one banquet to the next in his limo with the number plate LMO. Sleeves actually get rolled up. How about his 5am visit to Billingsgate fish market? That's a typical day. Generally his minder calls him at 6am for a working breakfast, perhaps with some captains of industry, maybe with some foreign diplomats. Then an outing to a school or a hospital for a presentation or the like. A formal lunch, at which he must give a speech. Afternoon tea with another petitioning group. Then a dinner at which again he has to speak. Back to Mansion House by 11.30pm at best. And wait for the minder's six o'clock knock. He keeps this up all year – and takes in more than a few foreign tours to promote the City. If it's value for money you're looking for, look no further.

"Well, that's most interesting, because I too have been to the Old Town in Hastings. I'm a good four or five inches taller than you – but still not tall enough to see over that wall."

Michael and his wife Diana lived in the Old Bailey too but they had a house in Norwich where Michael had been a circuit judge until his appointment to the London Recordership in 1998 where he presided over some of the most high-profile trials of recent years. He was an extremely popular figure at the Old Bailey, noted for his courtesy and humour, his diligence and his thorough knowledge of the criminal law.

Perhaps the best-known case which Michael tried was that of Jane Andrews, the former assistant and dresser to the Duchess of York who murdered her lover, Tommy Cressman, by battering him with a cricket bat and stabbing him in the heart. "Nothing can justify what you did," Michael told the defendant as he jailed her for life in 2001. "It was a brutal attack."

Also in that year, he presided at the trial of Mark Woolley, jailed for life for the murder of the BBC costume designer Liz Sherlock at Euston Station. He also sentenced the serial sex killer David Mulcahy to a total of two hundred and fifty-eight years and three life terms. In 2000 he heard the case of David Copeland, who carried out three bomb attacks in London, killing three people and injuring scores of others. He was given six terms of life imprisonment.

Michael's dispensation of justice was always guided by painstaking consideration of the facts. Where he thought it deserved, punishment was severe, but he could be merciful as well. In 2001 he showed compassion to a nineteen-year-old girl who had killed the baby she conceived when she was raped; placing her under an eighteen months community rehabilitation order and telling her: "This is on any view a tragic case. You have already suffered a great deal." Two years earlier he had put on probation another nineteen-year-old who had killed her baby, accepting that she had been suffering from depression at the time.

A trial in 1999 presented amusing problems when Stephen "Tosh" McCuish - a Glaswegian accused of conspiracy to rob and the murder of a Wolverhampton netball referee - decided to sack his barrister and conduct his own defence. McCuish's Gorbals slang occasioned Michael to remark: "I must confess I am having some difficulty keeping my own notes of evidence." Necessary translations included: "Spallomine" (he is a friend); "Swiboggin, man" (the place smells awful, your Lordship); and "Shooraboot at?" (are you certain?).

In 1990, Michael had published a book *Learning the Skills of Advocacy*, which went into four reprints. In his two-legged days he had been a demon spin bowler, irritating the batsman by changing the field after almost every delivery. He baked his own bread. He took to phoning me regularly after the day in court, picked me up at The Watch House and we would go for a bite at Carluccio's in West Smithfield. Later he introduced me to his club, The Garrick, where he threw bread rolls at his pals and generally made mischief, returning late for a nightcap in his apartment back at the Old Bailey. Michael was a Jew and took it seriously with a regard for the Law as heartfelt as that of any Old Testament prophet. Particularly affecting was my stay over with him, his wife and their three sons for the Passover meal at his Norfolk home.

The day after the Lord Mayor's Banquet in 2001, Michael called at The Watch House: "I was sitting next to the Chinese Ambassador and he has invited us to dinner. He meant it too. For we're not being asked to the embassy but to his personal residence in Hampstead."

So we went. That's Michael, me and the Common Sergeant – another judge of high esteem at the Bailey disguised by the lowliness of his title. Peter Beaumont was a senior man and there was certainly nothing common or non-commissioned about him. As the limo picked its way through the early evening traffic, Michael turned to me with a look on his usually genial face which I hadn't seen before: "Look, just a word in your ear – and a word in my own ear, if it comes to that. This is serious international diplomacy. We must be careful what we say. None of your Tiananmen Square stuff."

Dinner was exquisite. Seven small courses, each one in turn tastier than its predecessor. The Ambassador's wife was our hostess. Michael's caution in mind, I was punctilious all through in avoiding anything that might provoke a raised eyebrow, let alone be the cause of a diplomatic incident. Michael was seated on the Ambassador's right and I on his left. I steered the conversation resolutely in the direction of Ming Vases, the Great Wall and the Terracotta Army. But towards the end of the evening, I thought I would ask just one question that was at least not entirely anodyne. It was only two months after the 9/11 atrocities in New York and I ventured: "Your Excellency, what is the policy of the Chinese People's Government regarding the so called war on terror?"

On a perfectly articulated non-stress-based monotone, the Ambassador replied: "Oh you mean the Muslims. We send the army out in buses, arrest them, fill them full of whisky and hang them from lamp-posts to encourage the others!"

I still can't decide whether he was telling the truth or merely teasing, having achieved his triumph in the art of being more outrageous than thou. I looked past him to Michael whose face wore the look of a practised poker-player.

The Recorder and the Rector enjoyed six years of fun and games, until one night in the summer of 2004, Michael phoned to say, "I've finished my thirty thousand words summing up in this terrorist trial. It's been a strain what with my being Jewish – and you know what religion the accused are. One hint of partiality, his defence will pounce and the case will collapse. Anyhow, it's finished at last. How are you fixed for the Garrick?"

"I'd love to, but it's the bloody Parochial Church Council meeting."

"Never mind, we'll go later in the week – maybe Friday."

We never made it. On the Thursday evening, Michael attended the annual dinner of the Institute of Barristers' Clerks and, seated between the Lord Chief Justice and the Master of the Rolls – two of his affectionate sparring partners in the Law Courts on Lord Mayor's Day – he suffered a heart attack and fell dead into his pudding.

A few days later I was invited across to the Old Bailey to hear brief tributes paid by the Lord Mayor and the Common Sergeant. I was at the last minute and had to thread myself through the crowded court. Number One Court. Michael's Court. The only space unoccupied was the dock, so I went and stood there. There came a familiar voice – well, in my head anyway: "Ah Peter, I've got you where you belong at last!"

I loved him.

C.G. Jung and the physicist Wolfgang Pauli co-authored a paper entitled, *Synchronicity: An Acausal Connecting Principle.* It was an attempt to understand those familiar and unnervingly frequent experiences which look like coincidences but hint there must be more to the matter than that. You know, you're in the library and you read the words "red admiral" and just at that moment a red admiral butterfly flutters by. Pauli tried to account for this is=n terms of quantum mechanics and parallel layers of reality and Jung by recourse to his theory of what he called the Collective Unconscious. I thought of this at my interview with Chartres back in 1998.

The bishop said, "I'm asking you to be priest at two City churches: St Michael, Cornhill and St Sepulchre-without-Newgate. Patrons of St Michael's are the Drapers' Company and their Patroness is the Blessed Virgin Mary. You've just published a book *Shrines of Our Lady.* St Sepulchre is the National Musicians' Church. You've written another book *A History of the Promenade Concerts.* I think these jobs have your name on them, don't you?"

Synchronicity, or what?

In March 2000 Nicholas Kenyon, Controller of the BBC Proms, came to see me: "I'd like to hold the international press launch for the millennium Proms at St Sepulchre."

Just like that, out of the blue. And it wouldn't do our St Sepulchre's restoration project any harm either. So we hosted the launch and they all came – not only the world's press but musical virtuosi of all sorts: opera singers, pianists, orchestral conductors and cathedral organists of the highest esteem. They devoured the Olympian buffet lunch, drank the BBC's best wines and made music. And so St Sep's was on the telly!

A couple of weeks later Nick phoned: "I'd like to give you a little treat in return for letting us borrow your church."

"Well, Nick, the occasion was treat enough in itself."

"O come on – let me persuade you! What I had in mind was a night at the opera – any of the operas in the ROH's current season."

I felt I'd gone to heaven – without the prior inconvenience of having to die.

"Would *Parsifal* be OK?"

It was more than OK. Four hours long, so there were two meal breaks. I recollected – I think it was Mark Twain and his being asked to give his opinion about Wagner's operas: "Wagner has some wonderful moments, but some dreadful three-quarters of an hour!"

Meanwhile, the City Service at St Michael's was coming along nicely and established as the premier religious observation in the Square Mile to begin the New Year. Ann Widdecombe and Frederick Forsyth were followed by the Archbishop of Westminster, Cormac Murphy-O'Connor. He began with a story: "I was at a crossroads in Ireland and there were two pubs. I asked a local which one was preferable for lunch. He said, 'Well now, y'see, if you goes in the one, you'll wish you'd gone in the other!"

That got us off to a fine start. Cormac preached a straight-bat sermon and afterwards, as I walked him across to Drapers' Hall for lunch, he asked me what I'd thought of it. What do you say? I said, "The people were listening and that's always a good sign. Then you said, 'Money is a good thing, but money isn't everything.' You were speaking to an audience of liverymen and institutional bankers who know that truth pretty well already. These people spend many an hour in boring committees trying to decide how to give their money away."

Change the subject. I had heard of Cormac's having been given his Red Hat by the Pope, so he was now Cardinal Cormac Murphy-O'Connor. We were just walking through the ornate front door of Drapers' Hall among all the hundreds of others who had sauntered across from church: "Thank you for coming *Cardinal*. Now you see what happens to a chap when His Holiness hears you've preached at St Michael's!"

He enjoyed his lunch and stayed late among the liverymen and bankers. I wonder what he talked about?

VI

Before I shut up for good about my year with the Lord Mayor, I should mention, if only briefly, the most enthralling, exhausting, torturing, agonising – and as many other adjectives as you can think of – day of my life. It was the Lord Mayor's children's party, first Saturday in January 2001. There is no respite. This thing goes on for six hours. Three hundred predators aged between seven and eleven. Conjurers, snake-charmers, ventriloquists and, worst of the lot, head-banging pop music ceaseless. And there's our Lord Mayor, jumping and jiving, rolling around on the floor. Jelly. Trifle. Ribbons, bunting, loudspeakers – and existential despair. I shouldn't grumble for I was lucky. For the term of my Chaplaincy I had a room to myself on the third floor of Mansion House, at the back. O boy, there was no haven like unto my haven! Two hours of the riot and I left the Lord Mayor and the Sheriffs to it and went for a lie down. They all went home with goody bags while I went home with a hangover – and all I'd had to drink was lemonade from a plastic cup

All the City churches are so treasured – loved, even – and to be Rector of one of them is to acquire privileged access to prominent people in political life and the arts. And I was doubly blessed, having the two churches in my care. Very few notables turned down an invitation to come and speak. Michael Howard, former leader of the Conservative Party, came to St Sepulchre and gave a lecture about John Smith and the founding of the colony of Virginia – a miracle of bravery and enterprise, turning that wasteland into a fertile and prosperous state. To begin with, the colonists nearly starved. And courage was required to fight off the hostile native tribes. Michael gave an address at St Michael's City Service as well. The actor Edward Fox is devoted to Eliot's *Four Quartets* and has learnt that whole long poem so he knows it by heart. He tours the country giving recitations and at our Choral Evensong on Ash Wednesday he offered us *Little Gidding* – showing us a different side of his character from that so ruggedly displayed as the would-be assassin of General De Gaulle in

The Day of the Jackal. And Sylvia Syms who adorned that thirsty film *Ice Cold in Alex.* I recalled her from Tony Hancock's *The Punch and Judy Man* in which she played his wife, Delia.

"How did you get on with Hancock? You hear such stories – that he was rude, even violent, especially to women."

"He was always perfectly charming when he was with me."

And who wouldn't be!

On 10th September 2001 I caught the train to Oxford to attend a clergy conference called by Bishop Chartres in St Catherine's College, a horrible piece of pretentious, concrete brutalism. It was the standard fare. A trendy yet clichéd title, "Urban Ministry in a Time of Change." But what time is not a time of change for the go-ahead hierarchy of the Church of England? Oxford: dreaming spires over the legendary home of lost causes. Why does it prove so attractive to the unreconstructed Stalinists who lectured us on our duty to the so called poor and the so called alienated? And the only remedies they offered were the unholy trinity of taxation, taxation, taxation; regulation, regulation, regulation; intervention, intervention, intervention. I looked down from the back of the lecture theatre and beheld in these churchy academics a virulent hatred for all our traditions and institutions and a petulant ambition to remodel the world – and particularly our part of it in the Diocese of London – on the model of the Comintern. "Men," as Tom Eliot said, "dreaming of systems so perfect that no one will need to be good." The language employed by the Distinguished Speakers was straight out of the handbook of Marxian sociology: "developing structures," "alienation of the proletariat," "criteria of primacy" and so on.

The worst of it was the church services. Three each day. Picture the scene: the beautiful medieval church of Holy Cross, just behind Merton's playing fields. How would you have ordered these services? Some fine organ music. Ancient and familiar prayers. Sermons that gave off some whiff of intelligence. The natural rhythms and affections of English Christianity to express and delight in a sense of continuity with our forefathers. Come off it! We're talking about the contemporary Church of England. Not one service from *The Book of Common Prayer* in three whole days. Let me deal with the "music" first and get it out of the way. Over in the Lady Chapel an out-of-tune piano which was itself out-of-tune with an accidental oboe; a violin giving a good impression of an agonised feline; and a sempiternal, grinning clergyman with a shaved head. He wasn't wearing the dog collar, but I knew he was a clergyman, for he was wielding a guitar. We sang banal and meaningless choruses to plinky-plonky noises of the Jesus Goes to Toy-town sort. Then we sat through horrific sermons. The Bishop of Stepney told us, "Doctrine doesn't matter." Tell it to Thomas More and Thomas Cranmer. "All you need is love," he said – just like *The Beatles*. There is nothing more arch than an out-of-date trendy. Now I don't like to frighten you, but I should tell you what the bishop said next. "In a few minutes, we shall offer one another a sign of peace. I don't want to see handshakes. I want to see you hugging one another. And then I'll tell you something else I want you to do...." (Those of a nervous disposition please feel free to close this book now) This clown, by the way, is now Archbishop of York, Primate of England.

The so-called "peace" was announced and, as usual, all hell broke loose. Five full minutes of people sauntering around sacred space proffering more or less sentimental or lewd salutations. When I was set upon by a vast and enthusiastic lady. I did my usual escape act and fell to my knees and, when she tried to lift me bodily into the furnace of her embrace, exclaimed, "No thank you, madam, I'm English!" Now with trepidation I come to the "something else" which the bishop had promised to ask us to do. Well, it makes you think...I had been dreading the onset of this for six or seven minutes. Sentamu bawled out, "I want you to turn to the person next you, put your hand on his or her shoulders..." – his or her – funny isn't it how political correctness survives all atrocities? – "...and say three times, 'You are everlastingly loved!'"

Luckily, I found myself not next to Deaconess Blenkinsop with the hot lips and fiery breath, but Father Alan Griffin, Rector of St James Garlickhythe, national HQ of The Prayer Book Society. I clenched my teeth and whispered, "You are everlastingly loved, Alan." Alan placed his hands affectionately on my shoulders and replied reassuringly, "It's all right, Peter. I'll buy you a pint come lunchtime." But this was by no means the end of the embarrassment. The Bishop of Stepney went into full pantomime mode: "That's not enough. Louder! Louder!" And he cocked his hand behind his ear, as Bruce Forsyth used to do on *The Generation Game*: "Nice to see you; to see you, nice!" I feared this was going to develop: "Now where's the Archdeacon? Has any little boy or little girl seen the Archdeacon?" Followed by a great chorus of "He's BEHIND you!" All this folly could, I suppose, be overlooked – except that the date was 11th September.

After that ludicrous service – really a disservice – I ate a light lunch, thanked Alan for the pint of *Marston Pedigree* and ambled into Oxford. I went into *Blackwells*, browsed for half an hour, bought some books then returned to my room and read for the rest of the afternoon. At six o'clock I went, duty bound, back to Holy Cross again for another dose of the horrific Noddy liturgy. Only this time the priest – with his shaved head, designer stubble, leather jacket and lisp – was telling us about the attacks on the USA. Then guess what? Silence perhaps? Tears? The General Confession? Of course not. But straight into more of the plinky-plonky, happy-crappy music and Jesus Goes to Toy-town again.

The trouble is that this diminished sort of spirituality, this bankrupt, dumbed-down, blasphemous style of worship could not begin to do justice to the terrible events which were unfolding across the Atlantic. There were, however, two redeeming features: Chartres gave a pertinent, off the cuff short address which was a masterpiece in précis. He was less of the thespian and more of the Christian shepherd on that awful day. Then Fr Chad Varah, ninety years old, founder of the Samaritans and famous for an article he wrote in *Cosmopolitan* magazine about something called "telephone sex."(Don't ask me!) Chad had been a City Rector since about 1066, appointed before the synodical rule requiring our retirement at three-score-years-and-ten, so they couldn't get rid of him. Many would have liked to. Anyhow, all unprompted, Chad burst forth in a loud voice with, "In the midst of life we are in death, of whom may we seek for succour but of thee O Lord, who for our sins art justly displeased..." It cut through all that out-of-rune, plinky-plonky, shaven-headed, lisping, sentimental, you are everlastingly loved/bored charade like a hot sabre through the flesh of roast piglet.

In the college bar after dinner, news was continuing to come in from New York on the big screen. The clergy were entirely predictable: "Oh I do hope Bush doesn't retaliate!"

I said, "I bloody well hope he does." And so made myself more popular than ever!

Next day I escaped from that conference and came back on the first train to London. I put on a Requiem Mass at St Sepulchre at twenty-four hours' notice and two hundred and fifty turned out for it. City types, as I've been telling you, can be a bit raucous, insensitive, philistine. Not that day. I swear no one moved a muscle for the thirty-five minutes, start to finish. No mobile phone went off. There was an atmosphere of intense reverence and sympathy. Here were people, largely un-churched, with more than an idea of the holy than the cream of London's clergy at an Oxford conference. We had no jogging-for-Jesus music, no smarmy grins, no creepy introduction of the "We are living in tragic times,,," variety. No superfluous ecclesiastical chat of any kind. I started off with "Requiem aeternam dona eis Dominie et lux perpetuam luceat eis... I know that my Redeemer liveth and that he shall stand upon the earth at the latter day; and though after my skin worms destroy this body, yet in my flesh shall I see God, whom I shall behold and not another." The sun burst suddenly through the stained glass and illuminated the altar spectrally. When it was all over I stood out in the street by the porch as the City workers walked out, many sobbing silently, and went back to their desks.

The adjacent HQ of Merrill Lynch with its trading floor the largest in Europe – about a hundred yards long. Three of the bank's employees were killed in the attack on the twin towers and their chief executive asked me to put on a Memorial Service for them in St Sepulchre. For this, three tall candles dominated the transept and the church was again filled with City workers. There were prayers and readings and a couple of well-known hymns. A soaring soprano from our choir led us into the first verse of *The Star-spangled Banner*. Then all – all who could quell the lump in their throats sufficiently – joined in. Reverence. Resolve. Defiance. I bloody well hope he does retaliate... The Requiem Mass and that Memorial Service show that, even in the 21st century, you can still be authentically religious – providing you start by ignoring most of the Church of England.

Rowan Williams, Archbishop of Canterbury, happened to be in New York when the terrorists struck and he swiftly wrote a short book about it, *Writing in the Dust*. It's frightening stuff. Dr Williams said the West should not fight back: "If I decide the answer in the same terms, that is how the conversation will continue." This implies that the suicide bombing of populous skyscrapers was an opening gambit in a conversation! Besides, the Archbishop was confused, for we did not "answer in the same terms." The response of the West was a disciplined military operation designed to eliminate specific terrorists, while the attack on New York was the indiscriminate slaughter of innocent civilians. There was also confusion in the Archbishop's mind between revenge and justice. While I may seek on my own behalf to follow the teaching of Christ to turn the other cheek, I must not do this on behalf of those of my own people who have suffered innocently. It is my duty to take up the sword on behalf of the fatherless children and the widows. Not to do this is to concede victory to the aggressors, and that would be unjust. Would Dr Williams argue that the brave men who fought back against the terrorists in the fourth plane were wrong to do so? If they had not summoned up oceans of courage – and, by the way, said the Lord's Prayer first – and attacked the terrorists, then certainly that fourth plane would have been deliberately crashed into another densely populated target and the loss of life would have been catastrophically greater.

Dr Williams would not even allow us to describe the terrorists as evil men: "Bombast about evil doesn't help in understanding anything." Well of course bombast about anything never gets anyone anywhere, but if we are not allowed to describe indiscriminate mass murderers as evil, then the word "evil" becomes denuded of all meaning. The Archbishop wanted us to "understand" the terrorists' motivation. He reckoned they had no choice: "We have something of the freedom to consider whether or not we turn to violence and so, in virtue of that very fact, are rather different from those who experience the world as leaving no other option." This is nonsense on stilts. Not every disaffected Muslim thinks the cure for all his woes is to blow up skyscrapers. And if the perpetrators, for whom Williams had so much sympathy, really did believe that they had no other alternative but to commit mass murder, then they were psychotic as well as psychopathic. Williams' analysis is a high grade example of the obsequious drivel we have heard ever since 9/11 from those in the West who despise the civilisation which is their inheritance, while they give house-room to barbarism.

Once we have declared that the atrocities were not the fault of the terrorists who perpetrated them, what next? "We begin to find some sense of what they and we together might recognise as good." It is at this point that confusion and nonsense declines into lunacy. Is it really possible to make common cause between democratic freedoms and the rule of law on the one hand and psychopathic, nihilistic killing on the other? In any case the Muslim fanatics have spelt it out for us: "We shall win – because you believe in life while we believe in death." How would we go about establishing this "common cause"? "Do come in and sit down Mr Bin Laden, pour yourself another orange juice and let's discuss world peace…"

Then Williams proceeded to dismiss the war on terrorism as "a discharge of tension." And he added, "What possible guarantee could there be that the abolition of terrorism had been achieved?" Well of course, in historical matters there are no guarantees, as there are no inevitabilities – unless you are a Marxist. Williams' own perversions of logic and truth excited him to draw absurd conclusions. But worse followed. For it was at this point that the Archbishop's misapprehensions descended into irritable fantasy. He said that the bombing campaign in Afghanistan "…assaulted public morale by allowing random killing as a matter of calculated policy." That was just not true. The coalition forces gave the Taliban scores of warnings before the bombing started and took great pains to avoid civilian casualties. Williams amply demonstrated his – insane – belief that there was a moral equivalence between the Western powers and Al Q'aeda. In fact it's worse even than that: I think he actually conceded to the terrorists the high moral ground. Williams merely prated the old story again of the nasty capitalists' cruel exploitation of the Third World's picturesque poor. He wrote, "We could ask whether the further destabilising of a massively resentful Muslim world were really unavoidable." The question is of whether petulance and resentment are deserving of rewards. When children become resentful, they sulk and at this point the teacher dispenses smacks or a spell in the naughty corner – not packets of sweeties.

Williams' fantasy turns out to be paranoid: "Every transaction in the developed economies of the West can be interpreted as an aggression against the economic losers in the worldwide game." But it is only the likes of Williams and Soviet-style Marxists who would make this interpretation. The facts disagree with the Archbishop, for many of those Third World countries which have decided to hitch their economic wagon to the Western engine have massively raised the living standards of their people. And it is the capitalism of the free market which has been the most powerful force the world has ever known in the alleviation of poverty. Is it only the modern clergyman who can't see this? Paranoia usually goes hand in hand with sentimentality and we saw buckets of the stuff in *Writing in the Dust*: "As we protest at how the West is hated, how we never meant to oppress or diminish other cultures, how we never meant to undermine Islamic integrity, we must try not to avoid the pain of grasping that we are not believed."

What, by the way and according to the suicide bombers, is "Islamic integrity" – beyond the oxymoron?

Williams' conclusion is the exact inversion of the truth: "It is hard to start any sort of conversation when your conversation partner believes, in all sincerity, that your aim is to silence them." I thought it was *they* who silenced *us* in all those three thousand innocents slaughtered in the cowardly and psychopathic attack on New York? One thing above all else puzzled me at the time and still does. Prime Minister Blair, to his credit, took a very firm line against the terrorists and in his support for the American President. But it was Blair who appointed Williams – a man who described himself as "a hairy leftie." I can understand that Williams was Blair's placed-man apparatchik, but didn't Blair read *Writing in the Dust* first?

Williams has been praised all over the newspapers as a man who excites us to awe and affection. He is even exalted here and there as a saint. In fact, as his writings reveal, he is an old-fashioned class warrior. He dislikes our way of life in the West, even while he enjoys more than an ordinary share of its privileges. And he romanticises the Islamic world quite as much as the old Marxist fellow-travellers used to romanticise the Soviet Union: G.B. Shaw, H.G Wells, the Webbs, CND and all those others whom Stalin called "useful idiots." Williams is of that company. Williams' political posturing wouldn't have mattered much in normal times, but the period after 9/11 was not normal times and we now live on the edge of destruction. Someone should have warned the Archbishop in the words of that slogan from the Second World War: "Careless talk costs lives."

London felt eerie after the New York bombings and many wondered whether they were the shape of things to come – and in London perhaps? That's why I caught that early train back home from Oxford: I knew I belonged in my parish. The Square Mile fell into a twitchy silence. None of the scores of passenger jets which usually thundered above the capital every day. We were temporarily a no-fly zone. There wasn't the ordinary vulgar raucousness. People went about their daily routine quietly. More attended the weekday Masses at both my churches. Some asked questions, "What does it all mean?" Who knows? But after two or three weeks attendances at these services fell away. You could feel that people were beginning to relax and breathe again.

You felt you needed a period of quiet reflection, but the pace never let up. Activity at the two churches was accelerating wildly and this was exciting and encouraging. The restoration and revival projects coming on apace: only the trouble was that, because the parishes had been down and nearly out for so long, we didn't have the infrastructure of officers and institutions to sustain us. I was on the lookout then not only for money but for volunteers. We required vergers to open and shut the churches, cleaners, and we urgently needed to recruit a parochial church council that was not merely decorative and somnambulant. There was too much lack-a-day. For example, at St Michael's the PCC secretary, Ivor, a very senior civil servant recently retired, took notes at our meetings. Very nice – except that they were in pencil and illegible. So I had to develop the skills of Bletchley Park first to decipher them and then ask someone to type them up. Also I had decided from the start that, hectic as the parochial tasks drove, I must on no account neglect the interior life. I have too often seen the consequences of such neglect in my fellow priests: they become mere functionaries, ecclesiastical automata. I believe the Christian doctrines fundamentally and I regard the Mass as essential to life. I thrive on the work of pastoral care. I would say I am religious then, but not especially pious and I hope not at all pietistic. This aspect is nauseating where it appears. Parsons gazing into clerical suppliers' catalogues as though transfixed by pornography. High camp in the sanctuary. Fastidious, affected Anglocatholics in their cigarette-ash besmirched cassocks, knocking back the G&Ts and keeping a loving eye out for the choirboys. I think I once described the genre as "lacenick and old arse." To be avoided.

Conversation is necessary. I don't mean chatter – and especially not from the sort who think that the apogee of verbal communication is to provide the itinerary of their diurnal routine from early lav to bath time, not omitting to mention the vital detail that they had a cream bun (for once) rather than a croissant with their mid-morning de-caff. I abhor the forensic and paleontogical dust of most exhibitions, the museum culture generally and the chirruping of its touristy devotees who love to be associated, if only by default, with "people who matter." I cannot read academic books and regard them as the plague of the un-dead. I do read literature: Augustine, Johnson, Kant, Schopenhauer, Coleridge, Nietzsche, Wittgenstein and even Freud sometimes – one of the few men who could write beautifully while writing rubbish. I need music. Mozart, naturally. And I try to play the piano. Mozart, unnaturally. I enjoy – I think that's the word - the test of trying to write something sensible about the gospel every Sunday and I was still writing the weekly column for *The Northern Echo* and occasional pieces to the *Daily Telegraph* and *The Wall Street Journal* And I determined to write a book each year to help maintain the interior life – or, as I would rather say, to keep myself out of trouble. In short, I find it impossible to do nothing. But I cannot subscribe either to the prevailing supposition that *anything* is better than nothing. Believe me, it isn't. But that is as much confession as you're going to get out of me for a while. Let me talk about someone much more interesting...

I published that little book of sermons *Words from St Michael's* which they bought in good quantities over the after-Mass booze in the garden. And a small collection of poems *Words and Worse* which came to the notice of Sir Jeremy Morse, former Chancellor of Bristol University and Chairman of Lloyds Bank. Sir Jeremy also served on the board of the Bank of England and he invited me to a private lunch in that establishment. A wondrous place. Behind the stony façade there are the most elegant gardens. As you look out of the window on the courtyard side, you could think you were in deepest Sussex. Jeremy was a logophile if ever there was one. His record of success in the clue-writing competitions of Ximenes and Azed is such that Azed dedicated one year's competition puzzle to Jeremy's 80th birthday. He publishes puzzles under the pseudonym Esrom. He wrote a significant book called *Chess Problems: Tasks and Records* and he was a regular contributor to *The Journal of Recreational Linguistics.* Moreover, Colin Dexter named his fictional detective after him.

We sat over lunch for an hour and a half and Jeremy was generously nice about my verse, but he really wanted to talk about Eliot and I must say I was much more inclined to discuss *il migglio fabbro* than my own meagre efforts. He too seemed puzzled by the lack of interiority among the parsons, of what Denis Healey once called "hinterland" and he asked me straight out, "What do the clergy *do*? Do they ever *think*?" He was asking the wrong bloke. Then he took me down into the garden and presented me with a personal cheque for £2000 for St Michael's Foundation. Neither was it his last contribution to that cause.

There came a new diversion. I invited Christopher Gill, the Eurosceptic Tory MP to come and talk to us and he was eloquent about the sins, negligences and ignorances of his political masters. Christopher was Chairman of The Freedom Association, founded by the Viscount De L'Isle, Norris and Ross McWhirter and John Gouriet in 1975 as a non-partisan, centre-right, libertarian group in favour of our leaving the EU. Most restrained and gentlemanly in the reassuring old England style, Christopher was well-received. And a couple of weeks later came his invitation to a return match. Would I give a lecture to the TFA's London conference? Why not – it might be fun. I composed a piece called *The Twilight of Our Institutions* in which I argued that the bedrock of our society is not the vaunted and chimerical notion of "democracy" but the law, the church, parliament, the university and the monarchy, and that our understanding of these priceless assets had been degraded and dumbed down in the interests of political correctness and – Blair's persistent theme – modernisation. So I found myself invited to become Chaplain to TFA, a privilege I have enjoyed these last fourteen years. One of the treats of the year was to go to Stanway in the Cotswolds as the guests of the Lord of the Manor. Such a setting – the Cotswold stone of the great house glowing like a great ingot in the setting sun – and in the garden the fountain shooting rainbow colours a hundred feet into the air. Then give a talk in the medieval barn and retire to supper and the Lord's good wines.

I was driven to catch my train by the pulchritudinous twenty-three year old Christiana Hambro, daughter of the famous financier. Lovely ride through the countryside to Moreton-in-Marsh. I said, "It's very kind of you to do this."

"Not at all. We live nearby. We have a farm. Actually, we have three farms."

In fact the Hambro family owns virtually all the land between Moreton and Stow: a hundred and forty miles of the most fertile land in Europe. How many £billions is that worth?

Not long after I was asked to give the Hobart lecture at the Institute of Economic Affairs. What fun! I gave them a variation of the lecture I had presented to TFA and was thoroughly denounced for my pains. Geoffrey Howe was there and he had seemed friendly enough over lunch. I asked him how Lady Howe was getting on these days and he seemed to welcome the enquiry. But he walked out during my talk muttering the accusation that Mullen was "a latter day Savonarola." I took it as a compliment. Altogether, five walked out during the talk. And I was exuberantly congratulated by the IEA's director: "Best ever! Well done, Peter – you've got the record!" I gave another talk there sometime later which I entitled *Bishops' Tipple; Why is the Church of England Hierarchy Addicted to Welfarism?*. Well, you can imagine…I'll pass on without further comment. I was asked to talk to executives in a couple of City banks about capitalism. They seemed surprised when I said something along the following lines:

50% of Britain's GDP goes to the public sector. In so called communist China it is only 17%. At the height of their totalitarian tyranny, the Soviets were only spending 10% more than we do today. Never mind the anti-capitalist rhetoric, examine the facts. You are taxed on your wages. Then you pay 20% VAT on nearly everything you buy with the money on which you have already been taxed.

Fuel taxes are at an outrageously high level. If we have a car we pay road tax. If we drink or smoke, the price of our pints and fags are artificially inflated by taxation. Governments ask people to save, so to reduce the burden of taxation. But the prudent who do save are paid little or no interest. In fact, with rates as they are, savers - especially among the older generation - are actually losing money by their thrift. If we do save, we are taxed again on the meagre interest

If we do our bit by buying shares in British companies, we are taxed on our dividends. There are further taxes on share dealing. The state broadcasting propaganda department fiercely polices an annual tax called the TV licence. The industrial, commercial, financial and manufacturing companies which generate income for the country pay large sums in Corporation Tax and other business taxes. And, in the form of Inheritance Tax, we have to pay up again even when we're dead. British businesses which ought to be leading our economic recovery are prevented by labyrinthine corporate and state regulation.

Is this what the senior clergy call "capitalism"? These levels of taxation and regulation are combining to hinder economic recovery. And such taxes are required only because the government needs them to pay for its massively expanded army of civil servants, its quango mountain, its legions of useless box-tickers, its lousy education system, the failing and scandalously corrupt NHS, and its bloated state welfarism. Then there are the ecclesiastical protests against "the cuts." The truth is that the last government was borrowing and spending more when it left office than it did when it came in. Whatever economic and social system is currently being operated in our country, it is not by any shadow of meaning capitalist.

VII

By the summer of 2001, there was livelier life in both parishes – livelier anyhow than at the end of 1998 and for some considerable time before that. We inaugurated a sung Mass – usually to the music of Vittoria – at St Michael's, lunchtime on Ascension Day. A novelty was to take the choir and congregation up the tower afterwards for a prayer and a motet and for the Rector to bless or curse the City according to his mood. (Only kidding!) In later years we had lighting installed all the way up that treacherous spiral, stone stairway, but to begin with it was a case of feeling your way in the dark and quite beyond all the acceptable parameters of the religion of Health and Safety. I got Chartres' permission to celebrate a Latin Mass – the Tridentine, the real thing, not the modern doggerel version – each Corpus Christi. It is so tender and intimate, especially the bit in the Prayer of Consecration where it speaks of Our Lord taking the bread into his venerable and holy hands. I'm a devotee of *The Book of Common Prayer* but the Tridentine certainly beats Cranmer's bland, "He took bread..." In the same tone that you might say, "He took the *Daily Mail*." I loved the inclusion of all the saints' names in the Sursum Corda and Sanctus and I was told that I read the Latin like a member of the Mafia.

From the start, when The Guildhall School of Music and Drama reneged on its agreement to get involved with St Sepulchre, we were always struggling to find ways to make the church pay its way. Endless series of committee meetings then. The Diocese of London got involved, affecting to be on the side of the parish. But diocesan bureaucracies are always merely self-interested. The process was a scandal and a disgrace. Diocesan officials would turn up at The Watch House to discuss some new scheme. This might involve the re-ordering of the west end of the church or finding a way to utilise the dilapidated cottages in the courtyard on the north side. The diocesan architect would be present and assorted apparatchiks from Diocesan House, attended by surveyors, planners and lawyers – all charging their fees of course. Three hours chatter and never anything settled. "So let's meet again in September…" Same again. The myth of Sisyphus. But we did manage to install lavatories at the west end, assuring that the whole population of the City was not obliged any longer to traipse into my downstairs loo. And a nice kitchen, so we could let the place to various groups and societies and get some money in that way. I was ever nervous, though. I mean, could you trust them to look after the place, to turn off kettles, ovens and radiant heaters and to lock up securely at the end? No you could not. I went to visit Nick Fox and Fay Weldon in Shaftesbury – just for the Saturday – and left the Post Office Art Exhibition in charge. I returned about seven in the evening to find that they had contrived to set fire to the kitchen. Not a small conflagration either. As they say, "Many appliances were in attendance."

Then a stroke of luck, or Providence. A financial whizz called Tony Kench joined the good ship St Sep's and produced a proper business plan. I discovered what a spread-sheet is. There were many spread-sheets in the ensuing years. But this is what was achieved: a three-storeys luxury apartment in the ancient west porch tower, let to City businessmen for a rental of £700 per week. We were never short of tenants. How could we have been when we were offering all mod cons in a medieval church, with views of the Old Bailey and all the way down to Ludgate Hill? £700 per week makes it appear we were in the money. But not really, for we had to pay the diocesan extortion tax known as the Quota or Common Fund - £40,000pa. The Diocese ceaselessly complains that it can't do much to relieve the financial needs its clergy, but I read the Diocesan Handbook and discovered what it does spend our money on. I made a list and intoned it at Sunday Mass in lieu of a sermon. Here we go…

"We have a General Secretary, a Secretary, an Internal Communications and Website Officer, Press, Media and Public Affairs, a Director of Finance and Operations, a Head of Finance, a Head of Management Accounts, a Financial Accountant and an Assistant Accountant.

"And we have a Trust Accountant, an Assistant Trust Accountant, A Financial Support Officer, a Payroll Officer and three Financial Advisers. So many accountants and so little money. But then we enter the heart of darkness. There is the HR Manager, someone in charge of Reception, an Office Services Co-ordinator, a Synodical Secretary, a Head of IT. A Systems Manager, a Support Assistant, a Director of Property (who does not answer the phone) a PA to the Director of Property, a Property Accountant, a Project Development Manager, a Head of Environmental Challenge, a Head of Property Management, a Residential Property Manager, a Commercial Property Asset Manager, a Maintenance Manager, a Property and Maintenance Administrator, a Gutter Maintenance Programme Administrator, a Head of Care of Churches Team, a Church Buildings Support Officer, A Care of Churches Team Administrator, a Head of Strategic Development, a Strategic Development Support Officer, a Director of Ordinands and Ministry Portfolio, a Director of Personal Development, an Officer for Children's Ministry, another for Community Ministry, a Chaplain to Deaf and Deaf/blind People, an Officer for Youth Development, four Community Development Workers.

"The Diocese has a Chancellor and a Registrar, complete with backup staff; six Bishops and eight Honorary Assistant Bishops, plus six Archdeacons. Of the increase of their government there is no end. All an expensive and largely useless copy of secular bureaucracy. Useless? Yes, because while these apparatchiks increase and multiply, the annual church attendances are falling catastrophically."

I had a plan to reprise the thing and have the director of music set it to a Psalm chant, but we never got round to it. I was taken to task by the authorities but, as I replied at the time, "What's the charge? All I did was read out what you had printed in the Diocesan Handbook. If you really were ashamed of the extent of your bureaucracy, why print the full list for all to see?"

I think that what I was most pleased about was the way that we were beginning to give some shape and form to the Christian Year by establishing events that were fixtures and landmarks rather than one-off specials. The City Service every January. The Ash Wednesday Choral Evensong with the Allegri *Miserere* and a distinguished visiting speaker. Holy Week with Stainer's *The Crucifixion* on the Tuesday. Maundy Thursday Solemn Mass, concluding with the Stripping of the Altars enacted to the dramatic recitation of Psalm 22. Three Hours' Devotion with hymns, prayers and six short addresses on Good Friday. Lighting of the Paschal Candle and Renewal of Baptismal Vows on Holy Saturday, bringing to and end the Lenten Fast. Festival Mass on Easter Day – always *The Coronation in C K.317*. Up the tower on Ascension Day. The Latin on Corpus Christi. A parish garden party after Mass last Sunday in July. St Michael's Patronal festival at the end of September. The Remembrance Sunday Parade. The observance of All Saints and All Souls. And Carol Services innumerable. *The Credo Mass K. 257* on Christmas Day. And I managed to persuade our attached livery companies each to dedicate a Company Sunday when their members would come to the Choral Mass and the event would be, as they say, "themed around" the character and needs of each particular company. Drapers celebrated five hundred years of their patronage of St Michael's by greatly repairing and restoring the chancel and sanctuary. At the same time the bishop came and restored the Benefice: that is, he made me Rector for, though I was from the start accorded the courtesy title of Rector, I had previously been only priest-in-charge and on a three years' contract. For no bishop could have responsibly inducted a priest to the historic benefice while the church was as dysfunctional as it had been back in 1998. We were now paying our way at both churches and the congregation at St Michael's on Sundays was around fifty – not bad for a parish no one lived in and all who wished to attend had to put up with vagaries of public transport in London at the weekend, which was and is the period when repairs and maintenance are carried out on the tube, with the resultant line-closures.

I suffered a little local difficulty – but not local to the City. The Blackburn Diocese branch of the Prayer Book Society asked me to go up to Lancashire and give a talk. I spoke for about half an hour on the clear superiority of *The Book of Common Prayer* to the trite modern liturgies purveyed by the General Synod's Liturgical Commission. I drew attention to a few of the infelicities and desecrations of the modern rites – not especially from a doctrinal perspective, but as a matter of decent English. For instance, the *BCP* marriage service contains, at a key moment in the drama, six words of one syllable which perfectly describe, in impeccable rhythm, exactly what is going on. The bridegroom slips the ring on her finger and says, "With this ring I thee wed." Now why change that? Is there anything in those words that "ordinary people" can't understand? But the tin-eared illiterates have changed it to "I give you this ring as a sign of our marriage." Eleven word for six. A classic composition of the Circumlocution Office. "And", I added, "it's damn near meaningless. I mean if he has to *tell her* that the ring is a sign, it just means the sign isn't working. Imagine a road sign which said. 'This is a road sign.'" I criticised the mealy-mouthed, death by euphemism, funeral service too: no mention of "worms," no "vile bodies." "Oh yes, do let's have a nice funeral – but don't mention the corpse." By contrast, Cranmer's first Prayer Book of 1549 has the minister address the deceased directly and most lovingly. Well, these and other such things are obvious to all but the most obdurate and hidebound moderniser. I must say, it was a disgusting minor triumph as the audience cheered me on. Only the trendy Dean of Blackburn took offence. I didn't know this at the time, but discovered it when I met up with Chartres at an event in the City. He said, "All the reports from St Michael's and St Sepulchre's are golden. But not from the Dean of Blackburn. Don't give it another thought. I've replied to him and told him to lay off." At that time, Chartres was faithfully living up to his request that I should say the things which, by handicap of his office, he would find it difficult to say. This happy state didn't last forever.

And it wasn't all one way traffic between me and the bish. I got a message from his secretary just after Easter telling me that Chartres had been pilloried in the national papers for taking Easter off and going on a lecture cruise. Would I write a letter to *The Times* in his defence? I did. I wrote that the bishop had been working relentlessly for the last decade – and more – and that he was entitled to a break. They printed it and there came a murmur of thanks from Chartres' lair.

We were still trying to make ends meet at St Sepulchre's when suddenly we received a visitation from the sensational crime writer Patricia Cornwell. She turned up unannounced, with all her minders and assorted heavies, at The Watch House in the middle of Sunday lunch, asked to be shown the church and vowed zealously to do something in our support. I hoped for a cheque. It was the John Smith – Virginia connection which had drawn her attention to us. But a mere transfer of funds was not exciting enough for the multimillionaire lady novelist. She wanted a performance. OK, we're good at performances in the City. So I contrived to have the Lord Mayor and other dignitaries come to a reception in church. A brilliantly sunny late morning. Canapes and wine. Then the speeches. The extravagant Ms Cornwell informed the assembly that she wanted to pay for a new stained glass window. She pointed to all the plain glass windows in the place and exclaimed, "No – not just one window but *seven* windows." But we didn't want seven new coloured windows. We liked the plain ones that let in the light. She was unstoppable. Except nothing came of it. I think she just went off, returned her attention to the pathologist heroine of her rather brutal and semi-pornographic fiction, and forgot she had ever set foot inside St Sepulchre's. I did try a few times over the years to get in touch but, as they say where she lives, No Dice.

I was still trying to pursue what I believe is called, in more exalted circles, a writing career. The delightful literary agent Giles Gordon was interested in some of my stuff: the verse, the sermons and *Holy Smoke*, a book of short stories I was preparing about the life of a City Rector: "Give me the sight of it when you're finished and I'll see what I can do." He took me to breakfast at Simpson's in The Strand where he had porridge and a tot of *Famous Grouse* while I devoured scrambled eggs and kidneys with a glass of Champagne. He was much exercised by the doings of Tony Blair whose name seemed to bring out in him something close to an allergic reaction: "He's an utter b****** and a c***!"

Giles was very far from being an utter b****** and a c***, He was benign and charming, humorous, affectionate and kind. I say "was." For it was a shock to learn a few weeks later that, on returning home after a party, he had fallen down the stone cellar steps, hit his head and died.

As for *Holy Smoke*, I completed it and tried it on a few mainstream publishers with the usual run of rejections after the style of "We enjoyed your work very much. Unfortunately, it is not quite right for our current list." Grief – but you should see the stuff that *is* right for their current list! Another replied, "I don't really think there's a market in today's world for this sort of thing. We should have to guarantee sales of at least two thousand to make it pay." My friend

Digby Anderson, director of the think tank The Social Affairs Unit, advised me, "Publish it yourself. Our publisher Helen Esmonde will produce it for you." She did and made a very good job of it. We sold four thousand copies and even contemplated a second edition.

Through the Social Affairs Unit, I was put in touch with the US Liberty Fund. This owed its origin to the aspirations of a wealthy American oilman who, in the middle of the 20th century, got a taste for talking about things that matter – apart from oil. What he did was to invite writers, musicians and dons to his ranch and give them generous hospitality from Thursday dinner until Sunday breakfast. All they had to do in return was to turn up each day for three sessions of one and a half hours each and talk. I believe this is something very much like what John Henry Newman described as "the idea of a university." In his Will, the oilman endowed the Fund and the US stock market did the rest. The Liberty Fund is now run by trustees who arrange Thursday-Sunday Colloquia in American cities and in country hotels over here. I was invited to attend one of these in Tunbridge Wells where we were to discuss international relationships with particular attention to the Cold War. It was edgy and on the pretentious side of intellectual. Young bloods showing off they'd read their Foucault – I think that's how you pronounce it – their Althusser and, of course, Decontructionist of the week Jacques Derrida. I scribbled a verse about him, sent it to the *TLS* and was magnificently rewarded with a fee of £10:

D'y wanna know the creeda
Jacques Derrida?
Dere ain't no reada;
Dere ain't no wreida
Eida.

It was all very agreeable. Nice food and wine. Strolls out across the strays and down to the Pantiles in the afternoons. Late night laughter out on the hotel lawn. Professor Dennis O'Keeffe, in affectionate imitation of Sam Johnson, rolling down the hill into the flower bed. The Americans were the best. More English than English. Shades of T.S. Eliot and Henry James. There was one tall, gnarled philosopher with a broad moustache – George, I think - who actually said the best thing about England is the warm beer: "It's the main reason I come." There was a memorable moment in the plenary session, late on the Saturday. One of the young bloods was sounding off in the full flush of the arrogance of ignorance: "Well, the Cold War was a difficult time for us all. But now, at last after seventy years, the longest period of attrition the world has ever seen is over and done with."

Very quietly, Professor David Martin, formerly of LSE, concluded, "The longest period of attrition the world has ever seen began in Mecca and Medina in the 7th century, proceeded via the Crusades, the Siege of Malta, Lepanto, the Siege of Vienna – as far as 9/11."

They feed and water you generously for three days and send you away with a cheque for $750.

The most stirring, moving Liberty Fund conference I attended was in Malvern, ten years after the fall of the Berlin Wall, the collapse of the Soviet Union and the liberation of the Eastern Bloc. We were talking about totalitarianism and writers such as Kafka and Orwell. There were real men with us that week: young university teachers from Czechoslovakia, Hungary and Poland:

"We used to pass around copies of George Orwell samizdat. If you were caught it could mean death."

"How did you survive?"

"We kept meeting together and hoping. Said our prayers to the Virgin Mary, and she made sure we never lost hope."

It reminded me of a stay I had in Prague around that time. One evening after dinner I fell into conversation with the proprietress of the hotel where I was staying at the top of Wenceslas Square:

"What was it like under the communists?"

"My husband teaches at the university. Before the Velvet Revolution, the students knew the questions he set them were bogus. He knew their answers were bogus. And they knew the comments and grades they received in return were bogus too. It was a kingdom of lies. And when our little children went to school in the mornings, they were asked by their teacher, 'Did your mummy and daddy have people round for supper last night? What did they talk about?"

Darkness visible.

The old regime lingered on. First night I was there, I hardly dared believe the poster I saw outside the opera house: *Don Giovanni* by the lad himself and his considerable sidekick Lorenzo Da Ponte:

"Sorry, all sold out."

I went back to the hotel and consoled myself over Schnitzel and Riesling. I related my disappointment to a local:

"Nonsense. You could have got into the performance easily. They always claim it's a sell-out. What they actually do is give the tickets to the political nomenclatura who then don't turn up. So in Prague Mozart plays to near empty houses. And to think, this is where *Don Giovanni* received its first performance!"

The best nights out were with the Guild of Air Pilots and Air Navigators – now reconstituted as the Honourable Company of Air Pilots and awarded the Royal Charter. Lunches too. One in particular at Mansion House for Prince Philip's 80th birthday. He replied to our well-wishing by saying:

"I don't know how I've lived so long – except it's by your kindly toasting my good health so frequently."

Prince Philip was Grand Master of the Air Pilots for fifty years and now he is our Patron and Prince Andrew has generously taken over his father's role. The Prince is a pilot. And how. At a small luncheon given by the Past Masters, we presented him with a ceremonial sword with, on one side, inscribed the names of the fifty-nine types of fixed wing aircraft he had flown and on the other side the eighteen types of helicopter. Dick Felix, one of the Past Masters, was for many years the Prince's pilot. Dick told me: "We'd be twenty minutes into the air and he'd say, 'Come on, Dick – I'll take over now!'"

One of those Past Masters had his own port bottling-company and at the lunch he presented Prince Philip with the bottle labelled *Number One*. The Prince received it graciously but, on his way out after lunch, he handed it to me and said, "You'd better have this, Peter. Our house floats on the bloody stuff."

"Well, Sir, now I don't know whether to drink it or frame it!"

"Get it down y'neck!"

The Princes Philip and Andrew were lads on a lark when it came to aeroplanes. They had only to come into the room and the talk immediately would be all about flying after hours, low level, without lights. Embodiments of that joke, they were: Little boy says to his father who is himself an airman: "Daddy, when I grow up, I'm going to be a pilot!"

"Make your mind up, son. You can't do both!"

On Mayday, the Feast Day of Saints Philip and James – known in the trade as Phil and Jim – I was standing at the high altar in St Michael's saying Mass. It was the usual Friday lunchtime service for City workers and visitors. I thought I could hear some background music, or it might have been the wind getting up. Within a few minutes it roared like a tsunami. I could hardly hear my own voice, so I imagine the congregation could hear nothing at all. I finished the service and, still in my vestments, went out and stood at the top of the church steps as the slouching horde with painted faces lumbered by, snarling their politics of envy. One of these charmers stuck his chin right under my nose and enquired, "What are you doing for anti-capitalism, creep?"

"I'm Chaplain to the capitalists, Sir." I raised my right arm and began to declaim the exorcism service in Latin – or as much of it I could recall from *The Rituale Romanum*.

The reality was not funny. I had to fight my way through the mob to get back home. The police hadn't expected a demonstration on such a scale: really it was a riot. Vastly outnumbered, they were quite unable to keep order. Later that evening when things had calmed down, I walked along to church to see if any damage had been done to St Michael's. Fortunately not. But the whole area of the City around the Bank of England, the Royal Exchange and the Stock Exchange, including Mansion House (my parish in other words) was a waste land. The pavements and roads were littered with jagged shards of broken glass from the smashed windows. There was a trail of filth everywhere. Strange, I thought, how the preferred litter dropped by the anti-globalisation freaks consists of fast food wrappers and cans of Coca Cola. Later I learnt that the offices of the LIFFE building had been stormed by the axe-wielding mob. They actually managed to penetrate the first line of defence and break into the reception area. For years, business offices, embassies and other public buildings, anticipating outbreaks of savagery, located their offices on the ground floor but, as it were, went up higher. This was what saved the LIFFE staff form injury or worse that day. The murderous thugs tried to run up the elevators and break into the offices where the financial executives were at their desks and, presumably since the rioters were armed to the teeth with some very ugly weapons, kill them all. But they did not bargain for the entrepreneurial nous of the bank's security officers who, by pressing a button at the precise moment, reversed the escalators and turned the barbarians back down upon themselves in a heap.

That was potentially the most serious incursion of the day. If those security men had not kept their presence of mind, I'm sure there would have been fatalities. There nearly was a murder when outside the Bank of England the mob managed to manhandle a policewoman from her horse. Luckily – providentially! – again there were other officers on hand and the thugs were beaten back. Any sympathy one might be inclined to have for the political opinions of the anti-capitalists evaporates when one observes at close hand the full howling hatred of their *modus operandi*.

Three weeks later I went on a march myself. This rather resembled a march too and we tried to keep in step as we processed out along Fleet Street and towards Trafalgar Square, down Whitehall and back towards Piccadilly Circus, thence home again along High Holborn. It was organised by The Countryside Alliance in protest against the Labour government's politics-of-envy ploy in passing the Bill prohibiting hunting with hounds. Afghanistan was seething with jihadist violence, Iraq was on fire, but Blair devoted more parliamentary time than to both of these put together in his loathsome campaign of hunting the toffs. Our march didn't try to vandalise the City in the interests of socialist idealism and solidarity. No shop fronts were smashed. I didn't even see anyone with face paint and green hair. People could be observed picking up litter as they went along. And it was a good-humoured, leisurely affair – a nice day out combined with a no thank you gesture to ideological prejudice and class war. There was time to stop for a drink on the way and re-join the march. I enjoyed a pint of white beer at a pub in Whitehall. And there were ten times as many of us than had rampaged around the Square Mile on May Day.

An insistent Irishman – Paddy, of course – started to turn up at the Wednesday and Friday Masses at St Michael's and often to the Thursday Mass at St Sepulchre. He never gave anything away, but he was an avid theologian. No social churchgoer, our Paddy. He was sociable though and would often invite me for a drink at The Counting House pub or the Wetherspoons adjoining St Michael's churchyard. He lived alone and he was far from fragrant. But he was devout – the real thing. He knew everybody who had even the remotest connection with churchy things. An excellent and thoroughly reliable gossip. He was Roman Catholic but he went to Mass as you might say incontinently: High Anglican, RC, Orthodox. Paddy moved in a mysterious way in his response to God which, however, was as direct and sincere as that which Our Lord spoke about when he said, "You must become as a little child." About this time, a member of the Friday congregation asked me to think about giving a short exposition of the Gospel at the Friday Mass

"Just a minute, Peter."

"Without hesitation, repetition or deviation, I suppose?"

Anyhow, I did and eventually wrote them all down in a book and dedicated it to Paddy, It was published on All Saints Day and I was looking forward to seeing Paddy at the Friday Mass. No show. Three days later, I learnt he had died, alone in his library of theological books. What was Paddy? Some said he had been a priest and I could believe that. But now I'll never know. I thought of him as a mysterious figure, like unto Melchizedek – the word is Hebrew and it means righteous king. How strange therefore – coincidence, synchronicity or what? – that when I went to Paddy's funeral conducted at the Catholic church of St Etheldreda, Ely place - just round the corner from me by Bleeding Heart Yard and conducted by my friend the agreeable Fr Kit Cunningham - Kit should lay his hand on Paddy's coffin and say, "I thought of him as Melchizedek."

It was a fraught week. I was called to take the funeral of a City banker who had lived out in the sticks near the south coast. It was arranged at a crematorium, somewhere near Bognor Regis. Simple. just put on the clerical clobber, take yourself to Victoria station and enjoy a good hour's read on the journey. I arrived early and went for a cup of tea. When I came back from the snack bar, all the announcement boards concerning train times were blank. There was an explanation – of sorts: a bomb scare or something. No trains. Try to get to the south coast without a train. The only way was by taxi. I hailed three:

"No chance!"

"Are you joking, or what?"

Finally, "Right Father – let's go for it!"

Through the mess of south London's traffic lights and all the queues at the roundabouts. The police sirens and the snarl-ups. At last we hit the green belt and something like open country. And to arrive with three minutes to spare. Naturally, I didn't have with me the means to pay the fare for a sixty miles cab ride:

"Will you trust me?

"I think so, Father."

Next day happened to be Paddy's funeral and I went to St Eth's, leaving a note on the front door to say that the money for the taxi fare was at the reception desk at *Brewin Dolphin*, the stockbroker's firm next door but one to me in Giltspur Street. I wished Paddy had lived to receive his copy of my *Minute Sermons*. But, God knows, he had had more than enough books already.

Paddy: Requiem aeternam... God bless you – and thanks.

VIII

Chartres announced, in his adopted tone which was one part Old Testament prophet to three parts Henry Irving, "The Holy Spirit is on the move in the Diocese of London!" And he urged us to move with Him by showing our support for a new gimmick entitled The London Challenge. Here's the flavour of it:

When I was young and doing my training at theological college, we used to enjoy a summer review, a sort of pantomime to celebrate the end of the exams season. We did mildly irreverent things such as sing the words "Please don't alter the Psalter any more" to a Psalm chant. One year someone picked up the diminutive Chaplain and put him on a high mantelpiece from where he couldn't get down. There was a student, a man in middle years who, for reasons I could never quite work out, went by the name of Gloria; and he would put on a lot of greasepaint and come on and sing *Misty* and some of the other boys would giggle. The whole event did no harm, I suppose – and anyway it was only one evening, once a year. And we were very young. But the impression of today's Church of England, however, is as of a continuous pantomime.

The authorities are addicted to change. So we have perpetual change. They seem to forget – or do they? – that perpetual revolution was the chief means by which Leninists and Trotskyists aimed to destabilise the social order. And this depressing tactic works: if you keep moving the goal-posts and redrawing the boundary lines, it becomes impossible to play a game of football. Over these last thirty years, we have seen the deliberate abandonment of the *Authorised Version* of the Bible and *The Book of Common Prayer;* the altars moved; the traditional hymns replaced by empty-headed choruses; worse, the traditional teaching about sin and redemption rejected in favour of religion as psychotherapy, theology as mere wetness.

Now this pace of perpetual change has been deliberately accelerated and set to disco music. And this is what we find exemplified in the bishop's new – and still running - pantomime called The London Challenge. Glossy booklets; embarrassing admonitions to the clergy; a meeting of all the parsons at All Souls, Langham Place for a pep talk, a video presentation, more rock music and gallons of moral blackmail. But this is ancient history. The London Challenge next ascended into its phase two. Parishes were asked to receive visitors from other parishes to observe and evaluate the extent to which congregations are – in the jargon – responding to the London Challenge. The impression is of visits by the nit nurse or perhaps the thought police.

There are varieties of futility and then there are the Church of England authorities. Let me give you the craziest example. Clergy get asked to go on a great number of meaningless conferences and courses; all of them a waste of time; all of them merely aping the secular obsession with management techniques. But even I – who had long thought himself shockproof against ecclesiastical inanities - was astounded when I received an invitation from the diocese to go on a conference called *Work/Life Balance: Learning to say NO with confidence and compassion.* Unbelievably, the explicit purpose of this conference was to teach us all how to refuse to go on conferences. I simply wrote back and said, I replied, "I know – no thanks!"

Well, what sorts of things were being officially recommended as adequate responses to The London Challenge? Let me offer those of you with a high cringe threshold a few examples from the official (shall I say?) *literature.* On London Challenge Day – Oh yes, there really was one! – "Have your group decorate plain biscuits with icing, sprinkles and small sweets to share with the congregation at coffee time." Coffee time? What's that? It goes on: "Enjoy being able to have fun together!"

Well, if you get sick of *Playschool*, there are alternatives. For instance: "Why not try dancing for the Lord? It is a way to enhance worship by interpreting worship songs with movement. Using a sign language can help interpret the words of a song. Make the signs bigger to be more of a dance movement." This is *Game for a Laugh* translated to the chancel. That last recommendation is followed by some information which tells us a lot about how the church authorities assess our intelligence. They say: "Signing can be useful if you have deaf members of your church." Pardon? Gerraway! Then they say: "Some children learn through visual means." Can this really be true? Do they really expect the little darlings to go around with their eyes open? They add: "What about a worshipful line dance or a Christian conga or a jive-for Jesus?" I was relieved though to see the further advice: "The aim is not to shock people…be modest in what you wear so that people can focus on God and not be distracted by the dancers' attire." Or, presumably, by the lack of it.

Don't imagine the intellectual content of The London Challenge to be absolute zero. We were encouraged to "interview a parishioner as part of the service." Helpfully, they told us how to do this: "There should be eye contact between you both. A clip-board is permissible for the interviewer." Now the next instruction chillingly tells us a lot about the authoritarianism behind all this drivel: "If using a microphone, keep hold of it yourself. Even if your guest tries to take it, keep a firm grasp. This ensures that you have the control."

We were commanded not to value tried and trusted ways of doing things. It says: "Deepen relationships with one another, regardless of our own traditions." That is exactly how a revolutionary subverts a state or an iconoclast destroys a church – by abolishing its traditions. The London Challenge also instructed us as to what our politics should be: "Pray that all people, whatever their race, creed, colour or gender may live in harmony with one another and be in the forefront of promoting social justice…consider world development issues…a fair distribution of wealth…Pray for those who work in race relations." This is of course only political correctness tacked on to the failed collectivist social agenda which our rulers in the General Synod have tried to thrust on us for a generation in countless official reports on everything from glue-sniffing to the hydrogen bomb.

The hard politics sits awkwardly alongside the game-showiness and the general touchy-feeliness of the programme. But then psychopathy and sentimentality always go together. How about this: "Each member of the community will be bringing with them their (*sic*) story/history and culture…" Culture? Wot kultur is this? Jiving for Jesus? The decoration of small biscuits with icing while, of course, making sure not to lose your grip on the microphone? It continues: "Their culture and their family/work/situation/interests. If all these are valued and used, the image of Christ which emerges will have a depth of reality and vibrancy which will not be able to be ignored."

Apart from the atrocious grammar, what needs to be said about all that is that it has nothing to do with the Christian faith. In fact, it is its opposite. The Christian faith is the antidote to all this muck. The image of Christ does not *emerge* out of an oil can of psychobabble. Christ is proclaimed in the real Bible and received in the Blessed

Sacrament, and it is the vocation of every Christian to obey Christ's command and declare these things. The London Challenge's depiction of what human beings are is not merely demeaning, insulting and offensive; but, because we are taught that human beings are made in the image of God, it is frankly blasphemous and insane. Line dancing and cutting out little bits of blue paper and sticking them on larger bits of yellow paper has nothing to do with what we should be doing in church. The worship and apprehension of God has to be practised attentively, with dignity, with the best we can bring, with the beauty of holiness. You are here to kneel where prayer has been valid.

After thirty years spent destroying all our treasures and supplanting them with a never-ending series of mindless gimmicks and failed PR gestures, this, The London Challenge is the final shambles to which they hope to reduce us. Reading the glossy brochure and the pages of instructions you might feel justified in exclaiming," So the gates of hell *have* prevailed, then?" And, Bishop Chartres, if the Holy Spirit is really supposed to be behind this stuff, why is it all so fifth rate?

Well, I had hoped The London Challenge was the final shambles, imbecility's last Hurrah, but I had omitted to understand that what The Bishop of London instigates today, Archbishop Sentamu of York is very capable of improving upon tomorrow. I have already remarked on what this man is capable of in that performance in Oxford on 9/11 when he was yet Bishop of Stepney. Then as Archbishop of York he demonstrated that he was taking seriously his responsibility for the spiritual life of the nation. So he composed the Foreword to three booklets to guide us through Lent: one for "The Family"; one for "Adults and Youth" and the other for "Kids." Or is that last one for nanny goats?

These glossy booklets featured *Mr Men* style cartoon figures whom we must suppose are meant to represent the general public. Achingly politically-correct with all races represented - but no fat people or smokers. Dumbing-down beyond the farthest reaches of infantilisation, the booklets urge us to "Do fun things together. Create a space in your home...a corner of a room...an under-stairs cupboard... a shelf...make a prayer den using furniture and blankets...gather some objects that are fun to touch, feel and smell: a piece of velvet, feathers, a tray of sand, lavender bags or pine cones." These should have been enough to satisfy at least some of the more mentionable fetishists among us.

And what were we supposed to do in the prayer space? "Take in some pebbles, shells or feathers" – presumably to demonstrate our impeccable ecumenical relations with primitive animists and tree-huggers. And prayers are supplied: "Dear God, make wrong things right..." But this is not God; only the sentimental wish-fulfilment of Father Christmas or the Tooth Fairy We were even educated into the correct manual acts to perform while praying this desolate prayer: "Shake your finger from side to side for 'wrong' and then do thumbs up for 'right.'"

You feel there should be a caution not to do this near a window in case the neighbours see you and phone for the men in white coats.

Lent involves us in acts of practical devotion too. So, "Give a lollipop to your lollipop person."

Of course, as always in the Church of England these days, the sheer blithering idiocy only faintly disguises the right-on political hard sell:

"Email or write to your MP about a global poverty issue... Buy a Fair Trade Easter egg" But what, if you follow the advice of many leading economists who claim so called Fair Trade does nothing to help the poor, and recommend free trade instead?

The only orthodoxy we find in these booklets is environmentalist demagoguery and the pagan superstition of global warming: "Help lighten our load on the planet... defrost your fridge and find out how climate change affects poorer people...help stop global climate change: recycle your rubbish save trees, use both sides of the paper..."

(When doing what, by the way?)

Lent is supposed to be a time when we repent of our sins. But the only sins found here are those of not subscribing to the Christian socialist manifesto and being found guilty of global warming denial. Small wonder the pews are emptying faster than ever, when these booklets represent the mind of the Church of England. Lent is for deepening our understanding of the faith and for drawing nearer to God – for which vocation these booklets provide no nourishment.

What might the Archbishop have offered, if he had been in his right mind? That we should all begin and end the day by saying the Lord's Prayer. Read the Collect, Epistle and Gospel written in the matchless English of *The Book of Common Prayer* for each of the six weeks of Lent. Perhaps say the Psalms set for every day. Try to attend an early morning or lunchtime weekday service of Holy Communion. Competent shepherds of their sheep would also have recommended some spiritual reading.

These patronising booklets are worse than a joke, worse than useless. They ape the trite and gaudy language and images of a debased advertising culture, babyfied and debauched, and apply it to the Christian Gospel. But faith cannot be taught in this way. It cannot be communicated by the thing it is not, the thing that is actually anathema to it. People have to be taught. These booklets only insult the intelligence of the public. There is no Christianity in "Live Life: Love Lent" – only a blasphemous parody of the faith. But if the shepherds are hirelings?

I decided to avail myself of the antidote and try to perform a little innovation myself as an alternative to these *fleurs du mal*. There is a short service in the Prayer Book – about twenty-five minutes – called *A Commination: or denouncing of God's anger and judgments against sinners*. It is appointed to be declaimed by the minister or priest on Ash Wednesday. The reader pronounces God's curse on sinners, itemising the particular sins in sequence: "He that curseth his father or mother...he that removeth his neighbour's landmark...that causeth the blind to go out of his way...that lieth with his neighbour's wife." And so on. You get the idea? Of course this is not used in the contemporary church and hasn't been for half a century or more – except in outposts of regrettable reaction. It's far too judgemental for the modern parsons. Actually, it is perhaps the most tender service in the Prayer Book. It is about God's extreme willingness and desire to remove from us all these curses and those judgements which we deserve. In fact God has already done this through the sacrifice of his Son Jesus Christ. The service says as much:

"Let us not abuse the goodness of God, who calleth us mercifully to amendment and of his endless pity promiseth us forgiveness of that which is past, if with a perfect and true heart we return to him. For though our sins be as red as scarlet, they shall be made white as snow; and though they be like purple, they shall be made white as wool...

"For thou art a merciful God. Full of compassion, longsuffering and of great pity. Thou sparest when we deserve punishment. And in thy wrath thinkest upon mercy..." It gets Lent off to a cheerful start. Unlike the modern rubbish, it knows we can't be cheerful until we have been penitent. Christianity is about the joy which comes from confessing your sins and receiving ultimate assurance that you are a justified and redeemed sinner. It beats Jiving for Jesus and the fashionable ecclesiastical cult of the promotion of *self-esteem* – the sin of the self-righteous Pharisee for whom there was no forgiveness - because there was no sorrow for sin. The last thing I should esteem is myself.

I was back in Oxford not long after 9/11 but without that cloud. It came about like this. As the Patrons of St Michael's are the Drapers' Company – or, as they delight in being petitioned, The Worshipful Company of Drapers – so St John's College, Oxford are Patrons of St Sepulchre. The College Chaplain was Rev'd Dr Elizabeth, a lady of high academic achievement and repute but one of the most easily-provoked people I've come across. The irony was that she usually provoked herself. For instance, I replied to her invitation and addressed the letter to Rev'd Dr Carmichal. The eminent scholar, and I think they say "feisty woman" priest, wrote back to tell me I had misspelt her name and included with her correction the most tremendous bollocking. I sent her a photocopy of her letterhead: It said at the top not "Carmichael" but "Carmichal." I have found that those who are swiftest to take offence without cause are generally the last to apologise without conscience. I accepted her invitation only to find myself in the college chapel enduring the most long-winded recitation of intercessions I'd heard in my life. We prayed for the whole world, *by name.* An earthquake somewhere, a political summit somewhere else. Argentina, China, Mrs Emily Cater at number 54 Cheshunt Street had broken her leg. It was like the itinerary of places you called at on a long cruise, a world tour. Besides, this prayer-as-geography-lesson is incoherent and self-defeating. For as a matter of fact it is impossible to include everyone and everywhere in your intercessions: you would require infinity in order to do that. So extensive itemisation does not produce the desired *inclusivity* but only excludes by all the unavoidable omissions. Liz stayed often at the Watch House when she was "doing my research" in some dismal library and I once tried to cheer her up by taking her to a dinner at Merchant Taylors Hall. She noticed their image of St John the Baptist. She said, with more alacrity than I had seen from her in three days, "John is our Patron Saint. I wonder if Merchant Taylors might consider a donation to St John's Oxford?"

St John's Oxford, one of the richest colleges in the country and here comes Liz looking for a sub. I reflected that it was unfortunate St Sep's patrons St John's showed no similar generosity Jo our church.

Within the same month the Chaplain of Peterhouse invited me to preach at Evensong and then join the dons at High table before repairing to the Master's Lodgings for the port. I recall little out of the ordinary, apart from the long Latin Grace before dinner and the vinegary, arch and, I thought, at times vicious point-scoring and put-downs over the post prandial delights. Why do they feel compelled to live up to their own clichés?

I met Professor Antony Flew at a Reception in the House of Commons. I had always rated Tony since that remarkable book he edited – in fact two remarkable books – he had produced with Alasdair McIntyre in 1956: *New Essays in Philosophical Theology.* Full of disarming genius in their phraseology, "I have no expectation of catching empirical eels in my dialectical net." Tony was the atheist evangelical of the era. A hard case. Dawkins is like Old Mother Riley compared to Tony in his heyday. I liked him for it. Then he all of a sudden - as Enid Blyton used to say – was persuaded by the 18th century Archdeacon William Paley's so called Argument from Design. I make a parody but, briefly and crudely, "I'm walking along the beach and I discover an excellent watch. It didn't make itself. It must have had a watchmaker. It wasn't merely accidental. Humankind and the universe are fully finished like the watch, so we must have had a maker. Therefore God exists." Tony's conversion was occasioned by the writings of some prominent Christian apologists who applied Paley in the light of the new quantum mechanics and theoretical physics, and they argued that the physics of the universe is so finely tuned that if any of the constants – gravity, electromagnetism, the strong and weak nuclear theories – had been awry by as much as a Schrodinger's cat's whisker, then there wouldn't have been a universe at all.

Tony was a sheer treat: eighty-four yet the same schoolboy he had always been. And full of anecdotes which he used to pour out when I took him to The Arts Club for long lunches. Memorably:

"I was once at the Moral Sciences Club in Cambridge – in the late 1940s. Wittgenstein was there. The speaker was to talk to us about

Descartes. He began, 'I think, therefore I am.' To which Ludwig objected in a loud stage whisper, 'That's a f****** stupid place to start!'"

Not bad at all to receive a pertinent comment on the mistakes of the Enlightenment – and all before the Arts Club's fruit salad.

Life was a whirlpool of delight, but still there were devils to be exorcised and plenty of them. I will try to restrain myself and mention only one. Forgive me if the detail is, here and there, tedious and pornographic, but some evils are not dispatched in a hurry. A publisher sent me a book by the Archimandrite of Literary Nihilism, Professor Terry Eagleton: Catholic manqué, Trotskyist manqué and plain manqué manqué with the request for my review. His book was irretrievably uninformed and illogical. The reason I am making such a song and dance is that Eagleton is not the only literary nihilist. High culture in Western Europe today *is* nihilism. Another phrase for this is cultural Marxism. It consists of tenured, well-paid university teachers making their living by proclaiming that there are no elites – not noticing that in fact there is an elite and it comprises they themselves. They despise traditional values and one of their favourite expressions is that there must be "resistance" to these, to them, false standards and out-of-date and - another of their favourite words *oppressive* – customs and social habits but which most of the rest of the population takes for granted and tries to live by. "Resistance" is an odd description for what these narcissistic iconoclasts are up to. "Resistance", as I mentioned earlier in my account of that Liberty Fund conference, was costly in the former tyrannies in Eastern Europe during the Soviet era. There were those who resisted and by so doing really risked their lives. Whereas our academic elite merely fail to distinguish between "resistance" and "a cushy job." Bear with me while I quote from my review.

Terry Eagleton Presents Jesus Christ: The Gospels

This book deserves The Richard Dawkins Prize for Progress in Theology. I bet when God first read it he was rolling in the heavenly aisles with all the holy angels. Where it is not ignorant, it is banal and where it is not laughable, it is offensive. The first line sets the tone: "Jesus certainly kept some shady political company" – which is a bit rich coming from Eagleton the Marxist fellow-traveller, friend as he is not of publicans and sinners but of Leninists and Trotskyist riff-raff.

Jesus, according to Professor Eagleton, did not see many Roman soldiers when he was a boy except when he was "on holiday." I expected Eagleton to provide us with a colourful vignette at this point featuring The Holy Family heading off by charabanc to Bognor, young Jesus eagerly clutching his bucket and spade and demanding of his mother, "Are we there yet?"

It is pretty clear from early on in this book that Eagleton wants to construct, and even deconstruct – for he is of course a famous professor of literary theory – Jesus in his own image. So he tells us "Jesus was to the left of even the liberal wing of the Pharisees" – as if the terms "left" and "right" operated 2000 years ago in the land of Caiaphas and Pontius Pilate.

Rubbish abounds. He says that Jesus "makes no claim to be the Son of God in the Gospel, except once, implausibly, in the Markan trial scene." Why is St Mark's Gospel "implausible"? But this is just not true. Jesus declares himself Son of God in numerous places in the Gospels: for instance in his acceptance of St Peter's confession, "Thou art the Christ, the Son of the living God" (Matthew16: 16); when he promises the penitent thief a place beside him in Paradise (St Luke 23:43); "He that seeth me, seeth him that sent me" (St John 12:45); "Before Abraham was, I AM" (St John 8:58). And emphatically, "I and the Father are one." (St John 10:30)

Shouldn't it be the first job of the professor of literature actually to read the text before he opens his mouth?

Eagleton thinks that Jesus meant the Gospel to be only for the Jews: "He certainly admonishes his comrades…" I love that "comrades" bit, as if Our Lord were Vice- President of the TUC – "… to preach the good news he has brought to the house of Israel only." Then why does Jesus command them: "Go ye therefore and teach all nations" (St Matthew 28:19)? If the Gospel of salvation is for the Jews only, why does Jesus hand out its blessings indiscriminately to, for instance, the Gentile Woman of Samaria and the Pagan Roman Centurion whose servant was sick? Why does he make the godly helper of the man who fell among thieves a Samaritan?

I question Eagleton's authority for some of the judgements he makes here: "Jesus' popular support was probably by no means as massive as the evangelists make out." How does he know this? Were the evangelists telling porkies? Was Eagleton there on Palm Sunday when a great multitude cut down palm branches and strewed them before him? Was he there when they crucified my Lord? Naturally the communist Eagleton is used to people in authority telling lies and so he has no difficulty concluding that their estimates of the size of the crowds which followed Jesus were no more reliable than Stalin's weekly statistics of tractor production in the USSR.

He seems to think that Jesus was just a crazy mixed up kid: "The Gospels do not give us much access to Jesus' self-understanding, granted that he had any definitive sense of who he was in the first place." Is he really trying to make out that the man Jesus who went about dispensing sublime wisdom and testing friends and enemies alike with his profound insights had no idea what manner of man he was? Nonsense. Jesus understood himself in relation to the prophets and to his Father – and expounded these relationships explicitly and repeatedly.

Eagleton tells us that, because of his birth in a stable and his ignominious death, "Jesus is a sick joke of a Saviour." So the learned professor mistakes the Divine condescension – St Paul says, "He emptied himself" - of the Incarnation and the redeeming death, humbly accepted, for "a sick joke" does he? I wonder who is really sick here?

Misinformation abounds: "John the Baptist was an apocalypticist, whereas Jesus was not." So what are Jesus' prophecies of the end of the world in St Mark chapter 13, St Luke 21 and St Matthew 24 all about? How about the ecstatic reply to the chief priests when they ask him if he is the Messiah? – "I am: and ye shall see the Son of Man sitting on the right hand of power and coming in the clouds of heaven" (St Mark 14:62) It doesn't get much more apocalyptic than that. Oh but I forgot, this is the verse in St Mark which Eagleton dismisses as "implausible."

We are meant to think that Jesus was indifferent to vice and virtue, good and evil: "In the so-called Beatitudes…" – but why "so-called"? – "the poor, hungry and sorrowful are declared blessed, but not the virtuous." What of "Blessed are the pure in heart" then? That sounds fairly virtuous to me. Are not meekness and peace-making virtues too? (A few pages later he refers to "the so-called Lord's Prayer"). Metonymical irony perhaps? Synecdoche? Transferred epithet?

"The Christian movement begins in bathos. Its origins lie in a hideously embarrassing anti-climax…" Eagleton has to say this because of course, as a paid up dialectical materialist, he is not allowed to believe in the Resurrection. He adds, "Jesus has most of the characteristic features of the revolutionary activist, including celibacy." This shows that Eagleton doesn't know much even about revolutionaries: both Stalin and Mao were notorious womanisers.

The infelicities and desecrations are abundant: "The New Testament has scarcely anything to say about sexual morality" How about Our Lord's strictures on divorce and his telling the woman caught in adultery to go and sin no more? Astonishingly we come across the claim that Jesus had an "aversion to hard work". Put this beside what Jesus achieved in a mere three years – probably almost as much as a professor of lit crit. "There were no churches." Yes there were: they were called synagogues. And, within a decade of the Resurrection, house churches, founded by the Apostles themselves – "Jesus' comrades" - abounded all over the Middle East "The New Testament has nothing to say of God as Creator" Tell it to St John: "All things were made by him and without him was not anything made that was made (St John 1:3)

Oh I can't go on. It's all too silly. I feel sorry for Eagleton's students in the lit crit factory; for if he gets it all wrong when he tries to speak to *us* of heavenly things, why should *they* believe him when he speaks to them of things as mundane as literary analysis?

But in the end it's not his laborious dialectics, his galloping abuse of the English language. It's not even his antipathy to the faith that has been taught for two thousand years and which formed our civilisation in Europe and beyond. It's not finally even his spite and sheer nastiness. It's his colossal ignorance. I'll you what it's like: a man goes up to Terry Eagleton in the pub and says, "D'you like cricket?" And Eagleton replies, "O yes, I'm an expert on cricket. This is the game where men put on jerseys and shorts and run about trying for ninety minutes to put the ball in the back of their opponents' net."

I continued to try to slot in my writing in the interstices between all the other activities – not always very successfully or even satisfactorily. But an agreeable opportunity arose out of my membership of the Arts Club. Members were encouraged to practise their art, whatever form it happened to take. Bob Tear gave master classes to young singers, displayed his paintings on the Club's walls and sold copies of his mildly salacious novel on the bookstall. I was invited to give a talk on Dr Johnson and it made for a lively sociable evening: forty or so members and guests to the lecture at 6pm and then into dinner. I gave a talk every year for five years: after Johnson, came Coleridge, Eliot, Hulme and G.K. Chesterton. Eventually I extended and filled out these talks – adding the names of Newman, Collingwood and Sisson – and published it as the book *Prophets & Visionaries: Writers of Judgement*.

New Year's Day 2002, I began a sort of diary – not of my doings but each entry a philosophical remark, or a short argument on some topic in aesthetics, ethics or political philosophy. I tried to root these, whenever possible, in contemporary events but at the same time make them sufficiently detached as to hope they might retain their interest after the news of the day had turned into fish and chips papers. The book that emerged was *Everyday Thoughts* – a calendar of three hundred and sixty-six entries

Rabbi Professor Dan Cohn-Sherbok asked me to contribute a chapter to his anthology *Glimpses of God*. Here's a paragraph:

"Sunday morning and he entered St Bartholomew's church, Armley, Leeds, during the singing of the Introit. Here comes the gold cross, the Crucifer in his alb and starched amice and behind him the choir in red and white. Servers, acolytes, the Vicar and the two Curates in their vestments, green for the long season of Sundays after Trinity. They were singing *Blessed city, heavenly Salem* to Purcell's transcendent B-flat tune *Westminster*. It was as if he had died and gone to heaven and moreover had found the place devoid of Evangelical Retribution. The mighty Schultze organ, crowned with the carved angel of the Apocalypse, growled and roared. Then it all calmed down and we heard a single clarinet in Paradise over the ravishing lines:

From celestial realms descending
Bridal glory round her shed
Meet for Him whose love espoused thee
To thy Lord thou shalt be led."

IX

In the City it is always the most popular season for what Eliot called "fashionable weddings." But, the times being as they are, I got a couple now and again who wanted to do it themselves, compose the service, the whole lot. Once a young banker and a hair-dresser came in off the street and asked if they might be allowed to make "alternative vows". You wonder what's coming next: do they want to replace "Till death do us part" with "...until a week on Tuesday"?

For the lesson the favourite always used to be the miraculous chapter from St Paul ending with, "....and the greatest of these is love" Or else something luscious and sexy from the Old Testament's *Song of Songs*:

"Thou hast ravished my heart. Thou hast ravished my heart with one of thine eyes, with the chain of thy neck. How fair is thy love! How much better is thy love than wine, and the smell of thine ointment than all spices!"

They had to be brave to ask for that one.

But recent trends bear out G.K. Chesterton's warning that, "When men stop believing in God, they don't believe in nothing – they believe in anything." Couples sometimes ask if they might read the cringingly banal *Invitation* by Oriah Mountain Dreamer. This starts by hoping that the bride has not been "shrivelled and closed." No doubt the bridegroom hopes not too! It goes on to wonder whether the couple have "touched the centre of their own sorrow." This is at a wedding, mind you, not a wake!

It's *The Book of Common Prayer* at St Michael's, so there's none of that crooning, sentimental guff you find in the new *Common Worship* - hideously mawkish phrases such as, "Let them be tender with each other's dreams." It sounds like a schmaltzy song title by Andrew Rice-Pudding. I think there should be a rubric printed at this point in bold type in the margin of that godforsaken new worship book: "The congregation shall here throw up – bride's family's side first". The numbskull liturgical revisers never tire of telling the clergy that we have to *modernise* because the *BCP* wedding service is not relevant to our generation. That's patronising rubbish. How dare they tell today's young couples that this lovely, heartfelt traditional language is beyond them? It's not even true. In the three years either side of the new millennium we held eighteen weddings, all from the 1662 book, and most of the young couples stayed to become regular members of the congregation.

The old Prayer Book is not coy or sentimental about human nature, but tells it as it is. We *do* have "carnal lusts and appetites" which resemble those of the "brute beasts with no understanding." These incontinent appetites are the reason there are 200,000 abortions each year – for the most part abortion being used as a method of contraception. Marriage was ordained as a remedy against sin, for the procreation of children and for the mutual society, help and comfort that the one ought to have of the other. The *BCP* service makes these things plain and the Introduction to that service, read at the start to the whole congregation, by the priest standing on the chancel step. It is the best bit of marriage guidance the couple will ever receive. It does not suffuse itself in a pinkish glow like the new rite with its mush about "delight and tenderness," but outlines the couple's responsibilities: "...in sickness and in health...for richer for poorer" and "...keep thee only unto her so long as ye both shall live." Helpfully it then goes on to pray that by God's Grace the two of them will be given strength to keep their vows. So they are not left comfortless under the weight of impossible moral demands

The decisive thing about the *BCP* wedding is that it gives the lie to the accusation that the Christian faith is puritanical and anti-sex. In an ecstatic phrase the bridegroom says to his bride, "With my body I thee worship." And, whereas the supposedly *relevant* modern version is just one long catalogue of sentimental effusions and disembodied evasions of sex, the *BCP* is not afraid either to celebrate its joys or to condemn its misuse.

Things can go wrong and sometimes do. I've never actually had anyone shout their objection to the marriage when you come to that "...speak now or forever hold his peace." Incidentally, the only sustainable "cause or impediment" is if either of the pair is already married. Were the bride's mother to stand up and say, "'Cos I don't like the look of him!" it would get her nowhere. The late arrival of the bride is usually more of an irritation than a problem. In any case, it's a sort of unspoken concession that she might be five minutes behind time. The real snags start on those rare occasions when you have another wedding following in an hour and a half. I've never had a bride or groom not turn up at all, or anyone get as far as the chancel step then turn tail and run away. But I did once have a bride arrive full forty minutes late. The organist played his whole repertoire, the congregation shuffled and stared at the groom – most in sympathy but a few here and there in macabre curiosity to see what he might do. Poor lad was a wreck, red in the face, trembling, tears. Then at last all was well. I hope I'm not going to be thought "racist" when I tell you the plain truth: there is a phenomenon which all the City clergy refer to as "African time." Kenyan, Ethiopian and Nigerian wedding couples and congregations are the most cheerful, ebullient of all. But they don't go by clock time and for either (or both) of the principals to turn up half an hour late is not unusual. And this is even after you've warned them the day before when they turned up late for their rehearsal! I've stood through anxious minutes while the groom struggles (with his nerves and her digits expanded by excitement and the heat wave) to fit the ring on her finger. There's an easy solution: "Just slip it on her little finger for the time being." I've had them drop rings down heating grills – in which case you proceed without and go looking for it afterwards. And there's one bit in their responses that they hardly ever get right: "Till death us do part." Almost without exception they say, "Till death do us part" – because they've seen the old TV comedy show but they've (probably) not been married before.

After forty-odd years of splicing couples, I reckon I've seen it all. Literally, if I recall the number of times I've seen buxom bridesmaids in their gownless evening straps quivering outside church for half an hour in the January frost while the photographer does his bit. Bit? That's a joke: the photos usually take longer than the ceremony. Often I get asked to the Reception and that's nice of them, but it's a problem. For the only people the priest gets to know are the couple themselves, and if he does get to see their parents and the best man, it's only briefly on the day before at the rehearsal. I've learnt that the best reply to their invitation is to thank them for their kindness and say, "I can't stay for the meal, but I'll pop in before it starts and drink a glass to your health." The alternative is to find oneself stuck in an end seat in the draughty corner with only the great aunt for company – and she's deaf and a religious maniac.

It took me a long time to acclimatise myself to the character of the memorial service. Before I arrived in the City, I'd never attended one of these, let alone conducted one. Where I'd worked, in towns and villages, people died where they lived and the Prayer Book funeral was adequate for all their requirements. It was only in the City, where people worked but few lived, that these additional arrangements had to be made. Even so, I soon discovered that memorial services are not what they used to be in the City of London. Not many years ago, the church would be packed with dignified men in pinstripes and elegant ladies in hats and veils, come to pay last respects to such as Sir Robert, Chairman of *Bigbank Ltd*. They would sing with lusty restraint hymns such as *Jerusalem* and *The Day Thou Gavest Lord Is Ended*. The reading would be from the Bible, of course: something familiar and comfortingly apt such as "And God shall wipe away all tears from their eyes." It was rare to have a secular reading but if there was to be one it would be after the style of John Donne's matchless sonnet *Death Be Not Proud*. The Rector would give a short address. We would listen as the choir sang *Nunc Dimittis* and then everyone would repair to a local livery hall for drinks and canapes.

Occasionally, I got asked for a memorial service old style, but increasingly something - I am struggling for words - more pop and pagan is required. Dress multifarious informal. Organ music before the service might include "Some of Bob's favourite ballads: anything from *Singin' In The Rain*, or The Beatles' maudlin *Yesterday*; and now and then they will import the bank's audio system and belt out something off the top of the Richter Scale by Sid Filth that makes you think of a pile-driver screwing a score of metal dustbins.

New style memorial services are above all talkative. Three or even four of the deceased's family and friends will get up to "offer a tribute." I know we must all respect *De mortuis nil nisis bonum*, but most tributes would fall foul of the Trades Descriptions Act. We are asked to recall that Bob, "or 'Chuckles' as he liked to be called on account of his infectious giggle," was a married archangel with four children and fifteen grandchildren. He was brilliant in his work at the bank where everybody loved him. Like hell he was! Many in church wince as they remember how he used to growl at the juniors and make them cry. And if he was really so brilliant, why was he made redundant?

At home he had the *bonhommie* of Alistair Sim playing the reformed Scrooge. He kept a superb table, never failed to bring his wife flowers every Friday and he was always effervescently happy. Well, Solon said, "Call no man happy until he's dead," but I hardly thought the great sage meant that a man had to wait until after he'd died to effect such a remarkable character change - from curmudgeon to comedian, from reclusive skinflint to "life and soul of any party." As for constantly taking the children sailing, they, grown up now and sitting on the front row, remember cringingly that the only time the miserable bastard took them on a boat it was to threaten to chuck them over the side if they didn't stop whining. I suppose it's a blessing that most of the speakers haven't the faintest notion of how to project the voice and so the sentimental drivel cannot be heard at all beyond the third row.

But these schmaltzy eulogies are not the worst part of the service - not by any means. There is among modern, wholly un-churched mourners still the desire to "do something religious." Not *The Lord's My Shepherd* or *How Lovely Is Thy Dwelling Place, O Lord Of Hosts*. These mainstays of English religion are nowadays quite unknown. What is not unknown is some sentimental, vaguely middle-eastern, doggerel by someone with a name like Alhacca Armanaleg: "O look up to where the white night owl stares and think that this also will pass/ There's an ocean of grass so sit on your..."

Such sickly drivel that it might have been produced for a chocolate box by the combined efforts of Barbara Cartland and Patience Strong. I love it if, in the middle of this guff, a couple of mobile phones go off - especially when the tune they are bleeping happens to be *Jesu, Joy Of Man's Desiring* or the *Toccata & Fugue in D Minor* by Bach: ironically, the only bit of real religion in the whole hideous show provided by a post-modern icon of consumerism! The difference between the old services and the new is quite simply that, in the former, as befits a church service, the centre of reference was God; in the latter the centre of attention is the narcissistic, moonshine emotionality of the mob as it were at a *Diana-Fest*. Memorial services have become consumer affairs, part of the whole mindless, chuck-away me-ism of the contemporary junk culture.

There are moments so crass as to be unbeatable. A distant cousin might slouch to the lectern and remind us that "As well as being Master of the Guild of Confectioners, Bob was, in his younger days, something of a ladies' man." Cue for a woman in a flowery dress hinting at circumnavigation to step forward and warble, *If I Knew You Were Coming, I'd Have Baked A Cake*.

Since we're into consumerism, I'd like to offer a full portfolio of memorial services, including a parody – but truly the whole damn show is beyond parody. Here comes his elder brother: "I've known Bob all my life, of course..." (This works best if you can hear it in the voice of Alan Bennett). "...how he worked day and night to support his family. Straight home from the bank, and, after saying, 'Thanks for a nice bit of tea, mother,' he'd slip into his burglar togs and break into the LIFFE building.

"And, when he got too frail for organised crime and insider-trading, he'd still cheerfully contrive to fiddle his expenses every week. But this was when Bob came to rely on his many hobbies. As well as being a black belt *Canasta* player, he was, as some of his dearest friends know, a lifelong paedophile. After his retirement, and before his final illness rendered him too frail to operate the video remote-control, I'd go round to his house of an evening and, while we sipped *Dry Martinis,* Bob would show me his wonderful collection of literally thousands of photographs of little boys and girls in indecent poses."

But no, things have got so ridiculous that satire is impossible. Already, we've fallen a lot further than you think towards the everlasting bonfire.

The priest is called Father, but he is not meant to be the Father of lies. Bishops too must surely adjure all dissembling. But, as I discovered, there are liars even in palaces. In Bishopthorpe, for example, the riverside abode of the Archbishop of York.

There was something rotten in Bishopthorpe Palace.

When Dr John Sentamu was appointed Archbishop of York, I wrote in my column in *The Northern Echo* as follows:

"Today Dr John Sentamu will be enthroned as Archbishop of York in the great Minster. I sympathise with him because he will never escape the media tag "the first black archbishop". But some of his recent protests suggest he is enjoying the cliché. He has complained that the Church of England is "institutionally racist." The phrase is paranoid and meaningless and its absurdity is nowhere better demonstrated than by the fact that the new Archbishop of York is a black man. If the church is so colour-prejudiced, how come he gets to sit on one of its highest thrones today?

"But then Bishop Sentamu has sat in the best school for learning political correctness. He was a member of the Macpherson Enquiry which followed the murder of Stephen Lawrence. This is the enquiry which invented the ridiculous concepts "institutional racism" and "unconscious racism" and, when sceptics asked for a justification for these tendentious neologisms declared loftily, "We do not pretend to produce a definition which will carry all argument before it." In other words, we won't answer your awkward questions. Incoherence and bullying combined. Just like the secret police.

"Worse, the MacPherson Enquiry went on to define a racist incident as "..any incident so described by the victim, *or any other person*". This too is meaningless of course, but it is the catch-all, you're-guilty-even-when-you're-innocent terminology of the gulag. If *anything* can be legitimately described *by anyone* as a racist incident – the nonsense our new Archbishop put his name to – then when I ask you if you'd like a cup of tea, you can report me to the race relations authorities.

"It is a bad omen when a future Archbishop of York is seen to be giving his backing to the lying definitions of totalitarianism. I had hoped that his elevation to a position of high authority would make John Sentamu hesitate before he allowed his name and status to be abused by the gang of political opinion which operates coercion under the euphemism of "inclusivity."

"On the race issue Dr Sentamu is quite wrong: it is black bishops who are currently wielding the most power and influence in the Church. It is black African bishops who have got under the skin of the "progressive" English hierarchy by objecting to their wholesale surrender to secular nostrums and political correctness regarding homosexuality in particular. It was these secularising and modernising bishops and powerful apparatchiks in the General Synod who were delighted by John Sentamu's appointment – if not influential in it. It enabled them to say, "See, *we've* got a black Archbishop as well – and he's not a bigoted reactionary like those Africans causing all the trouble!"

"Dr Sentamu is wrong about the mood of the country too. People are not obsessed, as he is, with worries over the colour of bishops and priests. I know from my experience as an urban vicar, head of RE in a multiracial school, a country parson and now a City Rector that there is a great hunger for spiritual teaching. Secularisation has failed. But the hungry sheep look up and are not fed. Instead they see their new Archbishop as deeply preoccupied with social engineering as any member of Blair's cabinet. Help with the spiritual revival is what we need, not more obsessive social delusions – not another example of the kettle calling the pan black."

A few days later, I received a letter of complaint from the Archbishop's Media Officer, Archdeacon John Barton ALCD, who asked me to tell him "Where and when is Dr Sentamu supposed to have complained that the Church of England is institutionally racist?" As I suppose is appropriate for a Media Officer who was also my ecclesiastical superior, the Venerable Barton offered me some timely admonishment: "When writing or broadcasting, clergy are not exempt from the moral and professional obligations to verify their sources."

And Archdeacons, even one with such a lofty qualification as Associate of the London College of Divinity, – a sort of GCSE in Religious Studies - are under the obligation to tell the truth.

I thanked the Archdeacon for his advice and supplied him with a large dossier of reports from the national press and the *BBC* in which Dr Sentamu complains about racism in the church. For example, that he had told the General Synod in July 1999 that it must change from its "monochrome culture" and that "ethnic Anglicans must be more visible in the life of the church." Crucially, Dr Sentamu added, "The expectation of the historic, white, educated elite English norm is maintained regardless of the makeup of a congregation."

I made the point to his Media Officer that that last remark is as clear a definition of "institutional racism" as we could hope to find. Indeed, it was taken so seriously at the time that the then Archbishop of Canterbury gave over a whole speech in the Synod to reply to Dr Sentamu's concerns. I supplied the Media officer with many other such examples of Dr Sentamu's views on the race issue. But he was not satisfied and demanded that I apologise publicly for my original article. He accused me of writing that was "at best careless and at worst mischievous."

I stood by what I had said in my article and supplied the Media Officer with even more telling evidence of the Archbishop's views. For instance, as reported by the BBC in June 2005, Dr Sentamu had said "The Church of England contains institutional racism as a room full of smokers contains smoke." Dr Sentamu's allegation was also reported in *The Independent* in October 2005. These quotations have never been challenged as inaccurate by Dr Sentamu of what he had actually said. Still this did not suffice, and soon the Media Officer started to turn nasty and issue threats: "If you decline to withdraw these unwarranted slurs, I shall have to raise the matter elsewhere."

At this point I thought it appropriate to send all my correspondence with the Media Officer to my editor on the paper where my article had originally appeared and to my immediate superior The Rt Rev'd Richard Chartres, Bishop of London.

This was when the Archbishop's Media Officer started to lie to me. I had claimed, as part of my answer to his complaints, that Dr Sentamu had applied the description "institutional racism" to the Church of England in the Foreword he had written to the book *Rejection, Resistance and Resurrection* by Mukti Barton. But the Media Officer fervently denied this: "The Foreword to the book *certainly does not use those words*"

In fact, this is precisely what Dr Sentamu says in his Foreword: "Kinds of institutional racism are in society and so inevitably to some degree found in the churches, both in the Church of England and other churches." Bang to rights, Venerable Barton, I think. As a traditionalist priest I have become accustomed to being threatened and bullied over many years by the "liberal" – actually totalitarian – hierarchy, but I must say I was shocked to be so blatantly lied to by a senior member of The Archbishop's Staff.

This lying Media Officer then had the brass face to lecture me on standards of veracity: "Nor does something become true through repetition (contra Lewis Carroll) not even ad nauseam." So finally he was driven to quote *Alice in Wonderland* at me. I wondered which rabbit hole he was writing from? I mean, I questioned Dr Sentamu's constant harping on the race issue. He says the Church is "institutionally racist," while there he is a black man promoted to the second highest position in the worldwide Anglican Communion – and nobody laughs.

There is no institutional racism in the Church of England. But there was institutionalised lying and paranoia in Bishopthorpe Palace. So I wrote to the Media Officer asking him to explain why he had lied to me. He sent back my letter with a copy of his earlier letter – the one in which he had denied that the Archbishop had mentioned institutional racism in his forward to Mukti Barton's book or anywhere else. This explicit lying denial was highlighted in green felt tip, just as if the Archbishop's Palace were the office of a red-top newspaper!

Receiving no sense at all from the Media Officer, I then wrote to the Archbishop himself to ask him why his Media Officer had persisted in lying to me and in trying deceitfully to blacken my name with my employers on *The Northern Echo*. I received the following letter of reply from the Archbishop himself:

"Thank you for your letter dated 26 Marsh 2006.

"The difference between you and the Ven John Barton is over the use of two expressions. I have, as you know, used the expression "institutional racism" in the foreword of Dr Mukti Barton's book, *Rejection, Resistance and Resurrection*. Again, as you know, these words first came to public prominence in the Stephen Lawrence Enquiry report.

"The other expression is "institutionally racist." This expression has not been used by me. It was not used by me in the Foreword, nor have I used it in any reference to the Church of England.

"Mr Barton took up with the Editor of *The Northern Echo* the matter of your attribution to me of the words "institutionally racist" as a description of the Church of England. I am disappointed by the Editor not accepting (*sic*) the point – and even apparently suggesting that what was written in the newspaper was justified. It was not.

"I trust you will ensure that you do not attribute the expression "institutionally racist" to me again in anything you write. If you have thought that I have said or written material which can be interpreted as such, then you are mistaken. For anything you may write in the future, the position I trust is abundantly clear.

"Finally, of course, the suggestion that Mr Barton is a liar is wholly repudiated. Holy Writ admonishes us not to bear false witness, defame or flatter.

"I am not prepared to devote more staff resources or incur fees to take legal advice on the matter. The publication was now several months ago. This correspondence between you, me and my office is now closed.

"+Sentamu"

By the way, the reason Sentamu was not prepared to seek legal advice was because *The Northern Echo* had already done so on my behalf and their lawyers' opinions – of which I had been sent copies – showed perfectly clearly that the Archbishop didn't have a case.

The Archbishop headed his letter NOT FOR PUBLICATION and sent a copy of it to my Editor at The Northern Echo.

So I wrote to my Editor as follows and sent a copy to the Archbishop:

"Dear Chris,

I believe you have received a copy of the Archbishop of York's letter to me of 7th April.

Dr Sentamu's vainglorious climb-down is not mitigated by its incoherence. He clearly inhabits realms so tenuous where there can be "institutional racism" without there being anyone who is "institutionally racist"! It is not possible, of course, for moral qualities or characteristics to exist independently of anyone to whom they can be attributed. The Archbishop's distinction therefore is not valid.

Perhaps indeed Dr Sentamu even suspects it is not valid, and that may be why he is not prepared to ask his legal advisers to defend the distinction.

Although Dr Sentamu informs me rather loftily both that his letter is "not for publication" and ends with the sentence, "This correspondence between you, me and my office is now closed," you may be assured that my original complaint to the effect that Dr Sentamu's servant has impugned both the accuracy of my remarks and my good faith in making them still stands; and that I reserve my right to take such action as my own legal advisers recommend to me."

The Bishop of London's office phoned in a hot flush: "The Bishop does so hope you will not sue Dr Sentamu." I didn't. I let the matter drop. But years after these events I remain shocked and sickened by the fact that a very senior member of the Church of England hierarchy imagines he can lie with impunity and attempt to blacken the character of someone who told the plain truth and evidenced that truth with extensive quotations from the Archbishop's own writings. As I say, I didn't consult the lawyers, but my editor on *The Northern Echo* did, and I was pleased when they supported my version of events and declared I had no charge to answer. The bishops – with some noted exceptions – are well-known for their sordid and underhand ways of proceeding, but Barton's and Sentamu's is, of all their deceits, quite the lousiest trick I have come across. They should be made to wash out their mouths with soapy water.

Change the subject Peter...

Captain Ron Bridge of the Air Pilots was a child out in the Far East during the Second World War at the time of the Japanese invasion. Ron asked me if he might provide a book containing the names of the British, Canadian, Australian, South African and New Zealand civilians interned by the invaders and have it as a memorial to them and be available in St Michael's for those who wished to know more. The book was produced and I dedicated it at a commemorative service in the church. In this book appear the names of more than 19,000 British civilians, over 15,000 from the Commonwealth and thirty-two colonials.

Prisoners were often transferred from one prison to another and from one territory to another, usually to cater for the labour requirements of their captors. Many POWs were sent to Thailand and Burma to build the infamous railway. Others went to the Moluccan Islands to build airfields; to Sumatra to build another railway; to Japan to work in the mines, factories and shipyards. There was cruelty and deprivation but there were less unpleasant occasions – for some. Many of these prisoners were allowed to receive mail and send cards, and in some cases letters, albeit in very limited quantities. But there was a perpetual shadow. As one internee wrote in his diary: "You were always afraid of somebody or something."

There are many evocative personal stories and reminiscences. Some very moving, poetic. Another wrote: "Darkness came suddenly. There were only candles. The air hung thick. Our shadows dragged along the walls. For hundreds and hundreds of nights, this is how it would be."

Children were interned too. And some of them wrote revealingly, with a childlike directness about their time in the camp. One said:

"We experienced a wonderful sense of freedom with loads of time to idle away. This sounds rather odd as we were all prisoners. I enjoyed school there. I think it was the informality of it. We had lots of fun with the teachers. Nuns can be a bit scary though."

Survivors, their relatives and friends and the whole congregation went off after the service to a luncheon aboard the battleship *HMS Belfast* moored by Tower Bridge.

X

The famous organ at St Michael's was dead on its feet and its increasingly frequent faults and failures were making the Sunday music impossible or, as the director of music said, "Threatening to put a stop to the Monday recitals." The organ deserved its fame for it had been glorious. The sixty-three stop, three manual instrument contains many pipes from Renatus Harris' two manual organ – originally in the west gallery. The opening recital was given in 1684 by Henry Purcell and John Blow from Westminster Abbey and G.B. Draghi, organist to Chares II's Queen Catherine. Over the centuries it was many times enlarged and enriched so that it deserved its reputation as one of the finest in London.

The director of music became the creative force and the driving energy behind a project to raise something not much short of £500,000 for a complete restoration and rebuild. The City institutions gave generously and in this none excelled the Drapers who donated £50,000. Having shown that a great deal of money had been raised already, the director of music applied to the National Lottery Fund for a substantial grant. The meetings were interminable and complicated and the paperwork mountainous. Particularly amusing was the agenda of extreme political correctness pursued by the National Lottery people according to which our committee was obliged to describe what benefits the organ restoration would confer on ethnic minority communities. We had to frame our proposals in a variety of alien languages. Neither earlier nor subsequently had I ever espied one of the said aliens at a recital.

Much of the spade work was done by our octogenarian church treasurer Mollie Harris. To say that Mollie was indefatigable would be a gross understatement. Her mind as agile as that of any prize-winner of mathematics' Fields Medal. Punctilious, with the tenacity of a limpet. Churches notoriously have difficulty in finding and keeping an efficient treasurer and St Michael's had seen the coming and going of a couple in my first four years alone. We were betwixt and between treasurers when the thought struck me: "Why not ask Mike Dudding?" Colonel Mike Dudding OBE was Clerk to the Worshipful Company of Chartered Secretaries and Administrators and in that livery there were many highly qualified company secretaries, treasurers and accomplished admin people. Mike suggested Mollie who was a retired company secretary. I gave thanks for that she agreed at once and from that day on St Michael's finances – if not its resources – were in perfect order. Many others laboured manfully but our organ committee would have got nowhere without Mollie.

And so the Lottery grant came through and the organ was restored and renewed: God and the organ builders having made it mighty and mightier yet. Thereafter, we were never fearful that the Sunday music might be spoilt and the organ recitals were now guaranteed. Our greatest good fortune was to recruit Gregory Drott, one of the finest young musicians I have ever heard – one of the most virtuosic and sensitive musicians of any age I shall ever hear – to be our organ scholar and deputy director of music. Greg could get sounds from that instrument which no other organist could reach. His accompanying of the service was precise and imaginative and we were all exhilarated by his tremendous and often hugely amusing extemporisations – particularly of the last verse of the recessional hymn. He could play the piano affectingly too and I heard him accompany the gloriously bravura concert aria *Ch'io mi scordi di te K.505* which Mozart composed for himself and the soprano Nancy Storace, the first Susanna in *Le Nozze di Figaro*. It was like having Mozart himself, at a loose end, drop in for half an hour before going on to his game of billiards. Greg deservedly moved upwards and on to become director of music at St Stephen's, Gloucester Road where T.S. Eliot was once churchwarden.

I took a holiday and while I was away tried to go to church three or four times. On the train on the way home, I doodled the following:

On the Impossibility of Going to Church
Who are these with wings like frogs
Who flap around in churchy togs
And offer us a rusty saw,
As if we had not heard before
That money will not save our soul?
The preacher's dug himself a hole.
He tells us we should turn to God,
But never stops to think that odd:
We know we should be better men –

The problem is of how and when.
If we could be good by our will,
Then Christ need ne're have suffered ill.
The Creed they use is highly risible –
Changing "unseen" to read "invisible."
Then when it comes to intercede,
It's quite enough to make us plead
For silence rather than his manner
Of making petition for Havana.
Who lives in Dartford and prays for Fidel
Has a perspective unreal as Dingly Dell
He prays for parishes in consternation
Of "pastoral reorganisation."
What purpose in these weasel words?
Look, Father, tell it to the birds
And speak as we speak in the town:
You mean it's churches being closed down.
And that's not gospel, not even funny,
But Church Commissioners wasting money.
The sermon over and on our knees,
He offers us "a sign of peace."
And suddenly all hell breaks loose
With salutations lewd, diffuse.
They grab your hand, they slap your back
And squeeze so hard your ribs might crack.
These assailants don't even know your name,
But instant intimacy is their game.
So fall to the floor, cower, kneel
To dodge that smiley touchy-feel.
Then music: ah mein Vater, Mutter,
This schtinking schtuff is by John Rutter!
No words of judgement will afford,
It's like "Come into the Garden Lord."
I'll tear my hymnbook, run and hide
Rather than do this palais glide.
Now at this Eucharistic feast
We need the altar in the east:
But here they place it in the middle
(Surely a psychological fiddle?)

Declaring it's the proper thing
To have us standing in a ring,
Proclaiming this is "more inclusive"
When actually it's most exclusive:
To make a circle, to put it crude,
Is by circumference to exclude
Not only the traditional bod
But transcendence – bluntly, God.
Every cathedral, every church
Of which you care to make research
Shows this very same disgrace –
The abolition of sacred space.
All over Europe this is done,
And wheresoever, God is gone.
Now that there's no holy fear,
Satan is the victor here.
It's atheism, but by stealth –
Destruction to the soul's good health.
Where has true religion gone –
That mystery so near the bone?
The unutterable sense of the beyond
Turned into something fey and fond,
Banal, bathetic, bloodless, bland,
Bureaucratic, sentimental,
Euphemistic, detrimental
To the sense we covet most –
That haunting by the Holy Ghost.
How dare they still use words like "Lord"
When all their thrust, their every word
Is utilitarian, un-pneumatic
And God himself made democratic,
Preferring not an hierarch priest,
But a "president" at this dumbed-down feast.
He's reading from a PC Bible,
His every word a blatant libel
Of Christ, of God, our Prince and King
Served by some vain, elected thing.
But pause to ask, What is church for?
But to be on earth an open door,

A ladder leading up to heaven;
Its rungs the Sacraments, all seven.
Here we may hear the Holy Word,
But not from a version that's absurd.
Don't give us doctrine that's all wrong,
Or sermons out of Patience Strong
By parsonical, Pelagian chaps
Who would pull us up by our bootstraps.
No, we come to church today
To learn our sins are done away.
That is the gospel of Good News
To all who kneel in stalls or pews.
The beauty of holiness must abound
In silence, in ecstatic sound.
We should be like that Moses bod
When he looked on the face of God.
There should be joy; there must be fear
As we attend the Godhead here
Who gives to us who have no merit
Blessings by the Holy Spirit.
We leave as new, regenerate men:
Lift up you hearts and shout, Amen

It got published in some very minor ecclesiastical magazine – I forget which.

The parish of St Sepulchre includes Christ Church, Greyfriars, bombed out in the war with only the tower remaining. A City businesswoman called Kate bought it. Unique. Utterly wonderful. A beautiful home in the elegant remains of an ancient church, on seven floors and with a spiral stone staircase. One morning Kate called and asked me if I would come and perform an exorcism.

"An exorcism! Why should you want me to do a thing like that?"

"Because there are people buried there – a long time – their names carved in the walls."

"But Kate, what's wrong with that? They're not demons. Just ordinary folk like you and me who happened to live a long time ago and have now died. There's no need for an exorcism. You wouldn't want to exorcise your granddad, would you? Tell you what I will do though, gladly: I'll come and do a house-blessing."

I did too and did it with a flourish with a bell, salt and sprinkled water, "Peace be upon this house and all who dwell herein."

Splash the ancient walls then drink a glass of Champagne.

Kate said, "Well, that was as good as any exorcism."

Not long afterwards, she bought another redundant church tower down by Lower Thames Street and I gave a repeat performance.

When I returned to The Watch House from that blessing service, there was an aggressive tramp waiting by my door and demanding money with menaces and oaths.

"I haven't any money, but I'll make you a sandwich."

"I don't want no f****** sandwich you s****y-a**d c**t! You're a f****** lousy priest-c**t"

I dare say I am too.

In the old days the beggars were…well, you might say, poor but honest and they were grateful for a bit of nosh and a pot of tea. Not these days. A new species of indigent has arisen in the land, self-appointed victims, masters of the forked tongue and sly as Ulysses. One Saturday morning the doorbell went countless times. There was a young, fit-looking, well-turned out fellow:

"Father, all I want is the money for my train fair to Exeter. I must get home, you see and I'm skint."

"Why do you need to get home?"

"Because my mother has just died."

"What *again*?"

He'd forgotten he'd told me the same story a couple of months back. Off he disappeared into his petulance accompanied by many more profanities.

Looking after the beggars and down-and-outs is a tradition in the City which goes back to medieval times, to the early hospitals and hospices, the ancient guilds and livery companies whose purpose and function was charitable works performed in the name of God, Our Lady or one of the saints. For centuries this tradition was sustained and naturally in the course of time it changed and developed. For instance, until comparatively recently, if there was a problem with the church roof, the Rector or one of the churchwardens – often both together - would get in touch with a bank in the parish. One of the senior staff would invite them to a very good lunch in a City restaurant and ask, "How much do you need?"

And the cash would be forthcoming. Not now, not in this prevailing climate of political correctness. The big banks and finance houses operate a policy of "diversity" and "non-discrimination." As one manager told me when I'd asked for a sub, "I'd like to but I can't. You see, if I gave money to you, I'd have to give to the Muslims and Jews as well.

"Well, that's OK by me!"

But he didn't cough up.

I will give one example of this new mood which is so bizarre that you will think I'm making it up. But I'm not. You couldn't make it up. At St Michael's and St Sepulchre's we took health and safety seriously, so we asked our architect to design a handrail for our front steps. This received the approval of the Diocesan Advisory Committee and so I applied to the City of London Bridge House Trust which has a good record of funding these health and safety measures.

I spoke to Jenny over the phone. She described herself as a "small claims assistant" and she told me the rules. The upshot was that the Bridge House Trust just might sponsor our church for part of the cost of the handrail so long as none of this money was reckoned to support Christian worship. I mean they just might pay for that proportion of the handrail that is used by people who come to organ recitals or who drift in to gawp at the ceiling; but none of it can be reckoned against the usage by people who come to services on Sundays or weekdays. So it's all right to be the parish church – so long as you don't go in for all that praying and hymn-singing mullarkey!

This is just one nasty example of the way that institutions which originally and for centuries owed their identity and self-understanding to the Christian Faith are now active enemies of the Faith. So we see everywhere the Church under vicious attack from the secularists who wish to abolish us. And we see – as in the silly business of that Lent programme and the greater folly which discarded the real Bible and the real Prayer Book – we see the Church actually aiding its secular enemies.

The modern mood thinks that we can ditch the Christian faith but still retain all the social goods and benefits which were created by Christianity in the first place. We can't. If Christianity goes, the whole lot goes with it. As Eliot put in *Choruses from the Rock* (1934):

"Such modest attainments as you can boast in the way of polite society will hardly survive the faith to which they owe their significance."

The truth is that England is no longer a Christian country.

One afternoon I was working on my Arts Club lecture on Samuel Coleridge when a man I didn't know phoned from Nottinghamshire: "Peter, I'm a liveryman of several companies. I know something of your work in the City and I know you've been Chaplain to the Lord Mayor. Can I come and call on you next time I'm in town? There's something I think we could do well together."

Synchronicity strikes again, for when he arrived he handed me a present: a volume of Coleridge's notebooks. Geoffrey Bond is an interesting man who divides his time between his country home at Burbage Manor in Southwell - where Byron lived from 1803 to 1808 - and his multifarious activities in London. An enthusiastic and compendiously informed collector and antiquarian, Geoffrey sits on the Antiquarian Society of London. His lectures and books on heritage matters have long been popular and admired. Past-Master of more than one livery company and successful both in business and as a solicitor. A well-known broadcaster too as an original member of the *Antiques Roadshow* team. In the 1980s he had presented the long-running *Something to Treasure* for ITV. He is a member of The Athenaeum and The Garrick.

Geoffrey had been appointed Lay Sheriff of London and he wanted me to act as Chaplain for his year. Whereas, as the title suggests, the Aldermanic Sheriff is drawn from the Court of Aldermen and his term as Sheriff is usually followed by his appointment to the Mayoralty, the Lay Sheriff serves just for the year and then disappears...in Geoffrey's case certainly not into obscurity but back to Byron's old home and his full calendar of professional activities and extensive charitable work. He said, "You won't find the job as hectic as being Chaplain to the Lord Mayor."

And after my year with Geoffrey, I was again Sheriff's Chaplain to Past Master of the Air Pilots, David Mauleverer. And that's quite enough about my twinkly shoes and tricorn hat...

It was hectic enough because the Sheriffs accompany and support the Lord Mayor at all the principal City events which adorn the Mayor's term of office: The Lighting-up Dinner, The Show, the Lord Mayor's Banquet which I have described earlier. It was at a banquet in Mansion House that I found myself in the unusual position of being able to give Henry Kissinger some strategic advice. We were in the drinks reception before dinner. The gong sounded to call us in. Nobody ever takes any notice. People dawdle over another drink and are averse to curtailing their conversations until the chivvying of the Beadle gets too much for them. But at the first sound of the gong, I saw Kissinger march dutifully into the magnificent dining room. I thought I would keep him company. There he was completely alone, a singular tiny figure captured among all the brilliant white linen of the tablecloths and napkins, the blazing chandeliers and the rows of lighted candles. He looked puzzled, as if to say, "Where is everybody?" I told him that the apparent reluctance of the diners was traditional and that they would all be along in a minute. "In any case, Sir, as guest of honour, you will be asked to join the Lord Mayor's procession."

Clearly, they do things differently on the other side of the Atlantic.

These processions into banquets – not just at Guildhall or Mansion House – but all livery lunches and dinners is a tradition in itself. The host, whether the Lord Mayor or a livery master, and the principal guests pose for photographs in an adjoining room. The main body of guests, having finally heeded the Beadle's admonitions, take their places at table and remain standing while the procession enters. This is almost always to the piano or instrumental accompaniment to the march from Handel's opera *Scipio* composed in 1725. Rather disconcertingly, to me at any rate, the guests slow-handclap the procession in time with the music – a feature also, or so I was told, of the great military parades in Red Square during the Soviet era.

Since I have started name-dropping, let me finish with a big one. There was a memorial service at St Sepulchre in honour of a colleague and friend of Lady Thatcher. According to protocol, as the chief mourner she was last to make her entrance. As Rector, it was my place to meet her from her car at the top of Snow Hill and accompany her into church. Our former prime minister's brief had clearly included the name of the Rector of St Sepulchre and, as she descended from her car, she said brightly, "Good morning, Peter!"

"Good morning, Lady Thatcher."

As we walked the twenty yards or so to the church porch, I said, "Before we go in, I'd just like to thank you for all you've done for us."

She turned to me and smiled. then said with great intent, "I haven't finished yet!"

Everyone wanted to be at the New Year City service, for the distinguished preachers certainly but also for the old warhorse hymns the whole congregation belting out three verses of the National Anthem including:

> O Lord Our God arise
> Scatter her enemies
> And make them fall.
> Frustrate their politics
> Confound their knavish tricks…

Afterwards I was reprimanded by a discommoded liveryman in the gents across at Drapers' Hall:

"As a Christian, you should be praying for peace, not giving us this outrageous jingoism."

"All very well, but if you think Her Majesty has no enemies, look no further than *The Independent* newspaper and the BBC endemic."

But the preachers were outstanding. Peter Hitchens, the journalist and regular panellist on *Any Questions* spoke with mellifluous lucidity, so it was a pity he had to get back to his newspaper desk and was unable to come across to the buffet and hear his virtues lauded. Again I was hauled over by some soft left malcontent – not in the gents this time but in the main hall as I was trying to balance a plate of lamb casserole and my wine glass:

"We come to hear the Word of God, Rector, and not some right wing rant."

"Were you even listening? There was no politics in Peter's address and no ranting. He spoke for fifteen minutes about the glories of *The Book of Common Prayer*. There are ranters, of course – but Mr Hitchens was not one of them."

Dr Edward Norman, formerly Dean of Peterhouse and BBC Reith lecturer 1978 – one of the best historians and theologians in the country - spoke forcefully about the Church of England's neglect of fundamental doctrine. At least he looked as if he were speaking forcefully, but no one beyond the front two rows could hear a word. Edward merely whispered into the microphone, so faintly he might have been miming. I did get him to send me his script and distributed it samizdat and put the text up on St Michael's website.

Recorder Michael Hyam waxed passionate about the rule of law as the basis of civil society. But the best of all the sermons preached over the fourteen years of my stewardship was that by the philosopher

Roger Scruton. Slight, red-headed, Roger arrived on his bike and in good time. He went straight to the back of the choir stalls to finish what turned out to be quite the most evocative sermon I've ever heard. It was not at all discursive or abstract but dealt in *things*: his meaning was fully incarnated in his choice of imagery. For example:

"In our early English churches of flint and stone, a peculiar silence has been stored along with the sweet, damp smell of plaster, the mouldering prayer books, the embroidered kneelers and the Victorian altar cloths with their gold and emerald fabrics, like robes left behind by some visiting angel…At the Communion, the organist would improvise on muted pipes, whimsical, watery sequences, full of fifths and fourths in the manner of Vaughan Williams or Herbert Howells. It was as though the Holy Ghost himself were present, humming quietly to himself in an English accent…God, as represented in the sacred texts and liturgy of the Church of England, was an Englishman, uncomfortable in the presence of enthusiasm, reluctant to make a fuss, but trapped into making public speeches. God hid his discomfiture behind a solemn screen of words, using old-fashioned idioms which somehow excused the severity of what he was bound by his office to say."

The shyness and diffidence of Roger's delivery and manner, the sparseness of his physical frame and the gentle tenor voice in which he uttered these truths gave to his performance an extraordinary power and indubitability. It is rare that one is able to say of a sermon that it was *thrilling*. A retired parson with white hair but a boyish face said to me as we crossed Cornhill on our way to lunch: "He speaks with authority – not as the Scribes!"

We forever came under the denunciation that we were hidebound, reactionary and worse. I once heard an Area Dean from the East End refer to us affectionately as "fascist bastards." But then he was the sort of bloke who would have spelt "fascist" as "facist" – just like the lumpen intelligentsia in the class of '68. As a matter of record, we were ecumenical and interfaith. We even hired out St Michael's to the extreme Evangelical Proclamation Trust who would bring in their overhead projectors, screens and noise machines for a day's "conference" and pay the Church Council £150 for the privilege. Of course, I wouldn't permit a woman to celebrate Mass at our altars – but only for the good reason that there cannot be such a thing as a woman priest. The integrity which opposes the ordination of women is no mere misogynist whim. It is a theological integrity and it was outlined as long ago as the 1940s by the great Christian apologist C.S. Lewis. He said:

"Suppose the reformer begins to say that God is like a good woman. Suppose she says that we might just as well pray to Our Mother which art in heaven as to Our Father. Suppose that the Incarnation might just as well have taken a female form. Suppose the Second Person of the Trinity be as well called Daughter of God as Son of God. Suppose finally that the mystical marriage betwixt 'Christ and his Church' were reversed, that the Church became the Bridegroom and Christ the Bride. All this is involved in the claim that a woman can represent God as priest."

Lewis concludes devastatingly but incontrovertibly: "If all those supposals were ever carried into effect, we should be embarked on a different religion."

Well Mr Lewis, they have been and we are.

There is a profound shift in original mystical theology, in the psychology of ritual and in our beliefs concerning the Divine ontology when a female stands at the altar and declares, "This is my body." These things are not trivial: they go to the heart of Christian apprehension where they actually make the relationship between God and humankind a matter for experimentation .

There are a few things which must be made very plain so that there is no danger of misunderstanding. To claim that women cannot be priests or bishops does not deny ministry to them. Of course I do not wish to denigrate women's ministry. From the time of the gospels it was women who sustained the church: the women who stayed by the cross when the male disciples had run away. Women who took him down from the cross and brought him with spices to his rocky tomb. And a woman was first witness to his resurrection. But he didn't ordain any of them.

We frequently had women to preach at St Michael's: that Liz Carmichael (Carmichal) for example And not only Christian women. A lady Rabbi to preach at the Drapers' Installation Service. Jews, even of the unbelieving sort from the Reform Synagogue. Bob Tear himself, who was some sort of Buddhist mystic. I have invited humanists, atheists, pagans and nothing-in-particulars to ascend our pulpits. We are broadminded and broad-church. But we don't believe the impossible: that a woman can be a priest and celebrate Mass.

Mass calls to mind Mass vestments. We used them at both churches but we were not obsessed with their style, quality and other such minutiae – as Charles Sisson said, "There are clergy who pore over clerical outfitters' catalogues as heatedly as any pervert peering into his pornographic library."

But ancient churches can hardly avoid possessing a few treasures and at St Michael's we had an Elizabethan cope – the long garment which the priest wears in procession and discards when he puts on the Eucharistic chasuble. It was falling to pieces. Still, we used it on high days and holy days and I would tell our devoted parish clerk, Rupert Meacher to wear it at weddings. Rupert was the embodiment of elegance with an innate and incarnated sense of ceremony. Of course he should wear our best cope, even if it was in rags. Anyhow, I was coaxed into making enquiry as to how much it would cost us to restore this fabulous garment. We got the kosher antiquarians to come and give us an estimate. Guess what? The lady from the learned society of swish churchy gear – a pale, eunuchish creature, so brutish she might have been a minder on the wrong side in the Cold War - told us straight:

"To have it repaired? Oh well. This will be difficult, but it can be done. We're talking about £40,000. And of course, when it's finished, you must never use it. We can provide glass cases…"

I'm sure you can. Madam. Rupert carried on wearing it all the same.

XI

On the morning of 5th July 2005 Muslim terrorists – but should I follow Rowan Williams and refer to them as our "conversation partners"? – attacked central London. Two tube bombs and a bus bomb. The details are horribly familiar and I need not re-tell the story of what happened. It was a Thursday and on the following Sunday I reported as follows to the congregation at St Michael's:

"Last Thursday's events were sensational and, in an age haunted and afflicted by a sensationalising and instant mass media, made more sensational still. I spent some time down by Aldgate tube station at what was called *Red Incident Control.* The parish priest at St Botolph's had given his church over to care for the police, ambulance and rescue people; and we were on hand to pour cups of tea and to be of any earthly use in a hellish situation.

"One of the sordid complications of the terror was the repeated ringing of the telephone. The newspapers, avid for a closer acquaintance with the terror scene, had contacted the diocesan authorities. And those innocent lambs in the diocesan office kept phoning the Incident Control to ask if the press might be allowed to come in and do their work. Of course there is a legitimate place for news coverage, for searchlights in the fog of war. But the public interest is not "anything the public is interested in." And the gathering of lurid reports and horrific photographs are not part of it. There is a distinction between information and prurience; and it is one always blurred over when there is blood about.

"That is what I mean by the *sordid* aspect of the terror. And the sordid aspect does quite as much damage as the sensational and shocking aspects – because it lasts longer and it touches everyone. I met courageous men and women there, who had been down into Aldgate tube and so knew the worst. Police and ambulance. But also others you hadn't thought of: dozens of men in orange overalls who had been called to go down into the tunnel and put up emergency lighting. All were subdued and quietly horrified. Some were distressed, very shaken and somehow puzzled – didn't know where to put themselves.

"That is something else which terror does: it infiltrates and intrudes deeply into a person. It interferes with a person's heart and soul. It is an interference just as disorientating as a physical molestation. And more severe because it is more subtle. The devil is not always the demon king: sometimes he does his malevolence gently. St Thomas Aquinas said something about this. He spoke of *the banality of evil*. And so it is. The devil is one part dirty lecher and three parts petty thief. Evil spoils our days together, wastes our time by forcing us to have to do what ought to have been unnecessary. All those people at the Incident scene having to hang around, half-occupied for hours and days. All a perversion of their life's normal course.

"So what is a Christian to do? What can we do? First, we don't need the soapy explanations of Mr Slope the senior clergyman turning up to justify the ways of God to man – though there's no stopping him, I'm afraid. But what happened last Thursday was not God's fault.

"By the grace of God, there are things we can do – particular and specific things, given to us by the great teachers of the faith. And these are the old virtues. *Courage.* There was plenty of that in and under the streets, in the hospitals, and among the bus drivers who ferried the injured to hospital. Courage gives us the strength to do our duty. We must not be cowed or bowed by these events. Courage hand in hand with cheerfulness. The Spirit of God inspiring our spirits.

Fortitude is courage dug in. The bravery of the moment must become the habit of a lifetime.

"*Patience* – perhaps the hardest of all when the justice we long for does not arrive; when the guilty go free and unpunished; and when we have to listen every day to explanations and excuses for the terrorists, which are no explanations, no excuse. Patience is courage dug in for the long haul.

"*Prudence* governs all the virtues because it sets them in order and enables us to act in ways that are not only right but appropriate and timely.

"We do not possess any of these virtues naturally. We must pray for them. The terrorist attacks must not be allowed to get under our skin, to corrupt our judgement as to what the terrorist deserves. These attacks must not undermine our confidence and love of life. We must go about the daily round not just grimly determined but determined to rejoice. The antidote to fear is the love of God – our love for him and his infinitely greater love for us. And this love must be encouraged to spread out into our love and care for one another – not in some horrible *Schmaltzfest* or a plea for excuses - but in a renewed awareness that we belong to one another and that we are our brothers' keepers."

Three weeks later I gave a public lecture in St Sepulchre's which I entitled *Apocalypse Soon?* It was forty-five minutes in duration and I'm not going to repeat the whole thing here, but briefly...

I began with Samuel Coleridge's definition of Islam from his *On the Constitution of Church and State* (1830):

"That erection of a temporal monarch under the pretence of a spiritual authority, which was not possible in Christendom but by the extinction or entrancement of the spirit of Christianity, and which has therefore been only partially attained by the Papacy – this was effected in full by Mahomet, to the establishment of the most extensive and complete despotism that ever warred against civilisation and the interests of humanity."

Then Winston Churchill:

"How dreadful are the curses which Mohammedanism lays on its votaries! Besides the fanatical frenzy, which is as dangerous in a man as hydrophobia in a dog, there is this fearful fatalistic apathy. The effects are apparent in many countries. Improvident habits, slovenly systems of agriculture, sluggish methods of commerce and insecurity of property exist wherever the followers of the Prophet rule or live. A degraded sensualism deprives this life of its grace and refinement; the next of its dignity and sanctity. The fact that in Mahommedan law every woman must belong to some man as his absolute property must delay the final extinction of slavery until the faith of Islam has ceased to be a great power among men. Individual Muslims may show splendid qualities. Thousands become the brave and loyal soldiers of the Queen; all know how to die; but the influence of the religion paralyses the social development of those who follow it. No stronger retrograde force exists in the world. Far from being moribund, Mohammedanism is a militant and proselytising faith. It has already spread throughout Central Africa, raising fearless warriors at every step; and were it not that Christianity is sheltered in the strong arms of science, the civilisation of modern Europe might fall, as fell the civilisation of ancient Rome."

And G.K. Chesterton:

"There is in Islam a paradox which is a permanent menace. The great creed born in the desert creates a kind of ecstasy of the very emptiness of its own land, and even, one may say, of its own theology…A void is made in the heart of Islam which has to be filled up again and again by a mere repetition of the revolution that founded it. There are no sacraments: the only thing that can happen is a sort of apocalypse, as unique as the end of the world and again and again. There are no priests: and yet this equality can only breed a multitude of lawless prophets almost as numerous as priests. The very dogma that there is only one Mahomet produces an endless procession of Mahomets."

R.G. Collingwood described Islam as "a barbarism." Finally I quoted one of Osama bin Laden's own spokesmen: "We shall win because you believe in life but we believe in death."

There is an Islamic insurgency on three continents. Why should we not notice this? And in many parts of Britain militant Muslims are seeking, often corruptly, to govern and rule local institutions. Anyone who doubts this should simply take a stroll into Tower Hamlets or around the Midlands towns, or Bradford, Oldham, Rochdale, Burnley, Blackburn and Dewsbury. I don't blame Muslims for trying to become dominant in these places where they are populous. But if non-Muslims don't like what's going on, then they should not pretend it isn't. These periods of Muslim ascendancy have happened at intervals over fourteen centuries, so let me put the current insurgency in context.

In AD 732 a Muslim army of as many as 200,000 men was defeated by the Christian Charles Martel at Tours. If that battle had been lost, all Europe would have fallen to militant Islam .In 1565 the relief of the Siege of Malta, by a Christian alliance, ensured that the Mediterranean did not fall into Muslim hands and so give them a toehold in southern Europe

Then came the Battle of Lepanto on 7 October 1571 when a fleet of the Holy League, a coalition of Spain (including its territories of Naples, Sicily and Sardinia), the Republic of Venice, the Papacy, the Republic of Genoa, the Duchy of Savoy, the Knights Hospitaller and others, decisively defeated the main fleet of the Ottoman Empire.

There was that other 11th September – 1683 when Christian armies under Jan Sobieski arrived at the gates of Vienna and defeated the last substantial Muslim incursion: the last, that is, before the one which we face at present. There is no doubt that militant Islam's current aggression will have to be firmly suppressed if the character of Europe as we know it is to survive. If the European powers cannot bring themselves to act firmly, then the continent will be dominated by the Islamic ideology within a generation, with the resulting loss of all our freedoms.

Why is there a Muslim ascendancy in Europe at present? The most obvious explanation is that, owing to massive immigration over the last thirty years, there are enough Muslims in Europe to enact such an ascendancy. The next part of the explanation is simple too: Islam is strong; Muslims actually believe something and they practise what they believe. Whereas Christianity in Europe – by every measure employed from surveys, church rolls, vestry registers, polls, censuses – has been in relentless decline for a hundred and fifty years. Practising Christians are more numerous, and increasing, in every part of the world from South America to China, India to sub-Saharan Africa. But in Europe, the continent which for a thousand years was the cradle of the faith and the maturity of Christianity's classical formation, the faith is practically dead.

Our landscape, our statutes laws and customs retain unmistakable traces of what once was: a cathedral in every city and the parish church the most prominent – and most-used - building in every village. Universities throughout Europe created by Christian monks. Hospitals and hospices founded by Christian benevolence and dedicated to the saints. The trades guilds and the livery companies enshrining the cardinal virtue of charity. Almost all the people availing themselves of Christian rites of passage: Baptism, Confirmation, Marriage and Burial. The faith taught in our schools. Giotto, Dante, Aquinas, Bach, Pascal - The greatest efflorescence of painting, music and literature the world has ever seen created explicitly in the name of Christianity. All this is now abandoned and become a museum culture, something for the tourists to gawp at, a haunting of mere shadows.

But what has replaced European Christian civilization? We are urged to teach "values." And we do. We not only teach values, we put them into practice. And by our fruits we are known: a heedless, diverse, hedonistic, individualistic libertarianism in which anything goes. Non-judgemental. Anti-elites. Relativistic. If we have gods and icons nowadays, they are the idols only of a mindless culture of celebrity and a banal and garish entertainments industry.

This wasteland, this phantasmagoria, this gaudy shambles has its pathetic slogans: Democracy. The Liberal Society. Diversity. Secular Values. We speak glibly of values, but there are no values without discernment, criticism, judgement. But right judgement and criticism are abolished in a bedlam where it is said any opinion is as good as any other, and where governments license the opinions of the most foolish. Whatever else it might be, the culture we now inhabit is incapable of resisting confident, strident Islamification. Our secular consumerism is no match for militant Islam. Our Christian forbears had the faith and the courage to resist the various Muslim insurgencies. We have neither the faith nor the courage. We operate instead a policy of pre-emptive self-abasement and we appease those who seek our destruction. We have invented perverse slogans by which we neuter any adequate response: and the principal slogan is "Islamophobia" of which we relentlessly convict ourselves when we issue even the mildest criticism of this barbarism.

But many doubt that there actually is an Islamic insurgency on three continents. They claim that the fanatics and terrorists are very few in number. They are not. Professor Marcello Pera states the plain truth when he says,

"Is there a war? I answer, yes there is a war and I believe the responsible thing is to recognise it and to say so, regardless of whether the politically-correct thing to do is to keep our mouths shut.

"In Afghanistan, Kashmir, Chechnya, Dagestan, Ossetia, the Philippines, Saudi Arabia, the Sudan, Bosnia, Kosovo, the Palestinian Territories, Egypt, Morocco and much of the Islamic and Arab world, large groups of fundamentalists, radicals, extremists – the Taliban, Al Qaeda, Hezbollah, Hamas, the Muslim Brothers, Islamic Jihad, the Islamic Armed Group and many more have declared a holy war on the West. This is not my imagination. It is a message they have proclaimed, written, preached, communicated and circulated in black and white. Why should I not take note of it?"

What I have just written is a précis of my 2005 lecture. Writing today, nine years on, I see no sign that a Europe under the bureaucrats or an America led by a do-nothing, speechifying, isolationist, lame duck of a president has made any progress towards the rediscovery of its backbone.

Around that time, I was browsing through some theological dictionaries looking for information for a sermon I was preparing. You know what that's like: you open the English dictionary to find the meaning of a word and stumble across so many other words that are more fascinating, so that you end up forgetting the word you were looking for in the first place. I can't remember now what I was looking for, but I came across the word "Cainites" and I discovered the remarkable fact that the Cainites were a people living in southern Judea not long after the time of Christ. And they revered Judas Iscariot as their Patron Saint. I was puzzled. How could anyone revere Judas? I was intrigued and I did a lot more reading. The result was that over the next two years or so I wrote, as an historical novel, the story of Judas as seen through the eyes of the Cainites. I'm still trying to find a publisher for this novel, by the way.

What we do know – what is actually true and historical – is that the Cainites were one of many Gnostic groups around the Middle East at the time. Gnostics were religious and philosophical luminaries who claimed to be in the know. They were dualists – they believed that the universe is governed by two equal and opposite supernatural principles: light and darkness. If you ever go down into southern Judea, near the Dead Sea and the caves at Qumran where the Dead Sea scrolls were found, you can see why Gnosticism was popular. The climate. It is blindingly light by day and utterly dark at night. The Gnostics' extreme form of religion mirrored their environment. I think most people today are more or less unconsciously Gnostic, believing that good and evil are equal and opposite powers or influences. But this is not the religion of the Bible which is monotheistic and therefore teaches that the devil, Lucifer or Satan was created by God. In the enchanting prologue to *The Book of Job* it says that Satan was one of the sons of God.

The Cainite Gnostics also believed that all material things, including the body and the flesh, are bad; and that only spiritual things are good. They were apocalyptic. They believed that the end of the world was coming and that at the end a mysterious Divine Redeemer would appear from the realms of light, this world of material things would be destroyed and the true believers – themselves of course! – would all be transported to a spiritual heaven. All remarkably prophetic of the recent President Ahmadinejad of Iran who, with the aid of his hoped-for nukes, wished to provoke the Last Battle and reveal the mythological figure, the Hidden Imam

The Cainites believed that Judas Iscariot was the prophet of the Divine Redeemer. They thought that Judas saw Jesus as this figure. And Judas betrayed Christ in the belief that he would come down from the Cross and show himself to be this Divine Redeemer. Jesus did not do this, as we know. And Judas hanged himself out of disappointment. There might just be something in this. But the Cainite religion – Gnosticism – is not something that was limited to one particular place and time. Gnosticism is an all-pervading heresy and it is a constant threat to the life and very being of the Church, and thus of the soul. G.K. Chesterton says the Church has nearly died from Gnosticism no fewer than five times. St Augustine dedicated his life to fighting it – in the form operated by the Manichees. It emerged again with the Cathars or Albigensians.

It awakened again in modern times at the Enlightenment in the 18th century. Gnosticism thrives wherever Puritanism thrives. It is a form of bloodless idealism – the notion that we can escape from the things of the flesh and retreat into the pure world of spirit. It is present wherever people imagine that good can be achieved by abstract ideals, as the saying goes, "Putting systems in place." Well, what's the fuss about? Gnosticism and Puritanism actually sound quite nice – and there is something of it in all of us,

Writing *I Judas* – mostly in the very early mornings – was heavy and heady work and I needed a diversion. It occurred to me that I ought to devise a satire on the prevailing creed of political correctness – itself a sort of Gnosticism, teaching as it does that the evils of society can be done away with by the simple expedient of declaring that these evils are forbidden and inventing new and imaginary social sins such as racism, sexism, exclusiveness, elitism and the rest. How to produce such a satire? It dawned on me that this might be achieved by writing a parody of the Gospel, including a figure who was bound to remind us of Jesus but who, of course, was not Jesus but a politically correct guru. I called him BOSSY and throughout typed his name in capital letters to indicate BOSSY's importance and elevated status. My next bit of luck was the thought that the parody might be best achieved by writing it in the English of *The Authorised Version 1611* of the Bible. I had been steeped in this language for fifty years, hearing it spoken, reading it and reciting it myself every day.

It is three-quarters of a mile from the Watch House to St Michael's. I would make that journey at least five times in the week. That was two-and-a- half hours walking. So I would compose a section of *The Politically Correct Gospel* in my head as I walked along Newgate Street, down Cheapside and up Cornhill – and back of course – and then write it out on my return home. Just to give you the flavour:

"And seeing the multitude of the Great Unwashed, BOSSY went up on the hill which is called *Primrose* and, when he was set, calleth his groupies unto him. And behold, he openeth his mouth and giveth them a presentation, like:

"' Chipper are the poor Milwall supporters, for they have been drawn against the Arsenal.

"Chirpy are them that mourn, for they shall receive bereavement counselling.

"' Ecstatic are the bashful, for they shall get assertiveness training.

"'Buggered are they that do hunger and thirst after righteousness – 'cos there's not much of that around these days.

"' Right chuffed are the sentimental, for behold it's *Princess Di Day* next week.

"' In luck are the impure of heart, for there's tons of stuff for them on DVD and late-nite telly.

"' Perky are them that belong to the peace-keeping process, for they shall share the loot with their brethren in the IRA.

"'Right frisky are they which are laughed at for political correctness' sake, for they shall get to revise the compliance manual.

"'Happy are ye when the Fogeys and the Old Farts shall revile you and utter all manner of racist and sexist things against you. For great is your reward in Cloud Cuckoo Land, for so persecuted they the apparatchiks that were before you.

"'Ye are the salt of the crisp packet, but if the salt produceth high blood pressure then verily thou shalt take the statins.

"'Think not that I am come to destroy Standard Practice. I am come not to destroy but to fulfil. For verily I say unto you, Till Cloud Cuckoo land and Medialand, wherein dwell the multitude of them that are called *celebs*, pass away, one jot or tittle shall in no wise pass away from Standard Practice, till all be compliance.

"'Wherefore, whosoever shall break one of the least of these footling proscriptions and shall teach his neighbour to say, 'Bollocks to political correctness!' shall be called the least in the Nanny State. And whosoever shall do and teach total compliance shall be greatest in the Nanny State.'"

Surprisingly, I didn't have the trouble finding a publisher that I had encountered in the case of *I Judas*. Michael Mosbacher, director of the Social Affairs Unit brought it out in a handsome hardback edition and – irony of ironies – I was interviewed about the book on the BBC. While I sitting in the green room before the interview, I heard – or rather overheard – the poetry programme being broadcast at the time. I felt encouraged to draft a letter:

Letter to the poetry editor at the BBC...

Dear Madam

I have always admired the BBC's resolute commitment to equal opportunities and to the Corporation's determination not to allow even the most conspicuous lack of talent to be a bar to the making and presenting of its programmes. I am particularly pleased to see that you have devolved and divided the running of your poetry department between an adenoidal illiterate from Liverpool and a grunting dwarf from Barnsley with learning difficulties. You are to be congratulated for your consistent opposition to all forms of elitism and a positive commitment to mediocrity.

It is this awareness of your morally courageous support for rubbish which encourages me to advertise my own modest talents. I have written a long poem, rather like an earlier poem by Mr T.S. Eliot called, I think, *The Waste Pudding*.

I enclose the text and wonder if you will allow me to read it on the wireless, please?

Yours sincerely

Fresh faces continued to turn up at St Michael's. Ian Hislop read a poem one Ash Wednesday and stayed for a glass of Malmsey. Michael Portillo, formerly of the Falangist Tendency, came and gave an illustrated talk on Richard Wagner. There is no man more polished than Michael.

I rarely visited the other City churches, since I had enough services of my own to take care of, but one Sunday two bankers, man and wife, invited me to their church for the Christening of their daughter. I discovered I had stumbled across what I can only describe as a congregation of New Age bankers who had come to giggle around the font. It was a brisk experience of culture shock. As I came in, the huge congregation were singing and clapping to the words:

"Spirit of the living God, fall afresh on me;

Break me, melt me, mould me, fill me…"

The choir entered, almost at a gallop and clearly preferred to talk and laugh among themselves to singing the silly words to the babyish tune. Then here comes the Vicar, smile on full beam, vigorously joining in the clapping. It was not so much a procession as an outbreak of the conga. As he swung into the central aisle, I got a close up of his vestments which looked as if they had been designed by Walt Disney: cherubs with grins as wide as the Vicar's against an indeterminate symbol resembling a pop logo. The back of his chasuble was, I was told later, meant to portray the Holy Ghost descending to earth, but it was more like Monty Python's dead parrot falling off its perch. When he got to the chancel step, he spun round and the banana-split smile stretched wider still and wider. He raised his hands high and the gaudy chasuble opened so that he looked like a huge technicolored moth. He bawled a stentorian greeting, "Hello!" – a very long "hell" and a very short "o."

There was no opening prayer, as such. Instead the Vicar started to chat into his microphone: "We are here for a very special event. This is going to be an exciting day for Clive and Tracy…" (the said bankers) "…and a very special day too for little Sidonie Clarissa." Then he intoned a long emotional "Aaah!" And the congregation echoed in chorus. I noticed the family sitting in the front pew – Clive in suede shoes and white suit matching Sidonie's shawl. Tracey in a diaphanous dress that was more absent than present. The Vicar continued in his Noddy language: "After our special prayer, Sidonie Clarissa will be welcomed as a full member of our church family." And, in a very passable imitation of the sinister Jimmy Savile, he added, "How about that then?" The congregation howled. "But first," he said – just like a radio Four announcer – "...we'll all join together in another of my favourite songs." He bellowed the whole of the first verse as an example, in case the intellectual content of the words should prove too taxing for his congregation:

"Sing Alleluia to the Lord,
Sing Alleluia to the Lord,
Sing Alleluia, Alleluia,
Sing Alleluia to the Lord."

I'm not making this up. You can find this song, number S.22 in the numbskull *Hymns for Today's Church*. We stopped for a moment to get our breath back and then the running commentary was resumed: "Now we are going to tell God how sorry we are for all the things we have done wrong..." I felt like responding, "Yes, let's start with a suitably grovelling apology for the goings-on here this morning."

The Vicar chortled his way through the Confession "...which you can find on page 36 of the green booklet." A great rustling of paper among the penitents. "Now let us stand and express our faith in the words of the Creed. Turn to page 43. Today we're going to use the seventh alternative Eucharistic Prayer to be found on page 96 and the optional Thanksgiving, second part only, on page 123..." Religion by numbers

"But first..." we were going to witness Sidonie Clarissa's Christening. He asked us to sit down while the modern parents made their way to the font, grinning all the way at their fellow hippy-yuppies, and the hippy-yuppies grinned back and gave them a round of applause. It was then that I noticed the piece of paper on my seat. Everybody had one: grey and heavy like pretend parchment, with writing on in a script like the Indian rope trick. The Vicar stood beaming luminously at the font and began to read from the grey paper: "Introducing the godparents Emma and Steve..." A further round of applause. Step forward then the gorgeous couple: Emma in a kaftan and Steve bearded and wearing flip-flops and a single earring the size of the Koh-i-Noor diamond.

"Now, let me tell you a few things about this lovely couple who are to be Sidonie Clarissa's sponsors today. Emma is a senior producer with an independent television company making important films on social issues for Channel Four. She and Steve took the courageous decision to travel the world with their own three children, staying in spiritual ashrams before returning to England to live for a year in a special spiritual centre devoted to the idea that belief in God and atheism amount to pretty much the same thing. Steve, of course, is a top journalist involved in the production of technical texts and computer programmes for a management training company. They are both seriously committed to the counselling process, having been awarded their diplomas by The Guild of Pastoral Psychology. I know that Clive and Tracey will be glad to learn that Emma and Steve have a very positive and empowering attitude towards parenting. They have asked me to thank you all for sharing with them today and hope that we all in this service play a positive role in the life of Sidonie Clarissa. So let's hear it for Emma and Steve…"

Another minor riot. Then, taking the child in his arms and drooling his perpetual effulgence over her, he prayed – I think it was meant to be a prayer – "In the name of the Lord Krishna, Shiva, the great Buddha and of Jesus, whom many call Lord – and of all the prophets and masters everywhere who have taught peace and enlightenment, we welcome Sidonie Clarissa into this our family where true relationships are nurtured and celebrated." He poured water over the infant from a sea-shell, lifted her to his smiling chops and kissed her with an emphatic loudness which caused the congregation to laugh and the baby to cry.

A further quarter of an hour of this stuff before we were let out and into the nearby livery hall to partake of the New Agey food that was set before us and to hear speeches which the libel laws compel me to leave unreported.

XII

It was a great treat to be Chaplain to the Air Pilots. They live lives of nonchalant high drama, as when a Past Master turned up late for Evensong and said, "Sorry I'm late Chaplain – I've just been for a spin in my Spitfire." Prince Philip, then our Grand Master, once arrived for a Court reception and, seeing the men in their furry blue livery, exclaimed, "Ah, medieval airmen!"

I wonder if any guild or association of tradesmen has ever in the field of human endeavour had to counter so much scepticism and plain ridicule as the aviators? And not just from ignorant peasants either. A handful of years before the first flight, Lord Kelvin, president of the Royal Society, announced, "Heavier than air flying machines are impossible. I have not the smallest molecule of faith in aerial navigation other than ballooning." The Harvard professor William Pickering wrote in *Aeronautics Magazine* in 1908: "A popular fallacy is to expect enormous speeds to be obtained. There is no hope of competing for racing speed with either our locomotives or our automobiles." My all-time favourite is a quote from The National Academy of Sciences Committee on Gas Turbines in June 1940 – a few weeks before the start of the Battle of Britain: "The so called jet engine can hardly be considered a feasible application to air frames." Having been working on jet propulsion for ten years, Frank Whittle replied, "Good thing I was too stupid to know that!"

As one who has attended scores of the Air Pilots' Court meeting and receptions, I can testify that all the legends about the airman's fondness for dicing laconically with death are the plain truth. You think I've got some horrible disease, don't you?

Once I saw a man standing in the corner by himself. Remembering the etiquette about making sure no one is left out, I went over to have a word. He looked rather distinguished and about sixty-five. Having been informed that all members of the Air Pilots livery are or were hands-on airmen in the RAF or with commercial airlines, I asked innocently – very innocently, as it turned out, "Were you a commercial pilot or in the RAF?"

"Oh I'm still in the RAF!"

Well, I ought to have been warned, didn't I? But persisting in the digging of my own grave, I pressed on, "What is it exactly that you do?"

"Actually, I'm Air Chief Marshal."

Only the boss of the entire Air Force, the whole damned shoot!

Another chap had overheard and he relieved my discomfiture with a joke: "This plane's going to New York, you see. There's a blonde airhead sitting near the front in a seat she shouldn't be in. So the steward goes over to her and says, 'Excuse me, Miss, but this seat belongs to a VIP who happens to be talking to the pilot on the flight deck at the moment. Allow me to escort you to a seat a bit further back.'

"The blonde will have none of it. She says, 'I'm a blonde and I'm smart and I'm going to New York.'

"The steward's protestations are all unavailing. So he calls the chief steward who goes through the same routine with the same result: 'I'm a blonde and I'm smart and I'm going to New York.'

"By this time both stewards are out of their minds with frustration – and the VIP is back and asking why his seat has been taken. So they are all surprised a few moments later when they see that the blonde has of her own volition retreated to a seat nearer the back. Whereupon the pilot himself appears with a smirk on his face:

"'How the hell did you do that, Sir?'

"Easy. I just told her the front end of the plane isn't going to New York.'"

Talking about trying to make sure no one gets left out, I was once on the HQS Wellington at a reception provided by the Honourable Company of Master Mariners. I caught sight of a slender, upright, elegant lady standing in the corner all by herself. I did a double-take. Yes, it really was Princess Anne. I went over to her: "All on your own, Ma'am?"

"Yes, it's always happening. People don't like to push themselves forward."

Nonchalance isn't in it. After dinner one of the airline pilots told me: "…bringing home a plane from Nova Scotia, 30,000 feet over the Atlantic, a window broke – not the whole thing, otherwise the cabin would have been catastrophically depressurised, and that would have been the end of us. But the outer was shattered, leaving only a thin shield that could have blown any minute. I brought the speed right down and lost some height. We made it OK – though I'm afraid we were a bit behind schedule."

I got taken out and about by the Pilots, most thrillingly on a day-long visit to Fighter Command's wartime underground bunker operations room at Uxbridge. This was where the invading Luftwaffe, plotted on radar, were represented by counters pushed around across the table: "Bandits four hundred. Angels one-five!" Above was the gallery where Winston Churchill stood when he visited on 15th September 1940, the climactic day of the Battle of Britain:

"How many aeroplanes have we in reserve?"

"We have none, Sir."

At Uxbridge I met some of the pilots from that battle – elegant gentlemen in their eighties, their whole demeanour understatement: "I was nineteen and in a Spitfire squadron. On my first combat mission, I came out of the clouds and saw three or four hundred Nazi bombers heading for London. I must admit I gulped a bit as there were only eight of us. Soon cheered up though when our squadron leader came over the radio and said, "Come on boys, let's surround the bastards!"

Characters. John Hutchings, a Concorde pilot. While the AGM is going on in Merchant Taylors Hall, it's customary for the ladies to be entertained by a visiting speaker. I sat in with the ladies sometimes. One year John gave a talk about flying that great aeroplane. He began by asking, "Does anyone mind bad language?"

"No."

Does anyone mind *really* bad language?"

Slightly less certainly, "N-no."

John regarded that as *carte blanche* and went on to tell us of the time he invited a *risque* comedian on to the flight deck. "He was overcome with wonder and this came out in two words repeated over and over again, "F****** H***!" But John's talk was astonishing. He simply described a Concorde flight from take-off in London to landing in New York. So evocative you felt you'd actually been along on the ride.

Another year Air Marshal Cliff Spink invited me to Duxford Air Show. Cliff usually flew the Spitfire in the Memorial Flight, but this year he was piloting an ME109 while his Luftwaffe counterpart flew the Spit. They re-enacted dogfights for half an hour. The sound of that Merlin engine must be one of the most thrilling noises ever to enter the ears of an Englishman. Coming in very low at two hundred and fifty miles per hour, then pulling abruptly into a vertical climb to reach two thousand feet inside four seconds. Cliff told me that many years ago he was on a German airfield and an old Luftwaffe ace asked him if he'd like to fly the ME109 for himself. Cliff accepted. When he returned to earth, the German pilot said, "What did you make of it?"

Cliff was diplomatic: "Nice aeroplane but perhaps not quite as good as the Spit."

"I agree. You know, Cliff, I crashed three ME109s during the war. What do you say to that?"

"Oh, just thanks very much for your contribution to our war effort!"

They ask me to say Grace at their dinners and I can report I've had no complaints about "levity" such as I got from the Chartered Secretaries Company. On the contrary, these blokes would have taken me outside and shot me if ever I contented myself with uttering anything that was merely *safe*. So:

"Bold airmen stand o'er all the earth.
Post-Christmas cheer, extended girth;
This evening there's no chance we might
Try losing weight or gaining height:
So we who hurtle through the skies
Thank God for all those chips and pies."

And for the banquet in Merchant Taylors Hall after the pilots' Annual Service at St Michael's:

"There was a famous airman,
His wings they gleamed like brass;
He fell out of his cockpit
And landed…. in a tree.
He said, 'My word, I'm lucky –
Thank God that I'm still here
To raise a glass and hearty thanks
For all this evening's cheer."

We gave a dinner to mark Prince Philip's retirement as Grand Master after fifty years and his elevation to be Patron. The Wardens, Clerk and Chaplain gathered in a small room. Prince Andrew had agreed to take his father's place as our new Grand Master. The conversation was all about flying at nought feet over the sea at night without lights or navigation. When it came to dinner time, I had to stand beside Prince Philip and say my Grace. I thought it was probably not the occasion for the usual sort of thing, but something perhaps a little more, well…princely. I had cobbled together a pretend *King James Bible* verse, something a bit like a Psalm:

"Bring forth the best wine;
Let thy table be decked with all good things.
For the Princes are come in,
The Princes are come in, O Lord
Even unto the great feast.
Let all the company rejoice
And be exceeding glad. Amen."
Prince Philip leaned across and whispered, "Isaiah?"
I'm afraid I said, "One eye's 'igher than the other, Sir!"

There was a dinner at Rules restaurant to celebrate the fiftieth anniversary of the Pilots' first attachment to St Michael's. At the end of the meal, I read an extract from David Brown's excellent *History of the Air Pilots*:

"Flying tends to breed a philosophy of its own. In the beginning, from the time when the landscape first expands beneath the wings after take-off, and earthbound humans shrink to insignificance, there is a sense of pride and freedom. Later, as experience is gained, there comes a more lasting sense of detachment, and pride gives way gradually to humility born of the realisation of human limitations in the face of the elements and of a working environment which, by day and night, can be at times forbidding and at other times overwhelmingly beautiful – and sometimes both."

Per Ardua ad Astra.

The parish clergy are constantly deluged with communications from central church authorities – you might call it ecclesiastical junk mail. When I was a new priest in my first parish, the annual returns featured one sheet of paper on which the Vicar was asked to declare how many people had attended church at Christmas and Easter, how many had been baptised, confirmed and buried; how many names on the electoral roll. And that was it. Sign it and send it off. The whole thing took five minutes. Nowadays the return is a foot thick with millions of boxes to tick, the language opaque management-speak. Questions about low energy light-bulbs, carbon footprint and health and safety. I think the idea was that it should be impossible to complete. At any rate, I never finished it. I left pages blank and in other places I would answer "Gone away" or "Retired to the loony bin."

Just after the millennium year, there was a great deal of noise about the church's policies for the care of children. Along with every other clergyman in the Diocese of London, I received a forty-page glossy booklet called *Children: Promoting Their Welfare, Protecting Them from Harm.* It reads like jargon from the Circumlocution Office, peppered with bullet points and full of the same mixture of sentimentality and bullying we find in the MacPherson Report. At a time when the Diocese is pleading poverty and raising the amount the parishes have to pay each year in tax to central funds, it is surprising to see them lashing out on expensive publications of this sort. But the content of the booklet makes me despair for the mind of the Church.

It begins with portentous statements of the bleeding obvious: "Children need love, affection and encouragement; physical care and nurture; protection from physical dangers; security and control which is firm, clear consistent and kind…" The next sentence also looks as if it was generated by some Ecclesiastical Department of Tautologies: "Physical abuse may involve hitting, shaking, throwing, poisoning, burning or scalding, drowning, suffocating or otherwise causing physical harm to a child." I have yet to discover that our organist is a serial poisoner or that the parish clerk is just bursting to drown a Confirmation candidate.

But where the document is not pleonastic and banal, it is

meaningless. It goes on to say, "Those working with children and young people should be carefully selected." But by whom? As I understand it, the problem of child abuse in the Church takes the form of abuse by parsons and other church officers – the very people who are here being invited to select new colleagues. It's the old question of who will guard the guardians? Unabashed, it continues, "Team members should monitor one another in the area of physical contact." Apart from the fact that this injunction is sure to create group paranoia and institutionalise distrust, the obvious truth is that anyone who wants to abuse a child will do so when there is no one else watching.

It says that those who work with children should be "trained". Trained in what? Presumably Sunday School teachers can teach and choirmasters can impart musical understanding. The idea that there is something *additional* to their skills in which they must be "trained" is merely a superstitious fad believed like an article of faith by empire-building educational bureaucrats and social workers. It says, "Each parish is required to appoint a Children's Advocate who could be introduced and interviewed during the main Sunday Service." What, and ruin another act of Divine Worship?

And then, "Choirmasters, organists, bell-ringers and others who are likely to give individual tuition should follow their professional code of ethics." Well, what else? They'll be suggesting we should pay our taxes and not be cruel to small animals next. But, "Private tuition should not be given on church premises without another adult being present." It isn't always possible for another adult to be present, but in any case two adults can inflict twice as much abuse as one: Fred and Rose West made an efficient team, didn't they?

Under the heading "Confidentiality" it says, "Having a relationship with a grown -up who listens, encourages and affirms can be hugely valuable to a child…" (What would the denial of that statement amount to? But never mind). "…Such a relationship will allow for 'good' secrets." How is it that the self-appointed experts, the Diocesan Children's Adviser and the four "Child Protection Advisers", who have produced this piping hot slush don't understand that perverts know exactly – better than the Advisers – how to listen, encourage and affirm and otherwise manipulate a child's confidence? In the sickening jargon of child abuse the process is known as "grooming."

Incredibly the manual assures us, "Children should know that adults may be trusted not to betray confidences." Which adults? The statement merely begs the question which the manual sets out to answer – that of how to prevent child abuse by identification of the abusers. And, "Gossip and rumour-mongering are to be discouraged as inconsistent with the Christian life, but whistle-blowing is not." Unless the authors are first to abolish Original Sin, how are we to tell the difference? All this "monitoring" and "Whistle-blowing" reminds us of the Soviet system under Stalin.

The inanity of it all is stultifying: "Don't touch inappropriately or intrusively." Anyone who is not an abuser knows this without benefit of a bureaucratic, governessy lecture. "Don't give lifts to children or young people on their own. If this is unavoidable, ask the child to sit in the back." But this sort of unfriendly, antisocial behaviour is itself a form of abuse. Besides, if I saw a child standing alone in the churchyard in the rain and called out "Quick, get in the back of the car!" the poor mite would think he was being kidnapped.

I look forward to a new and revised Diocesan Children's Policy. To be fully compliant with modern mores it should surely read:

"And every year at the Vestry Meeting, the PCC should appoint the official Parish Paedophile. He/she should not confine his/her molestations exclusively either to little boys or little girls but, taking due account of diversity procedures, interfere with children indiscriminately without regard for gender, race or creed. Except, be it noted, little Jewish boys/girls must not be molested before sunset on Saturdays and Muslim children not until Friday Prayers are over. Choirboys/girls not to have hands laid on them suddenly until after the third Collect at Evensong..."

But no. In the face of such idiocy satire becomes impossible. There are many different ways to write nonsense – some of it very well paid. In 2001 Canon Dr Arthur Peacocke – a man who has written that "Jesus represents the pinnacle of evolution" - was one of the select winners of the prestigious £1million Templeton Memorial Prize for Progress in Religion. He is what's known in the trade as a Process Theologian, that is one who follows the scientistic mysticism of

Pierre Teilhard de Chardin. As founder of the Society of Ordained Scientists, he had spent decades, as he put it at the time, "...at the interface between science and religion." It is unfortunate, then, that his theological and religious opinions suggest not progress but regress.

Dr Peacocke claimed that Christians have nothing to fear from "...the beautiful and dazzling picture of science unveiled over the past five decades." Well, scientists are right to be proud of their achievements, but people generally are also right to fear the practical results of some of these achievements: the atomic bomb, for example, and other instruments of total warfare by which men have the capacity to destroy the world many times over. And the new discoveries in biology and biochemistry have their dark side, as Aldous Huxley correctly prophesied eighty years ago in *Brave New World*.

But in repeating these truisms I am only, as it were, clearing the ground for an exposure of the nonsense on stilts of Dr Peacocke's views. His "beautiful and dazzling picture of science" is, he says, what "has resulted in the first generation of human beings to have solid evidence of the origin of the cosmos and human life." This bizarre assertion not only damns creationists and biblical fundamentalists: why does Dr Peacocke not see that it also damns every generation of scientists before the current one? Scientists like to speak of scientific understanding as a form of progress - every generation always adding something to an accumulating body of knowledge. But it is not at all like that. What actually happens is that new experiments lead to new theories which falsify older theories. To put this epigrammatically: even the most beautiful hypothesis is one day killed by one brute fact. Or, as Bertrand Russell once remarked in the context of his famous doubts concerning induction, "The chicken that is fed every day eventually gets its neck wrung." Einstein supersedes Newton and quantum mechanics renders redundant the old mechanistic dogma that every event has a cause.

To claim, as Dr Peacocke does, that our generation is the first to understand the truth about "the origins of the cosmos and human life" is a breath-taking arrogance. Besides, this view entails also the view that the theories of earlier generations (each regarded as accurate in its own day) were false. If that was indeed the case, then *scientifically* we would be right to infer that our own present theory will turn out to be false too.

But there is an even more colossal hubris in the supposition that we can know the truth about the origins of the cosmos. Human beings have been doing science in the modern sense only for about five hundred years. Are we really being invited by Dr Peacocke to believe that, as such latecomers and apprentices, we can know about the origin of all things? As Ezra Pound said, "Pull down thy vanity!" There may be coherence and even insight in the Big Bang theory which fashionably dominates cosmology; but this theory too will in the course of time be discredited and replaced by something else. That is, after all, how science works. For the time being, our best bet is to regard the Big Bang theory as itself a creation myth alongside other creation myths - such as the first chapter of *Genesis* or the story of Marduk and Tiamat.

Dr Peacocke's argument develops its preposterousness as it gathers pace. From his assumption that the beautiful and dazzling picture of science is the only way by which we can correctly view the origins of the universe and human beginnings, he concludes that, "This new framework is something which the sacred literatures of 2000 years ago are hardly equipped to relate to." So much for divine revelation. Throw out the Bible then? Not at all. Oddly, Dr Peacocke proceeds to recommend yet more biblical criticism: "The church has not taken on board the impact of New Testament and biblical scholarship."

By this Dr Peacocke means the kind of forensic analysis of scriptural texts which reckons to tell us in what order they were written - the dry-as-dust "a missing consonant in *Deutero Isaiah*" school of pedantry - and the ideologically-conditioned principles of interpretation of, say, the demythologisers. And I for one am glad if the church has not taken biblical criticism on board. To try to construct religion and spirituality on the principles and methods of the higher biblical criticism is as if, when presented with a very good dinner, one were to refuse to eat it and instead spend the whole mealtime discussing the molecular structure of the meat and vegetables or merely reading and re-reading the menu.

Building religion on biblical criticism is like constructing a positivistic utopia - a thing which George Eliot refused to do, saying, to Auguste Comte who asked her to produce one, "We must not lapse from the picture to the diagram." Unfortunately, the church *has* taken on board the biblical criticism of such as Strauss, Ritschl and Bultmann, as well as the secularising theology of the last forty years, to the extent that the Kingdom of God is now widely seen only as a metaphor for the redistribution of taxes. Among the liberal elite who control the church, the secular meaning of the gospel is the *only* meaning of the gospel. After the demythologisers with their bulldozers have done their work, "gospel" means "social gospel," and without remainder.

This is why church attendances have declined catastrophically - not because modern men are being asked to believe six impossible things before breakfast, but because they are hardly being asked to believe anything at all. Dr Peacocke says, "There are moral, idealistic people who just cannot believe some of the baggage we hear {*sic*} in church". What baggage is this? The Virgin Birth, the Resurrection and Ascension? Yes, Dr Peacocke must indeed mean these doctrines - because biblical criticism, in the shape of Rudolf Bultmann, has told him, "You cannot believe the miracles and the Resurrection in an age of electric light and the wireless." Why not? What arrogance is it that makes us think that, because we own a wireless set and our privies are no longer dark, we can spit on the wisdom of the writers of ancient texts - men such as St Paul, St Augustine and St Thomas Aquinas who *did* believe in the miracles and the Resurrection?

Turning to modern people's experience of the church, Dr Peacocke says, "The images have gone dead on them." This is because two generations of positivistic, reductionist theologians and tin-eared liturgists have broken all the images. The banal modern liturgies and the vandalising re-ordering of church interiors have abolished spiritual poetry and sacred space. Why should a moral idealistic people - or anyone else for that matter - bother to attend to the etiolated teachings of the secularising iconoclasts? The Templeton Prize is a terrific reward not just for its winner but for yet another recitation of the clapped-out Enlightenment Project.

Despite Dr Peacocke's regressions, progress in religion is both possible and necessary. But, instead of regarding theology as a set of principles or a method by which the faith is explained - the awful school of "What Our Lord *really meant* by this parable" - we must take up again the techniques of the early Fathers, of such as Augustine, Dante and Newman, and seek meditatively to understand the faith *in its own terms.* You can invent a discipline for doing this if you fancy and call it the phenomenological analysis of religion. But really it is simply a case of entering a world - a world of images, pictures, lights, stories, holy words, dogmas and sacraments. This, rather than Dr Peacocke's "scientific framework" is the proper vocation for Christian theologian, priest, pastor and layman alike. The broken images must be restored. As Tom Eliot said:

> *The formed stone, the visible crucifix,*
> *The dressed altar, the lifting light,*
> *Light...Light*
> *The visible reminder of Invisible Light.*

Folly is not always as abstract and theoretical as Dr Peacocke's version. Sometimes it comes fully clothed in living examples of practical idiocy. Of such is the Corporation of the City of London's policy on trees in the Square Mile. I think the Aldermen and Common Councilmen who make the local laws must be descendants of the primitive animists. How else to explain the fact that pruning the trees is not allowed? Well, at St Sepulchre there were plane trees on the south side and they grew to overhang the high gutter. So in autumn the gutter became clogged up with the fallen foliage and water poured into the church, causing damage and mess that is easily imagined.

I applied – I asked nicely – if I might engage an expert to trim the trees. "Certainly not. We have to think of the environmental issues." And he added, as if boasting, "*All* the trees in the City are protected."

"But not the churches, apparently? I *am* thinking of the environmental issues: the colossal damage to a medieval church, a Grade One listed building."

"It's not allowed."

"Look, I'm not aiming to take an axe to them – not the full George Washington job. Just a little gentle pruning so that they don't overhang the gutters. It's costing a fortune in repairs – money we haven't got. And it's so unnecessary. During that deluge we had last Friday, there was a hell of a noise and when I went into church to see what was happening, water was cascading down the south wall like Niagara. It'll take thousands of pounds to put right."

Not a chance. I got on to the diocesan office to see if they could offer any advice. "Oh yes, we understand, Peter. The Bishop has a plane tree in his garden and he had a devil of a job to get it trimmed."

"He succeeded then?"

"Eventually."

"Obviously mere Vicars and Rectors don't rank highly enough to receive such concessions."

"Don't worry – we do have a scheme to help you. The diocese employs a team to attend the churches in autumn and remove leaves from the gutters before they can do any damage. There's an application form…"

"I'm sure there is. But who pays for this work?"

"It comes out of the budget, the diocesan fund."

"And where does the diocesan fund come from?"

"Well from the money paid into it each year by the parishes. But we think it's value for money and a good solution."

But how can bloody-minded, obsessive irrationality be a solution to anything?"

XIII

That in general the bishops are a pretty poor lot intellectually – and are therefore, inevitably, spiritually vacuous – is not in doubt. They cannot bear comparison with their predecessors of even fifty years ago, let alone with 19th century luminaries such as Westcott and Wilberforce. But there occasionally appears in our contemporary episcopal mediocrity a mind so crass and perverse as to persuade us that he is some sort of fifth columnist, working on behalf of that character described by C.S. Lewis as "The Enemy." Such an example is Richard Harries, former Bishop of Oxford

Over the last forty years, traditional believers have been forced to put up with the ruminations of many modernising iconoclasts but Harries surpasses them all. He was and is a champion of embryo research. He also turned his attention to cloning and wrote in *Church Times* saying that it is "right and necessary." He began, "Fundamental research needs to be done before any progress can be made in finding any cure for the range of serious diseases such as Alzheimer's, Parkinson's and others."

Towards the end of his life, Pope John Paul warned against this line of thought: "The results achieved in various fields of science and technology are considered and accepted by many as *a priori* acceptable. In this way, one ends up expecting that what is technically possible is in itself ethically good. But this is to perceive truth and justice as something modelled around the work of man himself – as in the attempt to appropriate the sources of life through experiments in human cloning."

There are two points to be made here. First, there is no guarantee that research using cloned humans will lead to the discovery of cures for *any* disease. If it were known that such research would lead to cures, there would be no need for the research in the first place. Harries tried to put his *a priori* eggs into an *empirical* basket. The result is the predictable mess. Secondly, the notion that the finding of cures for serious disease legitimates human cloning is a utilitarian argument which asserts that the ends justify the means. Whereas traditional Christian theologians, Catholic and Protestant, affirm that morality is *deontological* – derived from the fact of being and interpreted through the philosophy of natural law. By this ethical principle, some acts are *always* wrong. The destruction of innocent human life is one of those acts. Human beings – even in embryo – are not, as Harries believes, means to an end but ends in themselves.

Harries considers the assertion that "Either the early embryo is a person, or it might be" - and he denies that this is the case. This is a piece of philosophical illiteracy at a very exalted level. No philosopher would argue that the embryo is a person, for the word *person* is a term which connotes advanced human capacities such as self-awareness, rational thought, making choices and having conscious and meaningful relationships with other human beings. (For an excellent introduction to the concept of a person, we should turn not to Harries but to a thinker: see, for instance, P.F. Strawson's classic *Individuals* OUP 1959)

The point is that though by no means could an embryo be described as a *person* – neither could three-months'-old infants for that matter: would Harries permit lethal experiments on *them*? – it is certainly a human being; and it is on this basis that it has the right not to be killed. Or rather, forsaking the pretentious superstition of universal rights, let us say that adults have a responsibility not to kill it. Of course the embryo is not a person but it is a human being, a potential person. It is this human being that Harries proposes we should kill in the interests of some alleged future and greater good.

Harries' primary confusion leads him to make assertions which are truly bizarre. He further seeks to justify cloning on the grounds that, in any case, "There is in nature a very high level of embryo loss." This is an argument exactly matching the argument that because some people accidentally fall under buses it is permissible for us to push more of them in the path of the number 56 to Islington. You would think that even a man so deeply in thrall to bio-technology and utilitarianism as Harries is would understand that natural death is not the same thing as unlawful killing, murder.

But the hypotheses of bio-technology and the superstitions of scientism provide Harries with what he clearly regards as his most convincing argument in favour of human cloning. He informs us that, "Before the 14-day cut-off-point – that is the emergence of the primative streak or beginning of a nervous system – it is not obvious that you have an individual." From this statement we see that Harries is no better at defining *individual* than he was when he had a try at *person*. For whatever the status of the cell-cluster before the emergence of the primative streak, *it was always and nothing else but* the material out of which the individual could develop. No such surviving cell-cluster has ever gone on to become *anything else but* an individual. Christian moral philosophy clearly prohibits the destruction of innocent human life at *any* stage in its development.

Having classified the human embryo as a disposable piece of tissue whose only value is that of a commodity, Harries then turns his attention to the Real Presence of Christ in the Eucharist: "People who are groping their way into Christianity can suddenly find themselves shocked and horrified at the sacrificial, cannibalistic language of the Eucharist. Christians do not take seriously enough people's sense of horror at going to a Eucharist or Mass and hearing the imagery of sacrifice and eating God." He recommends that we use expressions such as "the food of angels" and "the bread of life" instead of Our Lord's words of Institution in which he explicitly told us, "This is my Body…This is my Blood." But we are instead to splash about among the sugary euphemisms of the Bishop of Oxford.

Eliot said, "You shall not deny the body." In his two ill-judged philosophical excursions, Harries denies both the Body Sacramental and our solid flesh. A man who holds such opinions can hardly be called a Christian –yet there was Harries, one of the most senior bishops in the land.

There was never any getting away from the contrast between the conspicuous wealth of the City and the squalor that rules half a mile away in Tower Hamlets and just down the road in Stepney. City institutions – especially the livery companies – have a conscience about this contrast, but what they do in response is frequently misguided, particularly their belief that the answer is to throw money around more or less indiscriminately. The General Synod labours under the same superstition.

There is no doubting that poverty is a problem in the sense that to be so poor as to have nothing to eat is a dire predicament. But this is not what is meant by poverty in the sense used by the ideological socialists in the Synod. These ideologues use a vocabulary derived not so much from the words of Our Lord concerning the poor in the New Testament, but from Marxist theory. The key document in modern times was the Synod's *Faith in the City* (1985) where there is much talk of "structures of power", "dynamics of economy" and "under-privilege." This last word is interesting because, though it is forever bandied about, it is quite meaningless. It implies that there must be "over-privilege." What then are we to aspire to – neither "under-" nor "over-" but just a moderate amount of privilege? This is clear nonsense.

In a direct reference to *Faith in the City*, Adrian Hastings wrote in his book *A History of English Christianity 1920-1985*, "Work among the poor is most effective when most professional and most carefully grounded within a homogenous and recognisably Christian strategy. It is least effective when too obviously amateur and over-ambitious or open to attack as neo-Marxist." Too often in recent times the response of the church to perceived poverty and "social deprivation" has been simply to chuck more and more money at the problem. As a policy this is about as good as endlessly tipping bundles of £10 notes into a raging fire.

So what is poverty today? I was sitting at lunch in the Stock Exchange between two knights of the realm who had both reached the highest rank in the City financial sector. Now semi-retired, they were giving their time and expertise to helping poor communities in the East End. They told me that there is no poverty in the traditional sense of not having enough to eat. How could there be when many people described as poor today go around in £70 trainers, drive motor cars, watch wide screen television sets and spend half the day ringing up their friends on their expensive portable phones? And it is not unknown for a few of them regularly to partake of even more illegal substances. Rather there is a poverty of understanding – a cultural lack of knowledge as to how to manage daily life.

Whereas fifty years ago there was genuine poverty. I know, because I was brought up in it. But poor people were aware and informed – because they had been taught by their parents – in the matter of knowing how to make a little go a long way. These people did not have motor cars and designer running shoes. Most didn't have washing machines, vacuum cleaners or electric cookers. The communal lavatory was outside and halfway up the street. What they did have was common sense. They would buy ten pounds of potatoes at a time; the cheap cuts of meat and "cooking cheese" – known affectionately as "mousetrap." They knew about the mysteries of baking bread, making stews and flavouring dumplings. They might brew their own beer and homemade wine. They would be careful to turn the light out when they left a room and shut the door behind them. These basic arts and skills no longer exist among those who are today defined as poor.

Today's so-called poor consists of an uneducated and untrained underclass whose members buy expensive (and inferior) processed food in the supermarket and send out for pizzas and curries which they eat while watching television. No wonder they soon run through what money they have. As Dickens remarked, "The twin of poverty is ignorance."

Ignorance breeds frustration and frustration breeds violence. So a great deal of what is regarded as poverty is really the brutalised yob culture which now defaces all our towns and cities. Those who live in the yob culture are not merely ignorant about how to make ends meet: they also have no concept of morals and ordinary human courtesy – let alone of religion. And this is because in the cultural decline which has overtaken this country in the last two generations, a great mass of humanity has never been taught anything. If they are now deprived, it is because they have been deprived by the very institutions which were historically set up to educate and civilise them – principally the church and the schools. And of course the sexual revolution, begun in the 1960s and run amok in more recent years, has resulted in the phenomena of the absent father, the single mother and the consequent breakdown of family life. So many parents are unwilling to train and discipline their children. Many more are quite incapable of doing so. The dependency culture is thus handed on from one generation to the next. That is the real poverty trap.

So far I have written only about the negative meaning of poverty; but there is in the Judaeo-Christian tradition a positive connotation as well. Christ said, "Blessed are the poor." The willing renunciation of material wealth has long been seen as the true path to spiritual enlightenment. If I may put this epigrammatically, there is the world of difference between two conditions which look alike: starving and fasting. We are urged, "Take no thought, saying, What shall we eat, or what shall we drink or wherewithal shall we be clothed?" It is a counsel of perfection, true enough, but it is surely preferable to the modern materialistic consumer culture which urges us through 24/7 TV advertisements and the colour supplements to take thought about nothing else except eating, drinking and dressing up in the latest designer clobber.

We have forgotten that there is such a thing as holy poverty, and its patron saint is St Francis, the holy fool, the court-jester in the kingdom of God. Chesterton reminds us, "In plain fact St Francis really was ready to live on refuse; and it was probably something much uglier as an experience than the refined simplicity which vegetarians and water drinkers call the simple life. He meant to strike the note of collecting his clothes like rags from a succession of dustbins. Ten years later, that makeshift costume was the uniform of five thousand men; and a hundred years later, in that, for a pontifical panoply, they laid great Dante in the grave."

St Luke quotes Our Lord as saying, "Blessed are poor." Jesus also taught that his disciples should visit the prisoners and captives. He went further and declared that he who visits a prisoner visits Christ himself. Arguably, it is the prisoners and captives who are the poorest of the poor because they are deprived of the richest of all riches, their freedom. At root, this is the deprivation of the freedom to choose and that is demoralising and even threatens to erode the captives' humanity.

Jail. Prison visiting. I was asked to preach at Wormwood Scrubs. It's not so much the smell as the noise. Prisons are metallic places where everyone shouts. But you can hardly hear the shouting above the clanging. It's as if everything is taking place inside a large tin box. The jail is a cruel place. I have listened to convicted child-molesters protesting their love of children and registering their outrage upon being repeatedly beaten up by their fellow inmates who regard sex criminals as beneath contempt. There is a hierarchy among convicts – just as there is a hierarchy among the clergy. At the top, the murderers and gangsters, with the ordinary thieves and burglars as the middle class, so to speak. Fraudsters are looked down upon as no more than pen-pushers. But everyone needs to think that someone somewhere is worse than himself. So they all despise the child-molester.

Are there any limits to self-deceit? I was "given the form" – brought up to date concerning the criminal record- of a notorious paedophile. He was a balding man with what little hair he had left a distinguished grey. Neat. Compact. An open, kindly face. You might have taken him for a scientist or a doctor on the edge of retirement.

He had for thirty years abused little girls – any child above the age of two might be his victim. His method was to give them sweets and presents and then rape them – or use his screwdrivers on them – and then get them to draw their childish pictures of the events. There is little one can imagine more obscene than the crude sexual words written in a childish scrawl.

He said he wanted to talk to me, "to put the record straight." He was under the unswerving impression that he had never done anything wrong. "I really loved them, you know – and they loved me." He sat there with his arms folded and sipped a cup of tea: "They lead you on, you know, Padre. Little mistresses they are. I never meant any harm – just touching. I loved them all, you see." His face was scarred where the other inmates had razored him more than once. He looked wary, glanced about him all the while we talked, like a small animal on the lookout for big predators. For all his cruelty, his deranged outlook, he was pathetic, banal. An assistant governor told me afterwards, "He'll never be let out. He was convicted on eight counts, and God only knows how many more kids he ruined. He had a stash of violent pornography bigger than the stack in the British Library."

From the pathetic to the tragic. I met a man in his sixties who was in for life. He was relaxed, nonchalant, elegant, calm. Resigned, you might say. "She nagged me for years. Wouldn't let go, not for a minute. Like a dog worrying a rat, she was. One day I just snapped and throttled her. I loved her. Still do. I'll be seventy-five when they let me out. And she won't be there for me."

How do you not weep for sheer bloody pointless misery?

Well, there's no doubt murder is wrong, but I felt sorry for him in a way I could not feel sorry for the child-molester. Perhaps I'm as bad as the inmates with their hierarchy of offenders? The murder he had committed was a catastrophe for him as well as his wife.. . The noise of the jail. And the atmosphere oppressive, threatening, always it seems on the point of exploding. I think it's a lot to do with the way the prison officers line the walls during free association, jangling their keys and making it very obvious that they are armed with huge, ugly batons. And the inmates watchful, resentful, always restless. There is no peace. There is no ordinary relaxed time – even in those free association periods. Everyone is on edge. From time to time, the inmates are rounded up – it might be for a meal, for work or for locking up – and they slouch off to where they are bidden with a mute contempt for the prison officers. They go to wherever they have to go as if they are doing so entirely of their own freewill – as if the officers were not there at all. As if they still possessed freewill.

I celebrated the Eucharist in the prison chapel. About eighty men turned up. Most of them sat leaning forward slightly as their act of reverence. There were no kneelers. The organ struck up with *Praise my Soul the King of Heaven* and they sang lustily, if not tunefully. It was again dismaying to see the prison officers lining the walls. But, as the assistant governor replied afterwards when I asked him if such a strong presence was really needed: "Well, Rector, would you prefer to live dangerously? We had fourteen murderers in there."

I preached on the mercy of God and took as my text Psalm 56:8: "Thou tellest my wanderings: put thou my tears in thy bottle; are they not in thy book?" There was no need to try to *explain* the imagery – there never is, and those who try always end up ruining the effect. Many of the men were plainly mesmerised by those words of the Psalmist. At the Communion about half of them came forward to receive the Sacrament, but once again their movements were accompanied by an uneasy shuffle on the part of the officers.

After the service some stayed behind to talk. One – he looked no more than a boy – said, "You know what, Father? It's boring in here. It's boring – that's the trouble. I ain't gonna come back in here no more when I gets out. It's so boring. Just boring and that's all."

The wife-murderer hung about when the rest had gone, so that the officers came across and told him to leave: "The Padre has to go now." It was obvious they wanted all the inmates back in their cells before the next mealtime. I said, "I'm in no great rush."

He had such a sorrowful, languid look. I said again, "Is there anything I can do?"

"You've already done it. Those words. Will you tell me where I can find them? It'll be my prayer every night. So tender, you see – the thought that God has a bottle for *my* tears. So tender. I used to feel like that about the missus. Still do."

He turned and walked off slowly down the wide corridor that led to the cells. The only prison officer left in the chapel gave me a look, then he followed after the wife-murderer, talking to him as if the two were old pals. I stood and looked towards the altar for a moment, then folded my surplice and headed for the security desk and a late lunch.

I persisted in trying to do some writing first thing each morning. As Anthony Burgess said, "Get up early, write your thousand words and you can have the rest of the day off." Not if you're running two City parishes – but I know what he meant. There are some very odd notions flying around concerning writing and writers. Frequently, it's said to me: "You must enjoy your writing." I don't. And I don't know any writer who does. But I know plenty – myself among them – who would agree with Burgess' other saying, "I enjoy having written." There is an element of purgation as well as creation. Another strange idea arises in that other frequent question, "What did you mean by that poem?" As if you have some sort of abstract notion which you then elaborate into verse. Nothing could be further from the reality. What the poem *means* is what the poem *says*. That and nothing else. Reminding me of a story about Beethoven who one day gave a recital of his *Appassionata* sonata. A lady who had been listening said, "All very fine, Herr Beethoven, but what does it mean?" So Beethoven went back to the piano and played it again.

So it is with composing poetry. As Sisson said, "There is a certain mental pressure which produces a very few words in a definite rhythm. You start to write and, if things turn out well, you find eventually you have a poem." Needless to say, things don't always turn out well. But no true poem is ever *contrived*. It's much the same with prose and longer pieces of writing, but not so intense. Eliot provides the best description of all this that I have ever come across:

"...that some form of ill-health, debility or anaemia may(if other circumstances are favourable) produce an effect of poetry in a way approaching the condition of automatic writing – though in contrast to the claims sometimes made for the latter, the material has obviously been incubating within the poet...it seems that at these moments, which are characterised by the sudden lifting of the burden of anxiety and fear which presses upon our daily life so steadily that we are unaware of it, what happens is something *negative*: that is to say not 'inspiration' as we commonly think of it, but the breaking down of strong habitual barriers – which tend to reform very quickly."

Exactly. So there is some sense in saying that the writer doesn't know what he's writing until he's finished the piece. Dante's "in a dark wood."

A practical example. For several weeks there was building up in me – what? – an inchoate urge, pressure, the need to write something substantial about the interior life of a priest – but not as a treatise on "spirituality" – whatever meaning can be attached to that strange word – but all bound up with the priest's daily life, the common task, his encounters with his people, the landscape he inhabits, music, the Sacraments. I baulked at the prospect for I knew from past experience that it would involve a long and merciless purging and rejection of all that did not belong to this particular...the best word I can find is *symphony*. And I knew also that, as Mahler said, the symphony must contain the whole world – the bad as well as the good, the banal as well as what is exalted and noble, So I began my novel *A Grain of Mustard Seed* – the title taken of course from St Matthew 17:20 –

"Verily I say unto you, If ye have faith as a grain of mustard seed, ye shall say unto this mountain, Remove hence to yonder place; and it shall remove; and nothing shall be impossible unto you."

Here's an extract:

"Hospital corridors are without fire buckets these days, so there was nowhere to stub his cigarette. He doused it on the underside of the notice pointing the way to PHARMACOLOGY and kicked it into the corner. If he walked round to Sister's office he could get a cup of coffee out of the machine. One o'clock – he thought he would have a cup of coffee at one o'clock. Smoke at twelve, coffee at one and pee at two. That was the way to punctuate the vigil with endless diversion. His eyes were already in that melted condition which makes all objects merge into a single badly-designed landscape, the floor stained brown and the walls painted cream: a deliberate ordinariness.

"But some funerals were not as ordinary as others - as once when the hearse passed slowly through the crem's main entrance and along the wooded drive, like an *adagio* introduction to a pantomime overture by Rossini. A glorious day, all cherry blossom and birdsong. The sunlight gleaming on the quiet and quality car as it pulled up outside the friendly door of the chapel. Half a dozen cars drew up just behind. Anne Shotton all in black, with a black veil and a bunch of yellow flowers in her hands, stepped unsteadily out of the first car. Derrington the undertaker smiled as he took her hand, like a patient father encouraging his tiny daughter towards her first dip in the big pool. A sickening orderliness of things: the *Prayer Book* open at the right page; the computerised musak playing a sugary introit; the people safely sitting. The chapel cosy, filled with dusty sunlight and the whole event going beautifully – until near the end.

"Anne Shotton began an energetic wailing which grew louder until it frightened the other mourners. She turned her eyes away from the ludicrously small coffin and towards me, shouting, *Why? Why?* And, *I want Gillian back - that's all!* Her sobbing became deep and rhythmical, then ceased at last and she vomited.

"Her husband came across and, by way of explanation, said, *She's upset..* His face was creased with embarrassment and guilt, like a tortured heretic leaping from the rack to apologise to his inquisitors for making too much noise.

"*Kindertotenlieder*? Mahler had nothing on Father Merrick who was a dab hand at kids' funerals.

"Suffer the little children. And now this child Alison. He went back into the ward and checked her condition as a punctilious sentry checks the state of his patch. Nothing to report. Even dying was routine, like the dawn that breaks gradually after the interminable night – as Schopenhauer might have said.

"And Pilate marvelled if he were already dead: and calling unto him the centurion, he asked him whether he had been any while dead.

"That was the Lord himself. Even the Lord had died. Fr Tom said it in the Creed every day. A funny thing the Creed, as he had pointed out from time to time. Nothing in it about the life of the Founder of the Christian religion, not a single puny miracle and positively no sermons on any mounts, no amusing parables or bollockings for the money-changers; no fishing and not so much as a single fig tree cursed: only that he was born of a Virgin and died at the hands of a Roman Governor. And the novel sequel of course to the effect that he rose from the dead. The bit in the Creed about that generally amused Tom – the line *according to the Scriptures* as if to say, *Well, that's what Scripture says anyhow – you can believe it if you like.*

"*Der Tod und das Madchen* had started up in his head again as soon as he returned to the girl's bedside and he was rather ashamed of its beautiful and presumptuous presence. For Alison, like the *damsel* in the Gospel *is not dead but sleepeth.* The satisfaction of having just smoked was offset by the fact that he now found himself with nothing to do. So he prayed again Archbishop Cranmer's prayer from *The Visitation of the Sick*, all the while recalling what a malicious iconoclast the author of *The Book of Common Prayer* had been and conjecturing for the umpteenth time whether literary genius could ever be an excuse for malice – in Cranmer's case the malice made explicit by his lusty hatred of the Catholic Faith and his single-minded desire to abolish it. And him an Archbishop too...

"All those lovely processions of vivid colours and exalted hearts, the Blessed Sacrament carried through the streets not just of Rome and Seville, but also through sordid and desultory places such as Oldham, Lancashire and the slag heaps of Wath-on-Dearne – Thomas Cranmer would have them all done away. In his first service for the burial of the dead, he had preserved the old Catholic bit where the priest addresses the corpse. Could there be a thing more tender? This lovely unity between the quick and the dead, heaven and earth arm in arm over the coffin. And no smiles forgotten, no need for memories even, for we and they are one in the timeless love of God. What does Cranmer do with this ecstatic tapestry? He rends it from the top to the bottom and makes the priest refer to the deceased in the third person. The language of the ecclesiastical bureaucrat. When he first wrote it down, he probably wrote it in triplicate. What was the matter with the man? Didn't he believe in the resurrection of the dead and the life of the world to come, or what? The soul of Protestantism, what is it but a failure of imagination, atheism in scarf and hood? Well, let them get out of the Gothic cathedrals and parish churches and leave them for the Christians! Go to hell! But is there any hell hot enough for a man who removes a people's religion?

"*Der Tod und das Madchen* and the bald girl and her waxy face: the countless drips and tubes, the sacraments of scientific medicine and techno-death. But D-minor and the little Schubert tune – could you hate even Cranmer with this going on in your head? Poor Archbishop C. – it was probably his wife put him up to it. He was married, they said, and he carried her to synods in a trunk. You hear her voice, as from someone standing behind him in all his prayers and egging him on to make them more horrible."

XIV

Is it possible to open a bank account in the City of London? We at St Michael's had a great deal of trouble over this – and St Michael's has been here a lot longer than the banks. I needed to set up a Music Trust to provide for our excellent choir, so obviously I would have to open an account in its name. Now dear reader, as they say, read on, preserving, if you will, that degree of imagination which is the temporary suspension of disbelief....

Our church already had an account with The Royal Bank of Scotland, and so for the sake of convenience, I decided to open the music account at their branch in Cheapside. I acquired the necessary forms and three other Trustees in addition to myself. These Trustees were all Christian gentlemen, professional men of good reputation in the City. The bank's application forms reminded me of the sort of tedious, overblown documents which Joseph K was repeatedly asked to fill in in *The Trial*. But I thought, it's all in a good cause, gritted my teeth and steeled myself to the alien bureaucracy – taking with me, names, addresses, one set of identification to prove our identities and another to verify our addresses. We completed the tautologically inane section which asked us to declare the purpose of the Music Trust: to provide for the church's music – and I felt like adding, "..but of course this is only a front to cover our involvement in the international drugs trade and money-laundering operations on the grand scale."

Bearing this sheaf of rigmarole, I turned up at the bank. The cashier leapt forward, all obliging smiles and, "How can I help *yew*?" I told her I would like to open a bank account. The look which spread across her face could not have been more startled if I'd reached for a sawn-off shotgun and yelled, "Stick 'em up!"

"But you can't open an account just like that, Sir."

"Well, I've brought all the documentation your colleague asked me to bring and several hundreds of pounds in cash and cheques to pay in straight away. And it's not as if it's an account on which we want to borrow any money – just to service the cheques in and out for the Music Trust."

She looked at me as if I were plumb dumb. To encourage her – I almost said to facilitate her, but that might sound indecent, coming from a conservative parson – I presented my two sets of identification, and similar papers relating to the other Trustees, and told her that our church already had an account with the Royal Bank of Scotland, and at this very branch too. She gave me the customs officer's stare and went away to take photocopies of the aforesaid rigmarole. Turning, Medusa-like, she enquired whether I had remembered to include my telephone number, "…plus your mobile."

"I haven't got a portable phone."

Her stare turned incredulous.

I tried to sound friendly and reassuring, "I think I've given you everything: date of birth, eye colour, position of mole under left foot, grandmother's date of birth…"

She was clearly one of those sort for whom jokes are no laughing matter. She said, "The manager will phone you today or tomorrow and arrange an appointment when you can come in and discuss your requirements."

"But I'm here *now* and I've told you what I would like."

"We don't do things like that, Sir."

"Well, how *do* you do them? You mean. If someone comes into your bank and wants to do some straightforward business, you say this is of course possible, but it will have to be done on another day? What's wrong with today, at this moment in time, *now*?"

"I'm sorry, Sir. It's a matter of security."

"What security? You know us. We're 'valued customers,' as your advertising section is forever telling us in a plethora of junk mail."

She merely shook her head and I was left to reflect on the phenomenon of the bank's refusing to take my hard cash. The manager did not phone that day, or the next day or the day after that. So, on the following Monday, I phoned the bank. By chance, the manager herself answered the phone and I reported the whole misadventure, or as much of it as I could recall. She was extremely nice and conciliatory, saying, "I'm afraid you were given some incorrect information: you don't have to make an appointment with me in order to open an account."

I was seized by a rush of euphoria, such as one might feel upon learning that one was not, after all, to be hanged the following morning. I was assured that the bank would "inaugurate the transaction – as soon as I identify the person who has your paperwork on their (sic) desk."

Next day a different cashier phoned to tell me I must make an appointment to open the account. It was like going round and round in a revolving door. I felt weak and dizzy by this time and said, "But I've spoken directly with the manager about this and she assured me – "

She cut me off and put the manager herself on the phone. She explained, "When you said your church already banks with us – and I have checked this of course..." She spoke rapidly and fiercely, as one instinctively suspicious of all Christian institutions. "...I thought the matter would be simple, but it isn't. Because the names of the signatories to your proposed Music Trust account are different to (sic) the names which appear on the church's regular account."

"Of course they are! I don't expect the same three people to do all the work that the church needs to do! But please tell me then, how can I proceed as quickly as possible to get this account opened?"

At this she began to rehearse the protocols of the gulag: "We shall need two sets of identification..."

"I've already given you three."

"...but for each signatory. Their passports and driving licences. And six months' bank statements for each."

The idiom was infectious. I said, "Will you put that in writing, please – in triplicate – so that I and my colleagues know exactly what is required of us, and then I won't be wasting any more of your precious time?"

"I'm sorry, Sir, but to engage in such correspondence is not part of the bank's policy. I will, though, contact you officially at a later date."

I was up early every morning looking out for Postman Pat. Nothing. In desperation, I rang a liveryman of the Chartered Secretaries Company.

"That should be easy, Peter. You have a bank account yourself, personally?"

"Yes."

"Well do it through them."

That same day, I wrote a letter to my bank and received – by return post! - acknowledgement that the Music Trust account had been opened.

I rejoiced, but the next day was the most sickening in all my fourteen years in the City. I went into St Michael's to celebrate the Wednesday Mass to discover that the Regimental Colours of the

Stock Exchange Branch of the Royal Fusiliers had been ripped from their pole in the nave and stolen. These Colours had hung in our church since 1919. You couldn't have a more poignant memorial: underneath where the Colours hung are two glass cases containing the names of the men who fell in the First World War: more than three hundred – and they just from one battalion. I often think that we lack a sense of proportion, that we live effete, attenuated lives these days – especially when, for example, we read that the journalists who went across to Normandy in 1994 to commemorate the fiftieth anniversary of the D-Day landings were offered counselling "for their ordeal." What ordeal was this? The soldiers who went across in 1944 and did the job received no counselling. No doubt they were better off without it.

St Sepulchre is part of a larger military tradition. At the west end of the church, on the north side, there is a monument to the Sixth Battalion, the London Rifles, and the names of their campaigns are inscribed prominently on a wooden screen. What thoughts and sensations arise when you walk into church on a winter's morning and read: "St Quentin…Loos…Amiens…Pursuit to Mons… Passchendaele…Somme…Ypres…Menin Road"! Close by there is a wooden cross, dilapidated now, almost rotted away. It was taken from the battlefield at Loos, where for three years it commemorated the hundred officers and men of the Sixth, the London Regiment, who fell there on 25th September 1918.

About this time, I was asked to preach at St Lawrence Jewry, the famous old church by Guildhall, used by the Lord Mayor and the City Corporation for their ceremonials. My address was to the veterans of the war in Japan. Afterwards at the reception I came across one of the most remarkable men I was ever privileged to meet. He was Neil Boyd. In the Second World War he was plucked out of the western desert and sent to fight in the Far East, where he was captured by the Japanese. He was kept half-starved in a cage underground and the passing soldiers urinated and defecated on him. Occasionally he was taken out and tortured. This continued for two years, then one morning he was put on a train, He hadn't a clue where he was being taken. Well, it turned out to be Hiroshima. As he told me:

"It was a morning of the most brilliant blue. I was awoken out of my dozing by a Jap soldier jumping up and down, shouting and pointing at the sky. Suddenly, a series of explosions rent the air and it seemed the whole universe was splitting apart. Fearful and brilliant colours, the like of which I had never seen before. Like an evil blossom enveloping me...

"It was like watching my own death in slow motion. The mists and darkness began to clear a little. I discovered I was blind in one eye, with only dim sight in the other. In this pitiful state, I began to look for my companion and fellow prisoner. All that was left of him was a shadowy imprint on the tower wall. And the tower was the only thing left standing except for two factory chimneys in the distance. I had survived only because I was sheltered by that wall and had been lying down...

"A ship of the US navy eventually took me to San Francisco where the liberated American prisoners were treated like heroes. The few English were incarcerated in an open prison while the authorities waited to decide what to do with us. I weighed just over five stone. I thought, I'm damned if I'm going to swap the Jap prison camp for a Yankee jail. So I escaped and tried to make my way across the States to New York, earning a sparse living by working on garage forecourts. The food I received was a banquet compared to what I had survived on in Japan."

Eventually, Neil got to London and the train from King's Cross to Hull where he found his street had been bombed flat and all his family were dead. He moved to York and took up painting – paintings which are startlingly evocative of his half-life in the camps. He also wrote an enthralling autobiography *An Englishman's Peace and War*. Finally, He told me, "I went back to Japan years later and asked the Japanese soldiers how they could inflict such torture on their captives. Japanese statesmen, soldiers and civilians have apologised to me." What Neil Boyd has received in this life could hardly be described as merciful, but his parting shot to me was, "God is merciful."

Fr David Burgess, Rector of St Lawrence, was the wisest priest in the City. All the City priests cover for one another at times when one gets double-booked, ill or goes on holiday. I used to love to say Tuesday lunchtime Mass at St Margaret's Lothbury when the petit, ebullient and charming Fr Jeremy Crossley was otherwise engaged. I was always well looked after by an eminent churchwarden who would eagerly bring me up to date on all the City gossip. I asked him, "Does Jeremy get other priests to help out, or am I his only stand-in?"

"Oh yes, we get others. David Burgess' successor at St Lawrence for instance. You know our Tuesday service is from *The Book of Common Prayer*. Well, this fellow came and began by announcing that he wasn't going to use the Prayer Book and that we could revert to that tiresome old text when Jeremy returned."

Where do they get these people from?

I was invited to breakfast at a café on the South Bank by Michael Gove. This was while his party was still in opposition and therefore long before Michael was appointed by the PR man Cameron to improve and reform state education – and, as everyone knows, subsequently sacked because he showed signs of making too good a job of it. He wanted to talk about philosophical theology – rare enough in a politician. When I asked why, he replied, "Because all morality, including public affairs, has to be rooted in absolutes." We talked about C.S. Lewis and R.G. Collingwood.   Michael had just published a clever book *Celsius 7/7* in which he enquired as to what Britain's response should be to the terrorist attacks on London. It is a lucid and brave book in which the author speaks directly, treating his readers as adults and declining to eviscerate his message according to the fashionable canons of Political-Correctness.

As Gove said, the beginning of the perils facing the West is that our political establishments will not even admit that perils exist. Meanwhile, church leaders have set up their ecumenical discussion group with *moderate* Muslims. This is futile for it is not the moderate Muslims who pose the threat, but the militants. Also the militants like nothing better that to murder the moderate Muslims. In the last chapter of *Celsius 7/7*, Gove asks the question, "What is to be done?" And on almost his last page, he answers his own question:

"We also need to rediscover and re-proclaim faith in our common values. We need an ideological effort to move away from moral relativism and towards moral clarity, as well as a commitment to build a truly inclusive model of British citizenship in which divisive separatist identities are challenged and rejected."

Well, you might respond, so far so good. But Gove stops short of spelling out what our common values actually are. I put it to him that we certainly don't need any more "ideological" efforts: during the last hundred years we have suffered from ideologies more than enough. So what precisely is required? I told him I am convinced the only "rediscovery" that can save western society is the rediscovery of our Judaeo-Christian civilisation and culture. Nothing else will do. We cannot work up a programme of resistance to the enemies who assail us by vague aspirational talk about "models." And to call for "moral clarity" without spelling out what constitutes that clarity is to leave the job half-done. What needs to happen is nothing less than a return to the practice of our faith. This is what the Jewish prophets in the Old Testament and the Gospels and Epistles in the New Testament consistently demand:

"Rend your heart and not your garments, and turn unto the Lord your God: for he is gracious and merciful, slow to anger and of great kindness" - *Joel 2:13*

"If we say we have no sin, we deceive ourselves and the truth is not in us. But if we confess our sins, he is faithful and just to forgive us all our sins and to cleanse us from all unrighteousness" – *I John 1: 8-9.)*

As Gove brilliantly pointed out, we face an uncompromising enemy and we must nerve ourselves to face it down. But I told him that I believe the way we live in the West today shows that we have lost our nerve. We have discarded the roots of our civilisation. In this sense we are our own worst enemy, for we constantly deny the only things that can save us. I remarked that the early 20th century poet and philosopher T.E. Hulme (1883-1917) wrote:

"We have been beaten because our enemies' theories have conquered us. We have played with those to our own undoing. Not until we are hardened again by conviction are we likely to do any good. In accepting the theories of the other side, we are merely repeating a well-known historical phenomenon. The Revolution in France came about not so much because the forces which should have resisted were half-hearted in their resistance. They themselves had been conquered intellectually by the theories of the revolutionary side. The privileged class is beaten only when it has lost faith in itself, when it has been penetrated by the ideas that are working against it."

"Our enemies' theory" is secularisation which involves, among other false doctrines, the belief that God is a primitive, outmoded idea, a delusion, and that modern man can devise his own ethical system, making up morals as he goes along on a merely utilitarian basis. I believe these suppositions to be destructive modern superstitions and that they constitute errors more deadly than anything they seek to correct. In fact secularism is fatal to western civilisation.

In March 2007, on the fiftieth anniversary of the signing of the Treaty of Rome which began the modern European movement, Pope Benedict criticised the EU as "godless." He spoke of Europe's denial of its Christian roots as "a form of apostasy" and he added:

"It is unthinkable that the EU could build a common European house while ignoring Europe's identity. Europe is a historical, cultural and moral identity before it is a geographic, economic or political reality. It is an identity built on a set of universal values which Christianity played a part in moulding."

Also, around that time, the Archbishop of Canterbury, the Roman Catholic Archbishop of Westminster and the Chief Rabbi met urgently to discuss the threat posed to British society and culture by aggressive secularisation. I determined to outline the progress of secularisation, how it has transformed Western society for the worse; how it has reduced us to impotence in the face of an alien fundamentalism which is confident and militant and which regards us as dross.

I wanted to show that what we are living through is a spiritual and cultural decadence and decline as deadly as that of St Augustine's day. It is not as if we have not had plenty of prophets to warn us about the many and great dangers to which our laxity and foolishness have exposed us. I mentioned, as principal among them, the philosopher R.G. Collingwood and some words he uttered before the Second World War:

"It is sometimes thought by people who have been reading historical thrillers that the Roman Empire died at the hands of barbarian invaders. That theory is amusing but untrue. It died of disease, not of violence, and the disease was a long-growing and deep-seated conviction that its own way of life was not worth preserving. The same disease is notoriously endemic among ourselves.

"From Plato onwards, Graeco-Roman society spent its life in a rear-guard action against emotional bankruptcy. The critical moment was reached when Rome created an urban proletariat whose only function was to eat free bread and watch free shows. This meant the segregation of an entire class which had no work to do whatever; no positive function in society, whether economic or military or administrative or intellectual or religious; only the business of being supported and being amused. When that had been done, it was only a question of time until Plato's nightmare of a consumers' society came true; the drones set up their own king and the story of the hive came to an end…

"Nothing could arrest the spread of amusement; no one, though many tried, could regenerate it by infusing into it a new spirit of religious purpose or artistic austerity. The vortex revolved, through manifestation now wholly forgotten except by a few curious scholars, until a new consciousness grew up for which practical life was so interesting that organised amusement was no longer needed. The consciousness of the old civilization, now bifurcated down to its very foundations, fell to pieces before the onslaught of this new unified consciousness, and theatre and amphitheatre were deserted by a world that had become Christian. The Middle Ages had begun and a new religious art was born: this time an art serving those emotions which went to the invigorating and perpetuating of Christian society…

"What we are *now* concerned with is the threatened death of our civilization. This has nothing to do with my death or yours, or the deaths of any people we can shoot before they shoot us. It can be neither arrested nor hastened by violence. Civilizations die and are born not with waving of flags or the noise of machine-guns in the streets, but in the dark, in a stillness, when no one is aware of it. It never gets into the papers. Long afterwards a few people, looking back, begin to see that it has happened…"

Thus I set myself to write a book about the subject and I entitled it *The Secular Terrorist*. In it I described how, in the words of Gertrud Himmelfarb, "The counter-culture *is* the culture now." I quoted extensively from the manifesto of the Frankfurt School, that coterie of Marxists who escaped Eastern Europe into the West and determined that the best sort of revolution was that which sought to undermine civilising institutions from within. The usual suspects; Marcuse, Adorno, Reich, Timothy Leary and the rest of the gang. *The Secular Terrorist* went into two editions and it's still around for anyone interested.

A signal example of the process by which ostensibly Christian organisations become penetrated by secular ideology is the charity Christian Aid. Along with all the parish clergy, I received an epistle from the Archbishop of Canterbury asking me to support Christian Aid. It was not an epistle, as St Paul would understand the word, more an exercise in jargonised sociologese sprinkled with "liberty", "solutions", "challenges", "awareness", "resourcing" and "empowering" – three times. The Archbishop deigned to mention God just once - which was a blessing, at least, as God does not feature at all on the Christian Aid website.

The clichés in the Archbishop's appeal were not merely verbal. With his letter he sent me a glossy brochure featuring pictures of Christians *a la mode* and the emblems of their faith. On the front is a black woman. She must be a priest, I suppose, for though she is not wearing the clerical collar, she has a purple stole about her neck. But without a surplice – which makes her improperly dressed. Behind her is a tramp with a guitar. In the foreground an obese girl aged ten looks as if she's about to swallow a large microphone. Inside there is that *sine qua non* of the modern Christian congregation, a drum-kit.

Well, when I was ordained I took the Oath of Canonical Obedience, so I suppose when the Archbishop asks me to do something, I should jump to it. So I went to look at what Christian Aid had to say:

"UK companies *must* declare their carbon emissions. Millions of the world's poor are suffering because of climate change."

Thus an organisation with a religious title slavishly echoes the secular cant of the age and accepts as dogma the pagan myth of global warming. And there is all the *ex cathedra* authoritarianism of the Totalitarian Left:

"Christian Aid has met *Barclays*. We are concerned..." they add loftily, "that they have not made public the very significant carbon emissions that result from their lending and investment activities."

This is not feeding the poor. It's only anti-capitalism and the snide politics of envy. If it's private enterprise, it's got to be wicked - even *Morrisons* supermarkets lorries, taking food to all parts of the nation, give off too much exhaust gas, they say. Then the Christian Aid commissars invite us all to email the government to "Stop Kingsnorth" – a new coal-fired power station in Kent.

Their counsels of perfection are no merely parochial affair. Next in line for Christian Aid's self-aggrandising condemnation is Israel for its "blockade of Gaza which was collective punishment, illegal and unacceptable." Yes, and if there were no blockade, Hamas would be daily importing weaponry, chiefly in the form of rockets to fire indiscriminately at Israeli civilians. But there is of course not even the attempt at fair-mindedness. Why try to understand an issue when a prejudiced rant is so much easier? So there is no mention of the fact that Israel withdrew from Gaza in a land for peace deal and was subsequently rewarded by Hamas' relentless barrage. There is no account taken of how, twice in the last fifteen years, a two-states solution was agreed, only for the Palestinians under Arafat to tear up the deal and launch fresh terrorist uprisings against Israel.

Christian Aid espouses every fashionable cause on the agenda. "Eradicate world poverty." (It was depressing to see that the Archbishop went along with this utopian fantasy.) "Fight poverty and injustice" – but only when poverty and injustice are defined according to the ideology of the Left which, however, has always impoverished – and often murdered – the population wherever it has been tried. And in any case, we should ask what such aid as is being distributed is worth when most of it does not benefit the poor in foreign lands but finds its way into the coffers of the corrupt dictators who rule them. So that a handy definition of foreign aid is the phenomenon of poor people in rich countries giving money to rich people in poor countries.

Naturally there is a demand for ever more "funding to address the needs of people with HIV in poor countries." This policy contains more *non sequiturs* than a Logical Positivists' picnic. There is the charity's "Stop Aids!" campaign, for example, which claims that sexual continence – faithfulness in marriage – does not work. (Now there's a piece of Christian teaching for you!) We are offered the case of a married woman who was faithful to her husband, but he went with prostitutes and infected her with AIDS just the same. This is meant to be an argument against the effectiveness of the faithfulness campaign – but nothing is made of the true cause of the wife's infection – precisely her husband's *unfaithfulness*!

No human activity, however apparently innocent, escapes the political police force that is Christian Aid – not even football:

"The Africa Cup of Nations is seen as a celebration not just of football but of Africa itself. But in dictatorships football is used to distract people from their problems." But perhaps a little distraction might be a welcome thing. Not to the totalitarian puritans in Christian Aid. Worst of all, "Football draws heavily on notions of nationhood and patriotism." And notoriously these virtues are anathema to international socialism. So it draws heavily on nationhood? For heaven's sake, it is the Cup of *Nations*!

The greatest enemy of prosperity for the poor is rightly identified as corruption, but the identification is made ever so selectively. Big business and national interests BAD: Politicised aid quangos and sentimental pop-stars' futile gestures such as "saving Africa" – and their own egos – GOOD. Christian Aid even quotes with approval the United Nations' Convention Against Corruption – omitting to mention that the United Nations itself is perpetually at the centre of a corruption scandal. You might think, Archbishop, that Christian Aid, a global anti-capitalist pressure-group masquerading as an ecumenical Christian charity, is the filthiest corruption of all.

Our treasurer Mollie died aged eighty-nine. I gave thanks for that she had lived long enough to see the organ restored. She was tiny but about as frail as a Sherman tank. I learnt over all the years that she served us so superbly a completely new meaning to the word "mollified." She was punctilious. She was charming. She was a lady. But like that other lady, Margaret Thatcher, she also had a handbag. And this handbag she manoeuvred vigorously against any person or institution she suspected of pomposity. Mollie was a great deflator of pretensions.

She was the original law unto herself. And I soon came to understand that "proper procedure" was exactly what Mollie decided it was – neither more nor less. She would come to church to the Wednesday or Friday lunchtime Mass, take the money from the collections from the safe, stuff it all into the famous handbag and march off militantly with it to the bank. I would have had the greatest sympathy for any mugger who dared try to relieve her of this loot.

Often on these Wednesdays and Fridays I would ask Mollie if she had time for a drink. I'm proud to say she never turned me down. So we'd go next door but two to the City University Club and to the bar on the second floor.

"Now, what would you like to drink, Mollie?"

"I'll have an orange juice, please."

"Well, I'm having a glass of white wine."

"Then I'll have what you're having, Rector."

She always called me Rector to begin with, but the next time she addressed me it was Peter – I'm glad to say. It made me feel like royalty: you know, the way you first address the Queen as "Your Majesty" but after that it's all right to say "Ma'am."

She was much respected and honoured at St Michael's. More than that, she was loved. Mollie Harris was a wonderful Christian lady. She was intelligent. I compared her to a Sherman tank and indeed she was indomitable. But the indomitability came with a very charming femininity. She was loyal. She was charitable and kind. She was generous. Her soul was as clean and bright as her smile. And she was an agreeably mischievous old – young - girl. I guess now the angels in heaven will be cringing with apprehension as she casts her punctilious eyes over the heavenly accounts.

Mollie Harris, helper and friend, may she rest in peace and rise again in glory

It was a delightful funeral. The Purcell *Thou Knowest* and young Wolfgang Mozart's *Laudate Dominum*. The lesson from St Paul about the resurrection with the brilliantly savage riposte to the sceptic: *Thou fool...*

The sun streaming through the south window and all the garden full of friends and pies and wine and laughter. Before that, *O Strength and Stay* by Ambrose, teacher of St Augustine

And *The Day Thou Gavest Lord Is Ended*

Nothing is ended: not with Our Lord

XV

At a City dinner I overheard someone say, "It's a good thing the Aldermen's robes are red. It doesn't show the blood."

He was referring to the rows and back-stabbings which are a feature of both the Court of Common Council and the Court of Aldermen. Of course they conduct their feuds most elegantly and rarely is there a deficit of politeness. But under that serene surface there are violent and dangerous currents and rocks upon which many a City career has foundered. Parochial Church Councils can be like this too. I have in mind one almighty shindig at St Michael's which went on for four years and drove me to the point of desperation. And I wasn't the only one. This is how it came about…

One summer Sunday in 2006. we were in St Michael's garden enjoying drinks after Mass.

"How would you like a new ring of bells?"

You could have knocked me down with a cocktail stick

"You mean the whole thing – all twelve?"

"I most certainly do. You must have noticed the ones you've got aren't up to much. Only three of them are ancient and the rest are no good. They're hard to ring too."

The offer came from a City businessman who was himself a bell-ringer, a member of the Ancient Society of College Youths.

"But the cost…"

"Around £175,000 at today's prices. I'll pay."

"You mean the whole lot?"

"I certainly do."

For once in my life, I could hardly wait for the next PCC meeting when I could give them the great news. We met in our fine oak-panelled vestry. Some of that ancient wood had actually survived the Fire of London 1666. Naturally they were all thrilled – except not all. There was one former churchwarden and Past Master of the Drapers who – I am choosing my words carefully – violently and persistently opposed the new bells for all those four years. All his life he had been used to throwing his weight about and getting his way. His manner was declamatory and frankly pretentious. He talked down to those he considered to be of the class of his inferiors

– which included almost everyone, with the possible exception of the Lord Mayor. I tagged him as a First Generation Patrician.

There was no rational argument against the new bells. The old ones were indeed a poor lot. And a magnificent new ring would cost the church not a penny. Gift horses and mouths leap to mind. That First Generation Patrician was an operator. He would have made a good dagger man on that Court of Aldermen or distinguished himself among the Borgias. He fought with his elbows and used all his kudos and his influence, particularly with the Drapers. His first move was to get the Clerk of the Drapers Company leading for the opposition. Then he gained the support of the director of music. From the start this axis filibustered at the PCC meetings I called to discuss the project. Of course they were trying to drag the thing out, while all the time metal prices were on the increase, in the belief that the cost would soon be beyond what our benefactor was prepared to pay. And here's another nice thing: the opposition got the Whitechapel Bell Foundry to oppose the project on aesthetic grounds – which was rather impudent of them, as they had themselves tendered for the contract and lost to Taylors of Loughborough!

The horribleness was not restricted o the PCC meetings, of course, but it really poisoned the parish. The devilish wonder was that one peevish and entirely self-centred man could subvert the whole community. It was like a four years toothache. I felt, walking down Cheapside, that any moment I might receive the blow of a half-brick to the back of my neck. I met the First Generation Patrician one day on my way to church. The street resounded to the uncertain music of a bells practice at St Michaels.

He collared me: "Peter, these bells rang for my wedding and they will ring for my funeral."

"Well, as you know, we're very busy at St Michael's. Did you have a date in mind?"

I got sick of it all. My parish felt contaminated by one man's corrupt ambition. So I decided to bring it to a climax and was almost past caring which way the result went. I asked the Archdeacon to attend a crucial PCC meeting. Wetter than the Tory wets under Maggie, this bloke was. But he was so constitutionally accustomed to watching his back that I knew I could count on him for seeing that all things were done in order. We went through all the crap again. The filibustering. That Clerk to the Drapers, a mean-spirited Rear

Admiral, dropped anchor. Never was the word *rear* so apposite. And its cognates resounded in my blistering desperation. He spoke for twenty minutes and concluded by saying that he was concerned only that "proper procedure" had not been followed.

For heaven's sake, we had been following proper procedure for four years!

Never mind the Clerk to our Patron Company: here we were suddenly blessed by a visitation from our patron Archangel, St Mike – or so it seemed to me at the time. He had not spoken a word in all out tortuous meetings, but now Alderman Sir David Howard, Bt, former Lord Mayor, spoke with quiet acerbity from his corner: "I've observed proper procedure all my life. This is not a question of proper procedure, but of one man's self-interest… "

The Rear Admiral's anchor dropped further than Davy Jones' locker. And that was the end of it. Except not quite. The Archdeacon, not really up to this sort of Punch and Judy show, said, "Very good. Now I'm sure Peter will want to convene an extraordinary meeting of the PCC and take a vote."

I said, "We've had more than enough bloody meetings. I'll rake a vote now."

Courage of convictions was not high in the ascendancy and no one opposed – though there were a couple of entirely predictable abstentions. I thanked Sir David and all my long-suffering friends on the PCC, wrote immediately to our benefactor and began to arrange a parish trip to Loughborough to watch the casting of our bells. Wondrous. The whole parish. Fish and chips. Ale. Molten metal and heartfelt prayers. The craftsmen pausing and taking off their hard hats while I intoned thanksgiving from the gallery high above the workshop. One moment of surpassing mirth. The bells were inscribed with the names of parts of the Latin Mass. A lady, on seeing the one marked "Agnus Dei," asked, "Is that the name of a donor?"

Well, yes, in a manner of speaking.

All that remained was to see the bells delivered by a crane, quarter of an inch either side of St Michael's door frames: and all twelve bells swinging into place like the sensational phenomenon at St Iago de Compostela. Chartres presided at the Mass of Blessing and he was a hundred per cent his usual persona. After the service, in the garden, an admirer exclaimed: "Such a man! He couldn't be anything other than a Prince Bishop!"

His companion replied, "Except a thespian."

But there they were at last, all twelve, and sounding miraculous. And it was such a relief not have to face each day with that chronic toothache, so to speak. Routine felt inhabitable once again.

George Cauchi retired from the high office of Secondary at the Old Bailey, to be succeeded by bright, dapper Charles Henty – an old Etonian and an officer in the Coldstream Guards. Charles had seen combat in the first Gulf War. Each year on the Thursday before Remembrance Sunday, I conducted a short memorial service under the dome in the Great Hall for the three members of the Old Bailey staff killed by a bomb in the Second World War. It was a dignified and moving occasion as the Sheriffs, the Secondary and myself as acting chaplain were led in silence by a policeman, along the corridors, down the long stairs and into the vast echoing space. The business of the Central Criminal Court paused and the tribute was attended by most of the judges and the other staff. One day Charles phoned and asked if I would have a cup of coffee with him and discuss amendments to the service:

"I don't know how to put this exactly, but some of the judges have suggested to me privately that it's too exclusively Christian. Quite a few of the judges are Jews, as you know. D'you think you could…?"

"Tinker? Of course. Our English Bible has an Old Testament as well as the New and this country is rooted in the Judeo-Christian tradition."

I think Charles had feared this matter might prove difficult, but actually the amendments required were simple, minor and entirely reasonable: mention Abraham and Moses along with Jesus Christ and the Prophets along with the Apostles. I was convinced this was a correct and generous application of a broad ecumenical principle. And the truth is that the God of Abraham, Isaac and Jacob is also the God and Father of Our Lord Jesus Christ and indeed of all of us.

The City rests – or rather doesn't rest – on the twin pillars of business and ceremonial. And when it comes to ceremonial occasions, one is sometimes asked to play an away match. For instance, I was invited to speak at an anniversary luncheon hosted by the Lord Mayor of Westminster in honour of some notables by whose talents the City had been enriched. This was a treat for me, as one of the principal guests was to be Sir Alec Bedser and, to come clean, my true religion is cricket. Astonishingly, it was another one of those occasions at which the most important participants find themselves left to their own devices. Kissinger, Princess Anne and now Sir Alec. I arrived in Westminster around noon and was directed into the bar. There was the tall, lean figure of Sir Alec standing all by himself. I don't think other guests were ignoring the great man. It was just that many – not being cricketing fanatics - didn't know who he was. This was a stroke of luck, for it gave me half an hour's conversation with him before we were called in to lunch.

My first recollection of this great fast-medium bowler was of the wickets he took against Lindsay Hassett's fine side which he brought to England in 1953: such resounding names as Arthur Morris, Neil Harvey, Ray Lindwall and the mercurial Keith Miller. Miller had seen action as a fighter pilot with the Royal Australian Air Force in the Second World War. Lithe, phlegmatic, courageous and amusing, Miller returned to England with another Aussie side long after his own retirement when a Journalist asked him a question about stress in the Modern game. Keith replied, "Stress? Stress is having two Messerschmitts up your arse. Cricket's a bloody game!"

Miller and Bedser belonged to that generation of players who had had their careers interrupted by six years of war. The young Bedser had played only seven matches for Surrey in 1939 before he was called up. He said, "It was a bit of a shock to wake up in 1946 and find my name on the England team sheet."

We stood at the bar and Alec was lugubriously entertaining about more than a few of the great names in cricket: "Len Hutton? Miserable bugger. Brian Close? Big gambler on the horses. Drinks."

I can't remember what I said in my speech that day, or even what we had for lunch. But I shall not forget my half hour with the great Sir Alec Bedser. At lunch I was seated next to a bloke who told me he was a practitioner of "Biodynamic Craniosacral Therapy and Core Process Psychotherapy." But, if that's the name of the cure, what words can be left to describe the disease?

Then blow me if it wasn't my turn to be in the middle of a little ceremony of my own. 2010 was the fortieth anniversary of my Ordination. Was it really more than half a lifetime since I had knelt in the chancel at Ripon Cathedral while the diocesan bishop John Moorman and a score of his clergy laid hands on me? The pressure is tremendous and you feel you are being pressed into the ground. And here I was, forty years on, surrounded by parishioners, family and friends at a Choral Mass of Thanksgiving for my priesthood in St Michael's. Mozart: *The Coronation K.317*. Nothing else would do. I didn't preach but read the close of *Little Gidding* from, "What we call the beginning is often the end…" to:

"And all shall be well and
All manner of thing shall be well
When the tongues of flame are in-folded
Into the crowned know of fire
And the fire and the rose are one."

Drapers generously gave me a reception across at the Hall – big as the bash following the City Service. The spot of bother over the bells was clearly all over with. And the following day I scribbled a poem about what's it's like to be a priest:

Forty years a priest, I do detect
That what my people most expect
Is that when crises come their way
I'll have the wisest words to say.
Vocation is to penetrate
Their fiercest ills and then to state
Not solutions, but insight
To help provide some small respite.
No motive is entirely pure;
There is no full and holy cure –
Not on this side of the grave,
So I pretend that I am brave.
And if I am to be of use,
There's nothing that I dare refuse;
No door through which I must not enter,
If I am to be their mentor.
To infiltrate all suffering's levels
I must do battle with the devils:
"The wounded surgeon plies the steel"
But that's not what my people feel.
They want their parish priest serene
And to remain perfectly clean;
Triumphant he must be and oughter,

Like Jesus walking on the water.
How to explain this cannot be?
Do not all sailors fear the sea?
The miner brings no ore of worth
Unless he burrows into earth.
Of this they have a fair conception:
The parish priest their one exception:
He must be wise and deep. Amen –
And yet as innocent as them
True the priest should not excel
In trying to chart the coasts of hell;
Nor make a virtue of abuse,
Claiming vocation as excuse
(Like Coleridge taking to the booze,
Claimed it demanded by the muse)
But listen, this word must be spoken:
The priest can't mend unless he's broken.
If broken, then he needs repair;
And will his people help him there?
So I think back to Easter Eve
When Our Lord his Cross did leave
Implanted in the courts of hell:
I wish I could do half as well.
His Cross still planted there to tell
The devil must suffer merry hell;
And so the priest must do as well
Until the resurrection bell.

There seemed to be no end to the celebrations. I was taken to lunch at Bucks, a gentlemen's club in the West End. But a club like no other I have ever been in. None of the extravagantly-upholstered armchairs into which jaded and world-weary men retreat to harrumph over their gin or port. No, Bucks was a stylish private house and the proprietors – if "proprietors" is not too vulgar a term for the hosts in such decent accommodation – decided to leave it just like that. I was the guest of my friend, churchwarden Michael Berry and his friend, the zealous and educated Roman Catholic Graham Hutton. Graham was trying throughout to get me to join the RC Church. We had some good banter: "Now why should I, an Englishman after the tradition of Andrewes, Johnson and Coleridge, wish to join an international sect?"

I think the notion of *patria* in religion is not negligible: the land, the people and the faith is one that goes back at least as far as ancient Israel.

Another of our parishioners threw a grand dinner at Dr Johnson's House, off Fleet Street. Good food and wine. Agreeable company and lively conversation. And of course, a magnificent setting. But that, for me, was the trouble – the setting. It didn't seem right, somehow, for it to be possible to hire out a place where the great man had sat and chewed the cud with the likes of Garrick, Joshua Reynolds, Edmund Burke and David Hume. It was all a bit National Trustish. Or am I just being an atavistic prat?

Also that mellow, lingering autumn we enjoyed a parish visit to St George's Castle, Windsor: the Queen's Chapel. In there, was a big sign saying that next year the Chapel would be CELEBRATING THE 400TH ANNIVERSARY OF THE KING JAMES BIBLE. I must say, it was a custom more honoured in the breach than in the observance. For at Choral Evensong, the lessons were both from some illiterate, god-forsaken modern version. I knew we were in for trouble from the start when, in the Old Testament lesson, King Solomon addressed the Almighty as, "You God..." – as if the deity were some miscreant fourth former on the back row. Of course it went from bad to worse. Thankfully, the pub lunch was splendid.

To notice yet again how the modern establishment – even in such venerable spots as St George's, Windsor Castle - constantly spits on its ancient liturgy is something we have had to get used to. But what were we supposed to make of the Archbishop of Canterbury's presenting himself at the court of the tyrant Robert Mugabe of Zimbabwe? He was allegedly there to protest about the treatment of Christians by the Mugabe regime. The first question to be asked is, "Why did Dr Williams address fifteen thousand Christians in a sports stadium?"

The answer we were given is that a renegade, Mugabe-supporting cleric had ousted the authentic bishop from the cathedral and so the real Christians were obliged to worship elsewhere. Has Dr Williams never read the Gospel of St Matthew where it says, "And Jesus went into the temple of God and cast out all them...and said unto them, 'My house shall be called the house of prayer; but ye have made it a den of thieves'"?

The cathedral in Harare is part of the Anglican Communion, of which Dr Williams is Head. He should have followed Jesus' example, stridden into that cathedral in full Archiepiscopal attire and commanded the renegade cleric and his lackeys to get out. But then those louts might have murdered the good Dr Williams. So what? As they were stabbing him, he could at least have fallen to his knees rejoicing in his martyrdom and repeating the words of the eighty-six year old Bishop Polycarp who was given the choice in AD 166 to deny his Christianity or be burned at the stake. Polycarp replied, "I have served my Lord these eighty-six years and he has never forsaken me. Why should I now forsake him?" Polycarp was duly burnt. But then there were men of faith in those days.

Dr Williams constantly displays a distressing innocence when it comes to involving himself in political matters, and often the one half of his "mind" does not seem to comprehend what the other half is doing: as when he described himself as "a hairy leftie" – but one who would like to see some aspects of Sharia law in Britain. This is a bit like some comely country yokel girl announcing that she wishes to remain a virgin for life, but also to beget seven children.

Moreover, Mugabe has not only terrorized white farmers and approved the wholesale rape of their wives and daughters, he has murdered 300,000 black Zimbabweans. To such a man, Dr Williams delivered the oxygen of publicity by his foolish and pointless visit. Williams constantly reminds me of a line by C.H. Sisson, "In the presence of folly, I am not sanctified, but angry."

A sad day at St Michael's. Churchwarden Jack Woodhead died aged ninety-eight. I struggled to find words to say at his funeral in his home town of Haywards Heath – because you didn't find out much about Jack Woodhead without using the techniques of forensic science coupled with the third degree. And that is because Jack was not a man to talk about himself. I managed to discover that, as a young man, he went to help in a French bank for a year to brush up his French. At the outbreak of war he joined the Queen's Regiment in the Intelligence Section and was despatched to Africa where he became Liaison Officer with the Belgian Colonial Forces. He received the Croix de Guerre with Bar. Other decorations from the King of the Belgians followed.

He was a member of the Stock Exchange and had a long and distinguished career in the City. But I knew him best for his long, consistent and outstanding contribution to the life of St Michael's Church, a place he loved. I met Jack on my appointment in 1998 and from the start he was a terrific help and an affectionate friend. He certainly was a regular. He became a churchwarden in the 1940s: as our recently departed Parish Clerk John Gaze often said, "Before I was born!"

Jack was at church every Sunday in his Sunday best and every Wednesday in his Wednesday best. His most outstanding and notable contribution was the way he welcomed everyone who stepped through the door – whether they were St Michael's old lags or casual visitors. I particularly appreciated his assiduousness on Wednesdays in his gentle proferring of the Collecting plate. Gentle, yes: but no one escaped. He was a natural at all the ceremonial and the livery connections such as Drapers' Installation Day. And I know he was particularly fond of Merchant Taylors' annual Vernon Service and delighted to go back to the Hall after the service and take lunch with members of the Company and with the boys who had sung in the choir.

On Ascension Day, while priest and congregation ascended the tower, Jack used manfully to make his way up all those steps – and that was in the days before we had any lighting and people leant against the whitewashed walls for support; the days before health and safety were invented. A measure of Jack's considerateness was that, when he finally decided – at the age of about eighty-eight, I think – that the climb was too much for him, he would stand by the tower door at ground level and dust people off with a clothes brush upon their descent.

He was very interested in the Bible and almost every Wednesday made a comment or asked a question about one of the lessons for the day. Jack had a particular bugbear: that parable in which Our Lord tells of the ruler who ordered his servants to go into the highways and hedgerows and command all and sundry to be invited to his wedding dinner. Then there was the one man who came in without a wedding garment. And the ruler of the feast had him cast into outer darkness. Every year Jack complained to me", I don't think Jesus was being quite fair." That was Jack all over: a deep sense of fair play.

At last there arrived that rather tearful day when Jack told me he thought he should retire as churchwarden. He was only ninety at the time and I told him I was not in favour of his early retirement.

I remember the occasion well. We were sitting together in the choir stalls after the Wednesday Mass. I refused Jack's resignation and, to his clear and bright delight, appointed him, there and then Churchwarden Emeritus – which position he rejoiced in for the rest of his life.

When he could no longer make the journey from Haywards Heath to church, we kept in touch by letters and by Jack's – I suppose about fortnightly – telephone calls, usually on a Wednesday morning. He would ask about life at St Michael's generally and of whether the churchwardens were behaving themselves. I'm glad to say that on some occasions I was able to reassure him that they were.

A director at *Investec* in Gresham Street asked me to give a talk about God and Mammon. As a City Rector I was pretty close to both. But it seems to me that there is a great deal of disinformation and resulting confusion about this....This what? I have been taught by my ecclesiastical superiors to call it a *debate*. But it isn't, not really. A debate in my experience is one in which protagonists take up their positions based on rational argument and above all after first establishing the facts. But in the hullaballoo provoked by the Occupy protest outside St Paul's, both facts and rationality were in very short supply.

More than once I took a look at the Occupy tented protest. I should rather say I took a sniff – for the place stank. You might even say, given its proximity to the great City cathedral, that it stank to high heaven. Certainly, the Bishop of London came close to canonising its occupants by saying that they should be given "some permanent memorial." Well, excuse me, but I always thought that to be given a memorial you have to be dead first.

But what does this Occupy camp deserve to be memorialised *for* – apart from making smells, interfering with the free passage of pedestrians, temporarily closing part of Paternoster Square and disrupting the worship and work of St Paul's? Perhaps it will be remembered for the early encouragement it received from Canon Dr Giles Fraser who, in those heady, hippy days when the camp was first set up, famously welcomed the protesters and cavalierly informed the police that their help in shifting the protesters was not required – and that they should "move on"? For this contribution Dr Fraser has since felt obliged to resign. Nevertheless, the Bishop of London says, "His is an important voice which must continue to be heard." But to be heard saying *what*? What rewards remain for such as Fraser who had welcomed the protesters into the cathedral? A regular column on *The Guardian* and frequent appearances on *The Today Programme's* dumb show *Thought for the Day*. And the living of the parish of St Mary's Newington, given to him by the bishop.

A senior policeman in the City said to me at the time: "God knows why the cathedral Chapter have got themselves involved in all this. In better days a mere wandsman or a caretaker would have phoned the station and said, 'Look we're having a spot of bother with some riff raff.' The police would have turned up and shifted them, and that would have been that."

The reason that such a happy solution could not be achieved these days is because the attitude of the Chapter is, to say the least, ambiguous, having committed themselves to "dialogue" with the people in Occupy. But dialogue can only take place between those who agree to attend to factual evidence and to abide by the principle of rational conversation. Occupy attends to neither. And the Chapter doesn't attend to them much. For example, the poverty and deprivation which Occupy claims to have discovered, and against which it protests, is not the fault of City financial institutions. The City of London earns colossal amounts of money and without its contribution to the national economy, we would all be worse off – and especially the poor with whom both Occupy and the Chapter claim to be in sympathy.

The Dean himself resigned and the new Dean announced his arrival by writing a letter to *The Guardian*. (Why is one tempted to ask, "Where else?") In this he boasted that the cathedral does much good charitable work among London's poor and that the Church Urban Fund has raised £60million for the alleviation of poverty nationwide over the last twenty-five years. This is rather disingenuous, for the Dean omitted to mention that the cathedral itself had recently received £40million from the same City banks of which it is hypercritical.

If we are to discuss the place and the vocation of St Paul's and its "dialogue" with Occupy concerning the poor, we need to put away fantasy and sentimentality and reintroduce the Reality Principle. To the fact that the City creates rather than dissipates wealth, should be added the other fact that St Paul's is able to continue its daily function as a house of prayer mainly because of the financial support it receives from City institutions. The Dean and Chapter, much occupied with Occupy, seemed to have forgotten that St Paul's is in effect the parish church of the City of London. It is patronised by Royalty for many grand occasions. It is supported by the Lord Mayor when he attends for a blessing on the day of his Show and at many other services throughout the year. The cathedral also receives enormous support from the ancient and modern livery companies of the City and from countless wealthy benefactors.

High-mindedness is no doubt a great virtue. I just wish the cathedral authorities had substituted facts and rationality for the economic cloud cuckoo land which they seem to inhabit. And they should stop biting the hands that feed them.

XVI

In 2008 the country was in need of comfort following the onset of the recession and the Chancellor's brutal Autumn Statement in response. Well, we can all take heart, for the Church of England rose to the occasion and issued a prayer for our financial crisis. It began with a casual remark to the Almighty – as if God and the bloke who wrote the prayer were just two old men chewing the fat on the same park bench:

"Lord God, we live in disturbing days."

It proceeded, as so many modern prayers do, to give spurious information to the Omniscient God:

"Across the world
prices rise,
debts increase,
markets are in turmoil,
jobs are taken away,
and fragile security is under threat."

Did you know that, God? Notice how the prayer is written as if it were a poem: the words not quite reaching the margins. I don't object to prayers for particular needs, but I wish the prayers would betray some evidence of thought and are not doggerel. Perhaps they should produce a prayer, for those tempted to compose a naff prayer? Why not, in a crisis – especially in an economic crisis - turn to the New Testament where we can find words pithy and apt enough even for the hated bankers in the Square Mile:

"Here we have no abiding City, but we seek one to come."

Thank God for light relief – though not for the sort of light relief that is heavier than heavy weather. You get all sorts and conditions turning up at the weekday lunchtime Masses. There are those who arrive late. And these are frequently also the same ones who leave early. Those who whisper gossip to their neighbours throughout. The rustlers of plastic bags. And of course the devotees of the portable phone – which many refer to as "mobile." I thought I'd seen and heard everything by now, but how about this? A curvy Italian woman in a

revealing outfit approached the altar to receive Communion. Her phone went off. So she answered it and maintained a conversation – while continuing to hold out her hand to receive the Sacrament. I said, "Turn that thing off!" And it was only by the grace of God that I remembered where I was and so avoided saying, "Turn that *******
thing off!"

At a carol service for The Fuellers Company, a tramp I knew to be aggressive walked up the aisle while we were singing. He shuffled slowly, pretty close to dead drunk. He stopped at the chancel step and I wondered for a minute what he might do next. I was glad when he turned and walked slowly back down the aisle and out. The hymn finished, I announced to the congregation: "That was one of the Wise Men. The other two will be along in a minute!"

We held a memorial service at St Michael's for John Gaze, whose funeral had been during the summer. As we were getting ready to process, a member of the choir remarked, "*The Guardian* wouldn't be pleased with the distribution of the sexes."

True enough, 90% of the congregation was male. Well, male-ish. A third was the deceased John's fellow parish clerks, a third members of the Carlton Club, and the remainder a flamboyant selection of his Gay friends, camp as a Girl Guides' picnic. There were two addresses by, as it were, camp followers – both brilliant displays of euphemistic circumlocution as they offered their brief biographies of John. It was rather like an episode of *Round the Horn* but without the jokes.

John was a good and kind man who had given much to St Michael's over twenty-five years. I thought it a pity that these recollections of him were all, by hint and innuendo, about his sexuality and his drinking. It reminded me of those Gay Pride marches where the protagonists are so blatant and explicit about what they would like people to think they get up to.

Saturday morning. A private Christening. I don't like them much. Why they couldn't have the Baptism in the middle of the Sunday Parish Mass, like everyone else, beats me. It's because they think themselves special. Really, they are snobs. They were late – this sort is always late. And so noisy and ill-mannered. No apology. They regard churchwardens and the parish priest with a disdain that would have disgraced an 18th century nobleman caught mistreating his bootblack. Fashionably expensive – that is tasteless, ugly clothes. ersatz, posh, intonation complete with bad grammar. I have found over the years that the industrial labourers of the working class and the farm hands who bring their children to the font are agreeable and polite. Moreover, they know what a church is *for*. They may not be schooled, but they are reverent. They speak quietly – not like the posh lot whose every utterance is self-advertisement and seems designed to test the church's acoustics to destruction. And the toffs are a pleasure to deal with. Like the workers, they too know what churches are for and they still retain some vestige of the notion that their meaning is retained by the phrase "in the presence of God." Both these groups know the meaning of the word respect

The private Christening party in church that day were neither humble nor grand: they were merely pretentious. They don't milk cows or fix rivets into whatever rivets are fixed into. And they don't sip claret serenely after a long day spent surveying their estate. No, there is nothing *real* about these people. They don't have proper jobs. She will be an Assistant Director working for an independent TV company making advertisements for cosmetics. He is setting up a consultancy to explore the interface between non-governmental agencies and the media

Not only do they allow their small children to chase noisily around the church: they themselves join in the gallop and so excite their shrieking offspring until, past hysteria, they collapse in tears. They live by a new infantilised yuppie Commandment: "Parents: obey your children." They have had expensive orders of service printed which set out clearly the prayers and – in a typeface bold enough to be read by a blind man - the very few responses the parents and godparents are required to make. When it comes to these, they are quite incapable, dumbstruck, and the priest is left in the position of having gently to coax them if he is to get them even to show a semblance of making their promises.

The booze-up and the cake: they're the real purpose of this pantomime. And the photographs – but photographs that will signify *what*?

In an uncertain world, we long for one or two things, at least, to be dependable. Thankfully, we could always rely on the former Archbishop of Canterbury to be one of these things. And so Dr Williams emerged to give us his views on the causes of the summer riots which broke out in towns and cities up and down the country in 2010. He blamed "massive economic hopelessness" among the rioters. Against this assertion, we need to understand that those who rioted were a very small minority of the youthful poor. So when the Archbishop cites material causes in order to account for riotous behaviour, he thereby cast a slur on the overwhelming majority of the poor who did not riot.

He added: "Too many of these young people assume they are not going to have any ordinary, human, respectful relationships with adults – especially those in authority, the police above all."

So the rioters don't like the police much? That does come as a revelation. Violent lawbreakers resent the forces of law and order – whatever next! There is more of this sort of wisdom:

"Too many of them inhabit a world in which the obsession with 'good' clothes and accessories – against a backdrop of economic insecurity or simple privation – creates a feverish atmosphere where status falls and rises as suddenly and destructively as a currency market."

Leave aside for a moment the fact that many of those who rioted appeared already to possess an abundance of "accessories" – if not quite so many good clothes – the fact is that most ordinary folk inhabit this ultra-materialistic and covetous world, and yet they do not take violently to the streets to commit opportunistic theft.

So: "We have to persuade them, simply, that we as government and civil society alike will be putting some intelligence and skill into giving them the stake they do not have."

But political policies should be decided by politicians. The church's responsibility is to provide spiritual and moral guidance. Of course, as the Archbishop rightly says,

"Demonising volatile and destructive young people doesn't help; criminalising them wholesale reinforces the problem."

I didn't notice any such "demonizing," but I did notice that far from being criminalized "wholesale," those accused were brought to trial individually to acknowledge responsibility for their own misbehaviour and they were not asked to account for the whole violent and thieving mob.

"We have the tools for something other than vindictive or exemplary penalties."

It seems, by this saying, that, while Dr Williams made every attempt to exculpate the criminal mob by the invocation of generalized economic causation, he turns his disapproval on those whose job it is to uphold the law. Are our magistrates and judges, public servants, really so "vindictive"? It was noteworthy, but not at all surprising that the Archbishop did not touch on one plain cause of the riots: and that was the reluctance of the police, immediately following the initial outbreak in Tottenham, to prevent the looters from going about their unlawful business. And we understand the police's institutionalized reticence. Since the Brixton and Toxteth riots of 1981 – and the incoherent Macpherson Report - they have been instructed to tread very softly when dealing with "communities."

Surely we should be thankful for the hard-working bureaucrats in the General Synod for their unstinting efforts to keep the clergy entertained? Along with every other Anglican priest in England, I received a copy of a thing called *Guidelines for the Professional Conduct of the Clergy*. It had the Church of England's trendy logo on the front – perhaps, after Tony Blair's rebranding of the Labour Party, we should all start to refer to the modern church as *New Church of England*? This logo looks depressingly like the symbol for the Euro. And the booklet is decorated in purple – which lets us know that it comes down from the bishops.

The *Foreword* says at once that what is being aimed at is "best possible practice" – so we might have guessed we were in for a tirade of management-speak and indeed we were not disappointed. But management-speak that was so scintillatingly hilarious. It began: "There is a risk in all pastoral work. The place of the meeting. The arrangement of furniture and lighting. The dress of the minister, especially for visits that he undertakes at night." I must say I didn't recognise myself here. "Furniture? Lighting? Dress?" It sounds like Lights. Camera. Action.

And it suggests the priest is some sort of amalgamation of interior designer, film director and catwalk model. The visiting at night bit conjures images of Count Dracula. There is more amusement to follow: "Improper questioning or physical contact can be emotionally and sexually abusive." What sort of parsons are they training these days? This booklet reads as if it had been written for investigative journalists and predatory sex-maniacs. It reminds me of the story about the woman who asked the priest to kiss her. He refused. She persisted: "O go on Vicar, give us a kiss!" He replied, "Certainly not! In fact I shouldn't really be in bed with you."

Then Lent was upon us and the parish got busy, so I was unable to accept all the invitations which so generously came my way, especially when one these invitations involved a trip to the USA. I was sorry to have to miss this…

"Dear Peter,

"I do hope you can come to our Sarum Seminar on Friday 16th March. Jennifer Borland will speak on 'Considering Women's Spaces: Architecture and the Bodies of Medieval Sheela-na-gigs'. Sheela-na-gigs, or sculptured bodies of women displaying exaggerated genitalia, appeared in a variety of architectural structures in the Middle Ages.

"This talk will investigate the connections between these images and some of the female audiences who may have viewed them. Dr Borland received her PhD in Art History from Stanford University in2006 and is currently teaching Medieval and Islamic Art History in the Department of Art & Design at CSU Fresno. This will be in the Learning Center, Foothills Congregational Church, Los Altos.

"If you'd like to 'brown bag' supper I'll have the room open at 6pm(signed) Mistress of the Revels, Ann Jones"

After receiving this invitation I did a bit of research on the web and found several sites about Sheela-na-gigs – many with pictures. One said "These Sheelas are quasi-erotic." Never did a "quasi" so amply demonstrate the art of litotes.

I wrote back: "Thank you but I can't come. I have passed on your kind invitation to Joan Bakewell."

The Episcopal Church of the USA is another country and they do things differently there. I read an article about Bishop Stacy Sauls, a recent candidate for the post of presiding bishop in ECUSA. Apparently, years ago when he wanted to test his vocation to the sacred ministry, he spent some time at Union Theological Seminary in New York. While in the West Village of Manhattan, he ventured into a strip club.

This is the report I read on what happened next: "A scantily-clad woman waltzed down the shoe-shaped runway and approached the wannabe priest, undressing herself as she strutted her stuff. By the time she reached the future Bishop Sauls she was naked and she squatted in front of him. At that poignant moment Sauls noticed not the naked charms of the stripper but the sequinned garter on her right leg on which were written the words GO FOR IT! And he knew he was meant to be ordained.

"As Sauls later told the story to several small groups of clergy, he marvelled aloud, 'Isn't it amazing how God speaks to us? '"Now ECUSA is to be renamed simply The Episcopal Church (TEC). The renaming has been savagely mocked, one wag saying TEC must stand for "The Episcopal Cult" and another "Trashing Everything Christian." The winner in this mocking contest must be our own Ruth Gledhill, Religion Correspondent on *The Times* who suggested TEC means simply "The Empty Church". I am indebted to Reverend J.M. Deschene writing in *Christian Challenge* for what he calls "The new TEC hymn":

"Our gospel is inclusive – the former one's passé;

We welcome all the sexes, transgendered, lesbigay;

And though we're loudly preaching our relevant good news,

It's more than disappointing with all these empty pews"

The modern Church of England is not to be outdone by the ecclesiastical avant garde across the pond. I was with the Bishop of London and the City clergy on a conference in the old seminary house at Merville in France. It put the pantomimes of my childhood in the shade. It was all jargon. Even in the loo and in French, of course. You stand there and read the notice that says "Ne pas oublier d'appuyer sur le bouton ci-dessous afin d'actioner la chasse d'eau." Or, as we say in English, "Flush!" A German academic spoke for an hour like Professor Teufelsdroch and actually said "Twenty-thirdly…"

One priest began the prayers, "Let us pray around the theme of hate. Think of a person in your parish whom you hate. Perhaps you hate yourself? Or you hate God?" In the debased canticles – presumably to avoid the modern sin of sexism - we changed "forefathers" into "ancestors" – as if ancestor worship were the coming thing in the C. of E. There were huge dollops of touchy-feely and the explicit hatred of tradition. For instance in a hymn we sang, "Preaching Christ and not our customs, let us build a bridge of care…" But what if Christ is mediated precisely through our customs?

There were vacuous choruses - the eleven-fold repetition of what was not worth singing once. All to dreamily mothballed tunes of the Joan Baez version of 1960s nostalgia. Pools of sentimentality. And then the feminisation of the church which has followed so swiftly on women's ordination: we prayed to the Holy Ghost as "Tender Sister." The climax was an act so spectacularly fatuous that it made you wish you hadn't come. It was called "The Symbolic Response."

We all had to leave our pews and be given little night-light style candles and put them on the floor of the chapel to form the shape of the Cross. All the time the creepy goo of the chorus droning on and on. Grown men - priests for God's sake - shuffling themselves into this mullarkey. It reminded me of *Blue Peter* and I wondered whether we were going to be shown how to make an Archdeacon out of egg boxes.

But seriously, we might all have been burned alive. On the last night I was asleep in my room at about 1am. Suddenly the fire alarms went and voices were shouting for us to get out. I pulled on my bags and peered out into the corridor to see the Bishop of London emerging through clouds of smoke like one of the Four Horsemen of the Apocalypse – sans nag. In a minute we were all out on the grass waiting for the French version of the Trumptonshire fire brigade to arrive which, thankfully, they did and we were saved. It had all begun with a faulty water heater in the Bishop's room. As he told us afterwards, "You are lucky to have a bishop who is so vigilant I don't sleep very well – or I wouldn't have noticed the fire in the closet."

There was another piece of vandalism at St Michael's to follow the theft of William Cowper's walking stick and the taking of the Fusiliers' Colours. Some thief with taste meticulously removed the magnificent wood carving of a lion representing St Mark from our pulpit, leaving only a hexagonal hole like a scar. It was a mess. The pulpit, the pew ends and many other parts of St Michael's were carved by the brilliant 19th century craftsman William Gibbs Rogers whose work can also be seen at Kensington Palace and Carlton House. Rogers was a pupil of the celebrated master Grinling Gibbons.

I was furious of course and the whole congregation with me. But beyond fury there's bafflement. I mean what kind of person – if "person" is the word I'm looking for – defaces church interiors and removes fine artworks of spiritual significance? The theft was well-executed too, so you might say the figure of the lion was exquisitely stolen and almost a work of art in itself. But do these church thieves take our treasures and sell them on or what? Or perhaps they belong to a band or guild of thieves who gather at one another's houses for drinks and canapés and boast, "And here's one I nicked from St Paul's… it contrasts nicely, don't you think, with the candlestick I pinched from Westminster cathedral…"

We discovered the theft and damage when we went in to prepare for the Sunday Mass. I was glad at least for something to take our minds off the depressing incident in the shape of Fr Gerard Stevens from Sevenoaks, our visiting preacher that day. He gave us a sound doctrinal sermon containing a couple of good jokes, including the one about the Irish bishop who told off one of his priests for constantly making fun of the English. The priest agreed to desist, but next time the bishop visited his church, he was preaching about Judas' betrayal. Jesus prophesies that one of the disciples will betray him and Judas says, "Oh my dear old chap, it is not I who shall do this is it?"

Then the one about Pope John XXIII's arrival at the pearly gates demanding entry. St Peter says, "Sorry, you're not on the list." John protests that Peter should appeal to the Holy Spirit and the Holy Spirit says to Peter, "Oh yes, you know John XXIII. He's the one who invited me to the Second Vatican Council – but I didn't go!"

I had to ask myself, do I look like "a poor honest young woman"? The Town Clerk's department of the City of London sent me a notice about Signor Pasquale Favale's Bequest which provides three dowries of £100 to poor honest young women born in the City. Signor Favale in his Will of 1880 bequeathed 18,000 Italian lire – then valued at £720 – saying he had been "…induced to make these bequests because his wife was a native of London and that he had passed many happy years of his life in the City." Whether in the first decade of the 21st century there actually are any poor women – I'm sure there is at least one honest one – in the thrusting plutocracy of the Square Mile is debateable. But what a heart-warming gesture by Signor Favale.

Alas it reminded me of another wedding story. I heard of a young man who went to his parish priest and asked to be married. He wasn't a regular churchgoer and he didn't really know his way about the various options. The priest asked him, "Do you want the old service or the new one?

He said, "Well, I think I'd like the new one please". On the day of his marriage this bridegroom was driving himself to church when there was a sudden downpour. The car leaked water in the engine and stalled. The bridegroom got out and tried to fix it. The rain came on harder and he got his trousers all muddied, so he rolled them up above his knees. Anyhow, he managed to fix the car and get to church – late. His bride was already at the altar, in tears. He ran straight to her side. The priest looked at his dishevelled state and said, "For goodness' sake man, pull your trousers down!

And the man replied, "You know Father, I think I'll have the old service after all!"

It was August and the City was quiet, the choir was on holiday, sermons were short and so I had time to think. I found myself thinking… It's a good job the gospels were written in an age before the exquisite sensitivity that has become political correctness set in. St Matthew and St Luke would never find a publisher these days. I mean, how dare the gospel-writers use all those offensive words such as "cripple," "blind," "deaf" and so on. Surely they ought to have lapsed into euphemisms "partially-sighted", "hearing impaired" etc – though it sure wrecks our figures of speech. You would have to say "As partially-sighted as a bat" and "As hearing impaired as a post."

It doesn't stop there. What about all those words Our Lord spoke about "sin" and "judgement"? Thank goodness we're progressed enough and advanced these days to know that there is no sin but only "lifestyle," and that one must on no account be "judgemental." St Luke tells how Jesus condemned self-esteem. Our generation promotes it. Or how about doing charitable works by stealth? Not in our celeb culture we don't. We shout it from the rooftops. And faithfulness in marriage, one man and one woman for life? That's just too restrictive for our enlightened sense of self-expression which understands that any act of human coupling (or tripling or more) is as good as any other.

I got to thinking it might be fun – and even a bit useful – to expose this euphemistic decadence in a satire, so I began to compile *The Politically-Incorrect Lexicon* which my publisher *Bretwalda* snapped up. The parliamentary sketch-writer and theatre critic Quentin Letts kindly wrote a Foreword and extracted from my book a selection which appeared in the *Daily Mail*. A few hundred definitons of words and phrases according to modern usage. If I'm allowed to have a favourite, it's one that appears on the last page:

"BURGLARY GONE WRONG: (police-spk)". A burglar violently assaults/murders a householder. This is described as a burglary gone wrong. It was going just fine until the murder.

Envoi

These fragments I have shored against my ruins…

I thought, "At least if I give the New Year City sermon myself, I'll be spared the worry of wondering if the preacher is going to turn up late." This is some of what I said,

"This is the tenth City Service for which it has been my job to find someone to give the Address. We have had many intelligent and distinguished preachers over the years. Well, you can see I've put a stop to that this morning.

"St Michael's is good for the careers of those who speak at this service. Archbishop Cormac Murphy O'Connor came one year and was immediately afterwards promoted to Cardinal. Michael Howard came and a few weeks later he was made Leader of Her Majesty's Opposition. I can't say I'm expecting the word from Lambeth this morning.

"Over the last ten years in the City I have heard some pretty odd things said about the Christian faith. I have heard Right Wing people say that they don't go along with the miracles and the resurrection and all that stuff, but that religion is good as a basis for morality. This seems to miss the point that to base your morality on a lie doesn't seem to be a good place to start.

"I have heard people on the Left talk about the faith as if it's a metaphor for social involvement. These people don't believe in miracles either. You must have heard this sort of thing from dozens of hairy Leftie clergymen: *The feeding of the 5000 was to teach us to share… if we all take just a little, there'll be enough to go round.* Well, if Jesus had said something as soppy and clichéd as that, why should the Gospel writers bother to record it? The feeding of the five thousand wasn't a socialist picnic: it was a miracle.

"The Archbishop of Canterbury – bless him! – told us at Christmas there were no kings at the stable, there weren't three of them and we don't know their names. No shepherds either. And if you don't believe the Virgin Birth, that's not a handicap. Why does he seem to think that the only criteria for truth are those of 19th century German biblical criticism? No kings? No shepherds? How do we know there is an Archbishop of Canterbury and not just some wraith-like political druid on his way to another debate in the General Synod?

"The Christian Faith is not an agreeable colour scheme for sectional interests of any hue. And the only reason for believing the Christian faith is because it's true. Most of its contemporary despisers know no theology or philosophy. Richard Dawkins is particularly vacuous: it's as if I should try to tell him that the whole of biology is contained in the book *Janet and John Look at Frogs*.

"Christianity is morally profound and intellectually vigorous. It was Christianity in the doctrine of The Trinity which corrected the metaphysical error which doomed classical civilisation. In the so-called Dark Ages, Christians invented the university and began to make possible modern science. Nothing has happened since that time to make our faith any the less believable. The problem is that our society seems to think we can give up Christianity, yet all the civilising and cultural benefits of the faith will remain: they will not.

"St Augustine has told us that God is love *and nothing else*. And this love is no abstract benevolence. God loves *you*. God wills only what is good for you. In fact *God so loved the world that he gave his only begotten Son that whosoever believeth in him should not perish, but have everlasting life.* Let us go then, you and I, let us return to him whose love can assuage all our fears. Let us return to the one who promised, *Come unto me all that travail and are heavy laden, and I will refresh you…Take my yoke upon you and learn of me; for my yoke is easy and my burden is light, and ye shall find rest unto your souls.*"

At the reception the Rear Admiral, Clerk to the Drapers, came across and said, "I don't much like your sermons."

Good, I must be doing *something* right then!

In May 2011 I wrote to the Bishop of London asking him to extend the period of my licensing to the parishes of St Michael's (where I had the Freehold) and St Sepulchre's beyond my 70th birthday on 11th January 2012. Here is a copy of the bishop's reply – six weeks later:

"Thank you for your recent letter, a letter which rightly prompts me to express my gratitude for all you have achieved at both St Michael, Cornhill and St Sepulchre. Your stewardship of these churches has been exemplary and I know from personal conversations how much your ministry is valued.

"In response to your request for an extension to you licence, I am afraid that I will be unable to grant your request. I know this will be a disappointment to you and I wanted to explain the reasons for this and to reassure you that this decision is in no way related to any unhappiness on my part as to your ministry or considerable achievements. Following the introduction of Common Tenure, I have taken the view that clergy should not have their licences extended beyond 70 where they are of incumbent or priest-in-charge status and I have asked the Archdeacon to begin looking at succession planning in all cases where a clergyperson is approaching that age.

"As I have enforced this in other places, I do feel I must do the same with all clergy colleagues. Of course, priesthood is for life, and I would be delighted to give you my permission to officiate, or to commend you to my brother bishops, wherever you decide to retire.

"I am sending a copy of this letter to the Archdeacon, and in doing so am asking him to meet with you to look at the coming months and to begin planning the transition. He will, I am sure, be keen to be guided by your wisdom and experience in the two parishes. We must also arrange an event to celebrate your ministry and perhaps you and Archdeacon David can put some thought to that as well."

Here is my reply:

"Thank you for your letter of 7th July in which you express your unwillingness to extend the period of my licensing beyond my 70[th.]

"You are right to suppose that this comes as a disappointment, but it also very much perplexes me. Your first paragraph is so exuberant in its praise for the ministry at St Michael's and St Sepulchre's that I blushed as I read it; but your second paragraph then declares that this ministry, still flowing in full spate, must on no account be allowed to continue.

"By extrapolation, if a bloke of 86 can still be deemed competent to run the Holy Catholic Church, why should another bloke, 16 years younger, be required to quit a job which, by Your Lordship's most generous tribute, he is presently doing so well?"

I asked Chartres for an interview, but he refused. Then how's this for cringeworthy? He wrote so say he wanted to give me a party "to celebrate your ministry" – which struck as being like the hangman asking what one might like for one's last breakfast. I was very touched when parishioners, liverymen and other of my City connections wrote to ask the bishop to extend my licensing to the two churches.

Immoveable, he composed a letter of refusal, made scores of copies and sent it out to all petitioners. Many were unsatisfied by the bishop's explanation for his action and so they wrote again – only to receive a further copy of the same letter.

My last weeks in the City were a cocktail of contrary emotions. The Christmas services were especially difficult. My people had always been affectionate and supportive, but I had never before experienced such kindness as the end drew closer. Tender words from individuals and families. A generous cheque from the church council. Another cheque from the Drapers. I went as I had arrived, so to speak: my last official duty being the New Year City Service. Quentin Letts preached. Here's a selection of the less embarrassing parts of what he said:

"Peter has been with you since 1998. In that time congregations have increased tenfold. St Sepulchre's has reopened. There has been restoration, a revival both musical and spiritual. This has been a remarkable ministry

"Is Peter in some ways a John the Baptist figure? He has a better wardrobe. To see him stride along Cornhill in priestly garb, with flying saucer hat, is a grand sight. Nor have I seen our man settle, of a lunchtime, for an improving plate of locusts and wild honey. He prefers something chateau-bottled.

"He has sometimes irked authority. Correction: he has *frequently* irked authority…

"The Obadiah Slopes who have found Peter a turbulent priest tend to approach life more warily, as zoo visitors will tiptoe toward the lion cage. These careerist dainties quake. Quiver. They lack the swagger - certitude is a better word – which marks men of real faith. Do priests have doubts? I am sure they do. If Thomas (which is called Didymus) had his reservations, we must allow our curates the occasional private wobble. But is it not their duty to keep those anxieties to themselves? Would not that be the stamp of leaders?

"In today's Church, alas, leadership and majesty and liturgical awe are regarded with suspicion. Leadership involves inequality, the led being, logically, on a lower plane than those who lead. If there is one thing today's off-the-peg Anglican vicar disowns, it is inequality. He is embarrassed by Establishment. He shies away from rousing 19th century hymns."

I retired to Eastbourne where in the mornings I write and take occasional lunch and supper with visiting friends at home or at The Pilot Inn near the top of Meads Village. I walk the shore and the Downs and ascend to Beachy Head and the lighthouse which has got under my skin and insinuated itself into the poems I try to compose:

"It is hard to look down on the lighthouse
From Beachy Head, instead
You feel you should look up to it
For guidance and its bright beaming;
But it stands mesmerising beneath the cliff
And its wayside shrines
To those who looked too far down.
"Your gaze must fall to where
It stands red and white like
The float of a drowsy fisherman.
"Beachy Head (as the Creed said)
Was made and not begotten
By the Second Person of the Blessed Trinity,
By whom all things were made,
And many unmade.
"Above and set in anxious twilight,
Five brazen trees askance,
Sparse, skeletal, frizzy
Like ladies emerged from the blow-dry.
On top of the tallest a rook rejoiced
In his sardonic tone as if
He had just won the tree in a raffle.
"I can see from here
Three of the Seven Sisters, pale,
Sniggering and speaking of rooks.
"The lighthouse is set like a chess-piece:
One of the bishops –
And it is easy to look down on them."

C.H. Sisson was my teacher and my friend. I shall end this memoir as he ended his:

"A septuagenarian may be allowed regrets, but they are no more to the point than the hopes of earlier years. One can hardly do better than to turn to the visible world, and here I am fortunate.

What it all means, God knows."

Shantih   shantih   shantih.